Turbo Prolog

Owner's Handbook

Borland International, Inc.
4585 Scotts Valley Drive,
Scotts Valley, CA 95066
USA

Table of Contents

List of Figures

List of Tables

Introduction

Turbo Prolog is a fifth-generation computer language that takes programming into a new dimension. Because of its natural, logical approach, both people new to programming and professional programmers can build powerful applications—such as expert systems, customized knowledge bases, natural language interfaces, and smart information management systems.

Turbo Prolog is a declarative language. This means that, given the necessary facts and rules, it can use deductive reasoning to solve programming problems. By contrast, Pascal, BASIC and other traditional computer languages are procedural: the programmer must provide step-by-step procedures telling the computer how to solve problems. The Prolog programmer need only supply a description of the problem (the *goal*) and the ground rules for solving it, and the Prolog system will determine how to go about a solution.

HOW TO USE THIS BOOK

This manual is designed to serve two different types of reader: those new to Prolog, and those familiar with the Prolog language.

If you're a new user of Prolog, you should first read Chapters 1 and 2. Chapter 1 tells you a little about the advantages of Turbo Prolog, and Chapter 2 describes how to enter programs into the system, how to have them compiled and executed and, finally, how to use Turbo Prolog's unique debugging facilities. You will then know enough about Turbo Prolog to get going with the tutorials, which are presented in Chapters 3–10. Each tutorial chapter includes a variety of exercises to help you check your understanding.

If you're already familiar with Prolog, you can begin with Chapter 2, which covers basic system operations, and then move on to Chapter 11, which describes how Turbo Prolog differs from other Prolog implementations.

All readers will want to refer to Chapter 12, which provides detailed information about all aspects of Turbo Prolog.

The tutorials cover all aspects of Turbo Prolog programming, except modular programming and interfacing with other languages such as C, Pascal, or assembly language. These features are described in Chapter 11, which also contains hints and tips on programming style and a wealth of other information about advanced system features.

For details about the files supplied on the distribution disk, installation, and Turbo Prolog menu commands, see Chapter 12.

THE DISTRIBUTION DISKS

Your distribution disk contains the main Turbo Prolog program and several other files. Information about each of these files can be found in Chapter 12.

Turbo Prolog is not copy-protected. Please note that Borland's no-nonsense license statement licenses you to use your copy of Turbo Prolog as if it were a book. It is not licensed to a single person, nor is it tied to one particular computer. The only restriction on using Turbo Prolog is that *it must not be used by two different people at the same time*, just as a book cannot be read by two people at the same time. And, of course, giving away copies of Turbo Prolog to others would be a violation of Borland's copyright.

MINIMUM SYSTEM REQUIREMENTS

To use Turbo Prolog, you should have the following:

- IBM PC or compatible computer
- 384K RAM internal memory
- PC-DOS or MS-DOS operating system, version 2.0 or later

ACKNOWLEDGMENTS

In this manual, references are made to several products:

- Turbo Prolog and GeoBase are trademarks and Turbo Pascal is a registered trademark of Borland International, Inc.
- WordStar is a registered trademark of MicroPro International Corp.
- MultiMate is a trademark of MultiMate International Corp.
- IBM PC, AT, XT, PCjr, and Portable Computer are registered trademarks of International Business Machines Corp.
- PLINK86 is a trademark of Phoenix Software Associates, Ltd.

1 About Prolog

Over the last decade, the price of hardware has halved approximately every fourth year, while the cost of writing software has increased annually, and now takes by far the largest portion of a total system budget. Software accounted for about 10% of total system costs in 1970, 50% in 1975, and more than 80% in 1985. This rapidly escalating cost has influenced the development of new programming tools to make it easier, quicker and therefore cheaper to develop programs. In particular, research has focused on ways of handing over a larger part of the work to the machine itself.

Prolog is the result of many years of such research work. The first official version of Prolog was developed at the University of Marseilles, France by Alain Colmerauer in the early 1970s as a convenient tool for **PRO**gramming in **LOG**ic. It is much more powerful and efficient than most other well-known programming languages like Pascal and BASIC. For example, a program for a given application will typically require ten times fewer program lines with Prolog than with Pascal.

Today, Prolog is a very important tool in artificial intelligence applications programming and in the development of expert systems. Several well-known expert system shells are written in Prolog, including APES, ESP/Advisor and Xi. The demand for more "user friendly" and intelligent programs is another reason for Prolog's growing popularity.

Unlike, for example, Pascal, a Prolog program gives the computer a description of the problem using a number of facts and rules, and then asks it to find all possible solutions to the problem. In Pascal, one must tell the computer exactly how to perform its tasks. But once the Prolog programmer has described *what* must be computed, the Prolog system itself organizes *how* that computation is carried out. Because of this declarative (rather than procedural) approach, well-known sources of errors in Pascal and BASIC—such as loops that carry out one too many or one too few operations—are eliminated right from the start. Moreover, Prolog teaches the programmer to make a well-structured description of a problem, so that, with practice, Prolog can also be used as a specification tool.

Although Prolog makes programming far easier, it can also make severe demands on the computer. Turbo Prolog is the first implementation of Prolog for the IBM PC and compatible personal computers that is both powerful and conservative in its memory requirements. It provides more features than many mainframe implementations. Turbo

Prolog is a full-fledged *compiler* with a pull-down menu interface and full arithmetic, graphics and system-level facilities. Turbo Prolog produces compiled programs that execute very quickly but do not gobble memory like other, less comprehensive micro-computer implementations of Prolog. Turbo Prolog also has a built-in linker (simply select .EXE from the **O**ptions pull-down menu and compile).

In 1983, Japan published plans for an ambitious national project involving the design and production of fifth generation computers, for which Prolog was chosen as the fundamental system language (corresponding to the use of assembly language in current architectures). Turbo Prolog runs on a computer costing about $2000 yet, in a comparison made in 1984 using an earlier version of the system, it produced programs that executed faster than those produced by the prototype of the Japanese fifth generation computer.

WHAT CAN TURBO PROLOG BE USED FOR?

There are a number of practical applications for Turbo Prolog. Here's a sampler of what you can do:

- Produce prototypes for virtually any application program. An initial idea can be implemented quickly, and the model upon which it is based tested "live."
- Control and monitoring of industrial processes. Turbo Prolog provides complete access to the computer's I/O ports.
- Implement dynamic relational databases.
- Translate languages, either natural human languages or from one programming language to another.
- Construct natural language interfaces to existing software, so that existing systems become more widely accessible. With Turbo Prolog it is particularly easy to include windows in such an interface.
- Construct expert systems and expert-system shells.
- Construct symbolic manipulation packages for solving equations, differentiation and integration, etc.
- Theorem proving and artificial intelligence packages in which Turbo Prolog's deductive reasoning capabilities are used for testing different theories.

HOW DOES TURBO PROLOG DIFFER FROM OTHER LANGUAGES?

Let's take a closer look at how Turbo Prolog differs from traditional programming languages.

Turbo Prolog is descriptive. Instead of a series of steps specifying *how* the computer must work to solve a problem, a Turbo Prolog program consists of a *description* of the problem. This description is made up of three components, with the first and second parts corresponding to the declaration sections of a Pascal program:

1. Names and structures of *objects* involved in the problem
2. Names of *relations* which are known to exist between the objects
3. *Facts* and *rules* describing these relations

The description in a Turbo Prolog program is used to specify the desired relation between the given input data and the output which will be generated from that input.

Turbo Prolog uses facts and rules. Apart from some initial declarations, a Turbo Prolog program essentially consists of a list of logical statements, either in the form of facts such as:

    it is raining today.

or in the form of rules such as:

    you will get wet if it is raining
    and you forget your umbrella.

Turbo Prolog can make deductions. Given the facts

    john likes mary.
    tom likes sam.

and the rule

    jeanette likes X if tom likes X.

Turbo Prolog can deduce that

    jeanette likes sam.

You can give the Turbo Prolog program a *goal*, for example

    find every person who likes sam

and Turbo Prolog will use its deductive ability to find all solutions to the problem.

Execution of Turbo Prolog programs is controlled automatically. When a Turbo Prolog program is executed, the system tries to find all possible sets of values that satisfy the given goal. During execution, results may be displayed or the user may be prompted to type in some data. Turbo Prolog uses a *backtracking mechanism* which, once one solution has been found, causes Turbo Prolog to reevaluate any assumptions made to see if some new variable values will provide new solutions.

Turbo Prolog has a very short and simple syntax. It is therefore much easier to learn than the syntax of more complicated traditional programming languages.

Turbo Prolog is powerful. Turbo Prolog is a higher level language than, for instance, Pascal. As pointed out earlier, Turbo Prolog typically uses *10 times fewer* program lines when solving a problem than Pascal. Among other things, this is due to the fact that

Turbo Prolog has a built-in pattern-recognition facility, as well as a simple and efficient way of handling recursive structures.

Turbo Prolog is compiled, yet allows interactive program development. A programmer can test individual sections of a program at any point and alter the goal of the program, without having to append new code. This would correspond to being able to try out any arbitrary procedure in a Pascal program, even *after* the program has been compiled.

This has been a brief overview of the unique features of Turbo Prolog. As you delve more deeply into this manual and begin writing programs, you'll discover more of its powerful abilities. Now let's turn to Chapter 2 and get started with the Turbo Prolog system.

2 *A Short Introduction to the Turbo Prolog System*

This chapter describes the basic operation of the Turbo Prolog system, including how to use the menu system, run a Turbo Prolog program, and create a program file using the Turbo Prolog editor.

Chapter 12, the technical reference, gives a complete list of the files supplied on the distribution disk and the files needed when using the Turbo Prolog system. Turbo Prolog comes pre-installed and ready to run on an IBM PC or fully compatible computer. If you aren't satisfied with some of the defaults (such as our choice of colors for the display) they are easy to change using pull-down menus. See page 168. For now, until you're familiar with the system, you can try out Turbo Prolog as is.

THE MAIN MENU

Once you have a copy of the system on your working disk and you are in the appropriate directory, type PROLOG. You should see the logon message shown in Figure 2-1.

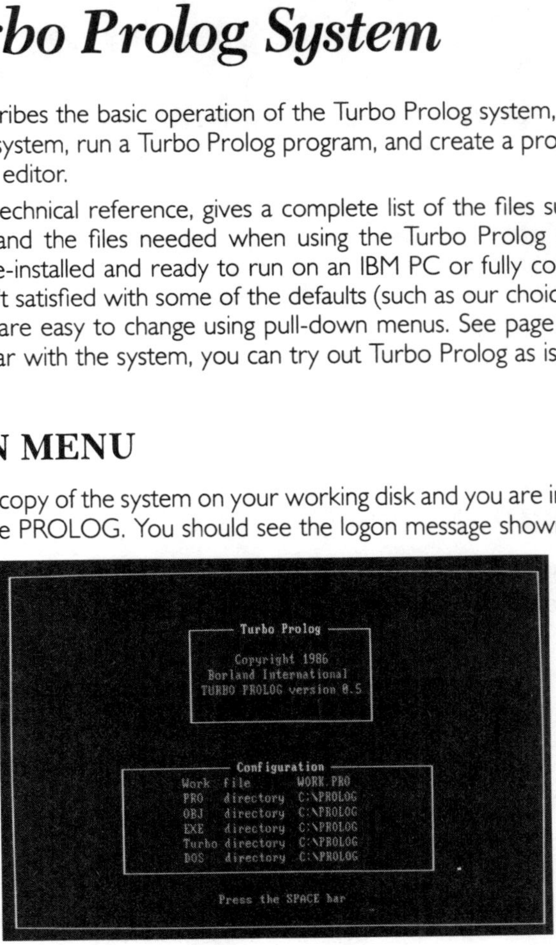

Figure 2-1 The Logon Display

In addition to the version of Turbo Prolog you are using, the logon message shows you the configuration for Turbo Prolog on your computer.

Now press the space bar and the Turbo Prolog main menu and four system windows will appear as shown in Figure 2-2.

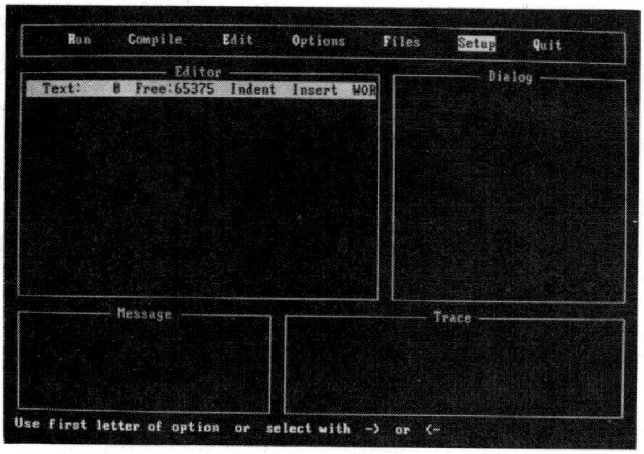

Figure 2-2 The Main Menu and the Four System Windows

The Main Menu shows you the commands and pull-down menus available. You select an item on a menu by pressing the associated highlighted capital letter or by first moving the highlighted bar using the arrow keys, and then pressing ↵. The use of each window is described throughout this chapter.

The bottom line of the screen contains a status message describing the use of the function or cursor keys. The meaning of these keys changes depending on what you are doing with the system at a given time: tracing, editing, or running a program, etc.

ENTERING YOUR FIRST TURBO PROLOG PROGRAM

Consider the following introductory Turbo Prolog program. We'll be using it to illustrate how to create, run, and edit Turbo Prolog programs.

```
predicates
     hello
goal
     hello.
clauses
     hello:-
         makewindow(1,7,7,"My first program",4,56,10,22),
         nl,write("  Please type\n  your name "),
         cursor(4,5),
         readln(Name),nl,
         write("  Welcome  ",Name).
```

Select the **E**dit option either by moving the cursor with the arrow keys until it is over the word **E**dit and then pressing ↵, or by simply pressing E. The screen should now look like Figure 2-3.

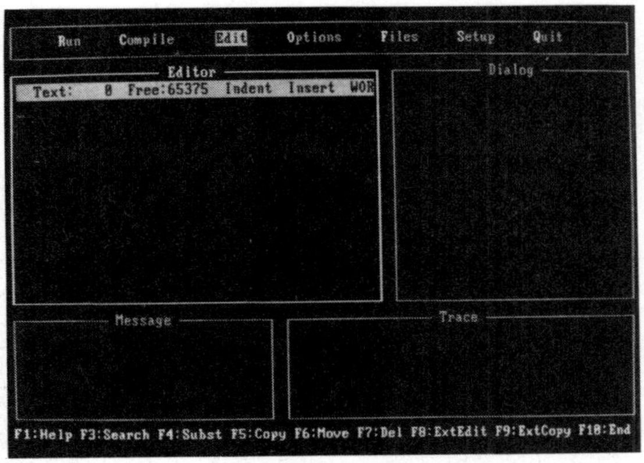

Figure 2-3 Using the Editor

Note that the editor window is highlighted and the status text at the bottom reflects the new meaning of the function keys.

To see how to correct a mistake, type in the first line of the above program as

```
predivates
```

To correct the mistake, position the cursor over the erroneous letter *v* and then press [Del]. Watch carefully what happens to the display. Now press [C] and look again. The mistake should be corrected. Now type in the first seven lines of the above program text, pressing [↵] at the end of each line.

When you type the end of the line that begins

```
makewindow.........
```

the rest of the text will scroll to the left inside the editor's window. Just to make sure it hasn't really disappeared, press [Home] after typing in this line, then press the [End] key. After you see what happens, finish typing in the program.

Once you are satisfied that the program text has been entered correctly, press [Esc] to leave the editor, then select the **R**un option from the menu. If you entered the program correctly, the program will be compiled and then executed and you should see the display shown in Figure 2-4. If you entered the program incorrectly, the cursor will appear at the error in the editor. Correct the program, and enter [F10] to continue.

Now type your first name and press [↵]. The program you have entered will respond

```
Welcome Alfredo
```

(or whatever your name is) and wait for you to press the space bar. The screen will then clear, leaving the main menu and the program text visible. Try running the program again and use an alias this time!

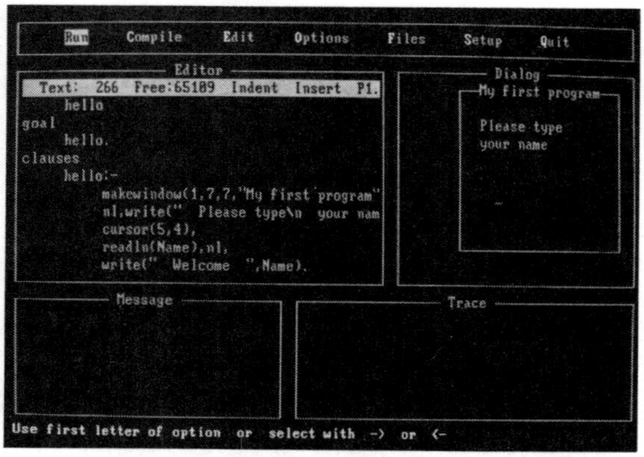

Figure 2-4 Executing a Program

To see what would have happened had you made a typing error in your text, let's go back and insert a deliberate one. If you aren't there yet, go back to the main menu by pressing the space bar or Esc. (If you've already gotten lost in the system, don't worry; pressing Ctrl Break—and the space bar whenever instructed to do so—will always eventually return you to the main menu). From the main menu, select the **E**ditor again, move the cursor to the line containing the word *goal*, and add a period (.) after the word. Now press Esc to leave the editor and select the **R**un option.

Because this extra period is a syntax error, you should see a message telling you so at the bottom of the editor window. The cursor will flash over the offending period in the text in the editor window. You are now automatically in editing mode. **DEL**ete the period, press Esc to leave the editor, and re-select **R**un.

To save the program on disk, select the **F**iles option and, from the pull-down menu it offers, select **S**ave. Type in the filename MYFIRST in response to the *Filename:* prompt, then press ↵. The contents of the workfile will now be saved, with the default extension for Turbo Prolog source programs (.PRO) added automatically.

To see a list of all Turbo Prolog programs on the currently selected directory of the currently selected disk, go back to the **F**iles menu and choose **D**irectory. Turbo Prolog will respond with a default current directory path name when you press ↵ and a default file mask.PRO (press ↵ here, too). A list of all programs with the .PRO extension in the default directory will appear on the screen, including MYFIRST.PRO. Press Esc to exit the **D**irectory option, and re-select the **E**dit option.

Now introduce two new errors into the program in the editor's workfile by replacing the second occurrence of *hello* with *howdy* and the third with *hi*. The first few lines in the editor window should now be:

```
predicates
     hello
goal
     howdy
clauses
     hi:-
        makewindow.....
```

Run the program and observe that, as before, the first error is detected and control returns to the editor so that you can correct the first "mistake"—*howdy* instead of *hello*. Do so now, but when you've finished, instead of typing Esc and **R**un, just press F10. F10 automatically exits the editor and causes the Turbo Prolog system to re-**R**un the program. But now the second error—*hi*—is detected. Correct it and press F10 once again. The program should compile and run normally this time.

The Turbo Prolog editor is a full screen text editor that uses the same key commands as the Turbo Pascal editor and the WordStar and Multimate word processor systems. The next section gives a short introduction to the editor; a complete description can be found in Chapter 12.

EDITOR SURVIVAL KIT

You need only read this section if you are not familiar with either the Turbo Pascal editor, WordStar, or Multimate. It's a good idea to familiarize yourself with just a few basic features at first, so that you can easily remember the necessary key sequences. This particularly applies if you are new to the Turbo Prolog language, since you'll want to be able to concentrate your efforts on writing Turbo Prolog programs. If you don't like the key sequences, one way to reconfigure them is to use Borland's SuperKey.

Basic Operation

Select **E**ditor from the main menu. If there is already text in the workfile, delete it using the Del key. Type in your name and address in the format you would use on an envelope, for example

Jeff Stoneham
32 E 24th
New York
NY 12345

Terminate editing by pressing the Esc key. Save the contents of the workfile by selecting **F**iles, then **S**ave. Save what you have typed in the editor under the filename ADDRESS.

Use Del to delete what you have typed into the editor, and type in a list of your five favorite foods, each on a separate line. Now finish the editing session again (press Esc) and select **F**iles from the main menu, then **L**oad. When asked for a filename, type ADDRESS followed by ↵. The system now asks if you want to save the text in the workfile. You do not, so press N and notice what has happened in the editor window—your favorite foods have been overwritten by the ADDRESS file.

Block Operations

When deleting your name and address from the editor window, you may have wondered if there was a better way to delete than pressing Del all those times. Well, there is a better way, thanks to the editor's block operations: first, you mark the block of text to be deleted, and then you delete it. Once marked, you can also make a copy of the block in another place in the text, or move it to another place in the text.

Marking a block is easy. To try it, first re-select the **E**dit option. With your name and address still in the editor window, use the arrow keys to position the cursor at the top left corner. Mark the start of the block by pressing Ctrl K B. Now move the cursor to the last character in the last line of your address and mark the end of the block by pressing Ctrl K K. Observe what has happened to the text display.

Let's make several copies of this block so that we've got more text to play with. Move the cursor to the end of your address and copy the block by pressing Ctrl K C. Move the cursor to the end of the newly created text and make another copy of the block. Repeat the process until you have a total of ten copies of your address in the editor window. Use the arrow keys and PgUp and PgDn to move around the text inside the editor window.

Now let's mark a new block. First we must un-mark the old block by pressing Ctrl K H (notice that the original block is no longer highlighted). Insert a new line 4 into the file consisting of 20 letter X's. Now make line 11 a new line of 20 letter Y's.

Our new block will be lines 5 to 10. Mark it with Ctrl K B and Ctrl K K as before. To delete the block, press Ctrl K Y and you should now have a line of X's followed by a line of Y's.

Next, mark a new block that consists of these two rows of X's and Y's. Move the cursor to the end of the text, then move the new block here by pressing Ctrl K V (check that it has been moved and not copied using PgUp and PgDn).

Block operations can be carried out with fewer key presses by use of the function keys. As mentioned earlier, explanations about the function keys are listed at the bottom of the screen.

Press the Help key, F1, to display a pop-up menu containing information about the function keys (and all the built-in standard predicates, but more about those later). Press F1 now and select Help Information from the resulting menu. Browse through the information using PgUp and PgDn. When finished, press Esc.

F5, F6, and F7 are used to copy, move, and delete blocks, as well as to actually mark the beginning and end of the block. To use them, first move the cursor to the beginning of a block, then press the required key to mark the beginning of the block. Then move the cursor to the end of the block, and press the same key again to mark the end of the block. If you want to delete, press F7. If you want to copy or move, move the cursor to where you want to put the text, and press either F5 or F6.

Search and Replace

Search and replace comes in handy if you decide to change the name of something in your program after you've written it. To use it, delete everything currently in the editor and type in this well-known phrase

> To be or not to be
> That is the question

Now let's replace every occurrence of *be* with *be,*. Press F4 and you will be prompted for a search string. Type *be* and press F4 again. You will now be prompted for the string to replace the search string with. Type *be,* and you will be asked if the search and replace is to be *global* or *local*.

A global search will find and replace every occurrence of *be* in the text, one by one; a local search finds the next occurrence only. Select a global search. Now you will be prompted for whether or not you would like to be asked before each replacement is actually made. In this case, press N. The search and replace will now be carried out and the text transformed to

To be, or not to be,
That is the question

If you simply want to find a string in the text, you can use the search command (as opposed to search *and* replace). Press F3 after which you will be prompted for a search string. Use the search function to find the first occurrence of *he* in the above text.

Notice that the search text in both search and search and replace operations is terminated by pressing the same key that was used to initiate that operation. This means that the search string can include the "new-line" character and that the replace string can be used to insert new lines and to change the layout of the text (for example, the indentation). For example, try replacing T with T ↵ in the above text.

Note also that if a search or local search and replace is selected, that operation can be repeated with the same choice of options by typing ⇧ F3 or ⇧ F4, as appropriate, once for each desired repetition.

Table 2-1 Summary of Editor Keystrokes

Keys	Purpose
Esc or F10	Exit the editor
Arrow keys, PgUp, PgDn, Home, End	Move the cursor
Del	Delete the character at the cursor
Ctrl K B	Mark the beginning of a block
Ctrl K K	Mark the end of a block
Esc K H	Un-mark a block
Ctrl K C	Copy a marked block to the position indicated by the cursor
Ctrl K Y	Delete a marked block
Ctrl K V	Move a marked block to the position indicated by the current cursor position
F1	Help information
F5	Copy block
F6	Move block
F7	Delete block
F3	Search
⇧ F3	Repeat last search
F4	Search and replace
⇧ F4	Repeat last search and replace

TRACING

In this section, we'll show you how to make a trace of a Turbo Prolog program. We'll be using the same example program we used earlier. If you have already saved it on disk, use the **F**iles command to enter a copy into the editor's workfile; if not, type in the program again.

To trace program execution, we must add the *trace* compiler directive to the beginning of the program so that the program begins

```
trace
predicates
        hello
goal
        hello.
        ...
```

Now select the **R**un command and notice what happens on the screen. In the editor window the cursor flashes at the end of the goal *hello*, and in the trace window, the start of execution of this goal is shown as

```
CALL:  goal()
```

F10 can now be used to execute this goal in single step mode. Press F10 once and the trace window will now show

```
CALL: hello()
```

to record that the goal should satisfy the predicate *hello*. Another press moves the cursor on to the definition of *hello*. Press again and notice in the trace window that we have now CALLed the *makewindow* predicate. Another press causes the *makewindow* predicate to be executed, which is displayed in the trace window as

```
RETURN: makewindow(1,7,7,"My first program",4,56,10,22)
```

Notice that the window is drawn at the top right of the screen.

Now press F10 repeatedly and watch what happens in each window, until the trace window displays

```
CALL: readln(_)
```

Press F10 again. The cursor should now be flashing at the place in our execution window where we are to type a name. Type TOM, then press ↵. The trace window now shows

```
RETURN: readln("TOM")
```

Finally, press F10 repeatedly until the trace window shows

```
RETURN: hello()
RETURN: goal()
```

at which point execution of our program has finished. Press F10 one final time and the system instructs you to press the space bar to return to the main menu level.

ALTERING THE DEFAULT WINDOW SETUP

Turbo Prolog provides four windows—four views on the programming environment:

- The *editor* window
- The *dialog* window
- The *trace* window
- The *message* window

These windows can be used in any configuration, and any window can take up the entire screen or only a small part of it. At any time, you can switch your point of view and reconfigure a window's size and position. The size of the four system windows can be changed either during a program's execution by giving a **S**etup command, or permanently, so that each time the system is booted, your own preferred window layout is used.

While any window is active, it is possible to toggle the window size between its current size and the full screen by pressing Ctrl F10.

Temporary Changes to Windows

Remove the *trace* compiler directive from the example program, run the result but don't reply when asked to type in a name. Instead, press ⇧ F9 repeatedly and observe that each system window is highlighted in turn.

Highlight the message window. Now try out the effect of the arrow keys and make the window as near a square in shape as possible. Repeat this for the other three system windows so that they are all square. Next, select any window, then use the arrow keys while holding down the ⇧ key to move the window around the screen. Reposition the system windows so that they appear in these positions:

```
MESSAGE        TRACE

EDITOR         DIALOG
```

Let's assume these are where you want to put the system windows. To resume execution of the program, press the space bar and type in your name as requested.

After the program has executed, control returns to the main system and the reorganized window display remains (until new changes are made, or the system is rebooted). To verify this, use the editor to alter the first *write* so that it reads

```
write("  What is   your name")
```

and re-run the program.

Select **W**indow from the **S**etup menu to restore the system windows to roughly their former positions. Select each window in turn and, having done so, use the ⇧ and arrow keys to re-size and move the windows.

Saving a Window Layout

Select **S**ave from the **S**etup menu to record a window layout in a disk file. By default, this file is called PROLOG.SYS and if changes are saved in this file, the new window formats will be used whenever the system is booted.

To avoid erasing the supplied defaults or to keep several window configurations filed away, the new settings should be saved under a different name, for example WINDOWS1.SYS. To use a different layout, select **L**oad from the **S**etup window.

3 Tutorial I: Five Simple Programs

This is the first of eight chapters giving a step-by-step tutorial introduction to the Turbo Prolog language. It begins with a study of the structure of a Turbo Prolog program, first by means of a simple example and then by examining the fundamental components of a program, one by one. In every case, our starting point will be a motivating example with the threads drawn together a little more formally at the end of the chapter. (Chapters 11 and 12 contain very precise definitions of all Turbo Prolog features. At this stage in the tutorial it's getting started that matters.)

Apart from program structure, the two other important ideas introduced in this chapter are *backtracking* (which is how Prolog searches for all possible solutions to a goal) and how to make Prolog check if something is *not* true—at least as far as the available information makes it possible to determine.

THE STRUCTURE OF A TURBO PROLOG PROGRAM

Consider the following example program:

```
                /* Program 1 */

domains
    person, activity = symbol

predicates
    likes(person,activity)

clauses
    likes(ellen,tennis).
    likes(john,football).
    likes(tom,baseball).
    likes(eric,swimming).
    likes(mark,tennis).
    likes(bill,X) if likes(tom,X).
```

The `clauses` section contains a collection of facts and rules. The *facts*

```
likes(ellen,tennis).
likes(john,football).
likes(tom,baseball).
likes(eric,swimming).
likes(mark,tennis).
```

correspond to these statements in English:

ellen likes tennis.
john likes football.
tom likes baseball.
eric likes swimming.
mark likes tennis.

Notice that there is no information in these facts about whether or not

```
likes(bill,baseball).
```

To use Prolog to discover if bill likes baseball, we can execute the above Prolog program with

```
likes(bill,baseball).
```

as our *goal*. When attempting to satisfy this goal, the Prolog system will use the *rule*

```
likes(bill,X) if likes(tom,X).
```

In ordinary English, this rule corresponds to:

bill likes X if tom likes X.

Type the above program into your computer following the method outlined in Chapter 2 and **R**un it. When the system responds in the dialog window,

```
                    Goal :_
```

enter

```
                    likes(bill,baseball).
```

Turbo Prolog replies

```
True
Goal :_
```

in the dialog window and waits for you to give another goal. Turbo Prolog has combined the rule

```
likes(bill,X) if likes(tom,X)
```

with the fact

```
likes(tom,baseball)
```

to decide that

```
likes(bill,baseball)
```

is true. Now enter the new goal

```
likes(bill,tennis).
```

The system replies

```
False
Goal :_
```

since there is neither a fact that says bill likes tennis nor can this be deduced using the rule and the available facts. Of course it may be that bill absolutely adores tennis in real life, but Turbo Prolog's response is based only upon the facts and the rules you have given it in the program.

Variables

In the rule

```
likes(bill,X) if likes(tom,X).
```

we have used the letter X as a *variable* to indicate an unknown activity. Variable names in Turbo Prolog *must* begin with a capital letter, after which any number of letters (upper or lowercase), digits, or underline characters ("_") may be used. Thus the following two names

```
My_first_correct_variable_name
Sales_10_11_86
```

are valid, whereas the next three

```
1stattempt
second_attempt
'disaster
```

are invalid.

Careful choice of variable names makes programs more readable. For example,

```
likes(Individual,tennis).
```

is preferable to

```
likes(I,tennis).
```

Now type the goal

```
likes(Individual,tennis).
```

Turbo Prolog replies

```
Individual = ellen
Individual = mark
2 Solutions
Goal :_
```

because the goal can be solved in just two ways, namely by successively taking the variable *Individual* to have the values *ellen* and *mark*.

Note that, except for the first character of variable names, Turbo Prolog does not otherwise distinguish between upper and lowercase letters. Thus, you can also make variable names more readable by using mixed upper and lowercase letters as in:

```
IncomeAndExpenditureAccount
```

Objects and Relations

In Turbo Prolog, each fact given in the `clauses` section of a program consists of a *relation* which affects one or more *objects*. Thus in

```
likes(tom,baseball)
```

the relation is *likes* and the objects are *tom* and *baseball*. You are free to choose names for the relations and objects you want to use, subject to the following constraints:

- Names of objects must begin with a lowercase letter followed by any number of characters (letters, digits and underscore ["_"]).
- Names of relations can be any combination of letters, digits and underscore characters.

Thus

```
owns(susan,horse).
eats(jill,meat).
valuable(gold).
car(mercedes,blue,station_wagon).
```

are valid Turbo Prolog facts corresponding to the following facts expressed in ordinary English:

susan owns a horse
jill eats meat
gold is valuable
the car is a blue mercedes station wagon

(Notice that a relation can involve one, two, three, or more objects). You may be wondering how Turbo Prolog knows that *susan owns a horse* rather than *the horse owns susan*; we'll discuss this in the next chapter.

Exercise Write the following facts and rules in a form acceptable to Turbo Prolog:

ellen likes reading
john likes computers
eric likes swimming
david likes computers
marybeth likes X if john likes X
gina likes anything eric likes

Domains and Predicates

In a Turbo Prolog program, you must specify the domains to which objects in a relation may belong. Thus, in our example above, the statements

```
domains
    person, activity = symbol
predicates
    likes(person,activity)
```

specify that the relation *likes* involves two objects, both of which belong to a `symbol` domain (names rather than numbers).

Enter the following goal:

```
likes(12,X).
```

The system responds

```
type error
```

and places the cursor on the error (under the 12) indicating that the number 12 cannot be invoked in the relation *likes* since 12 does not belong to a symbol domain.

Similarly,

```
likes(bill,tom,baseball).
```

will give an error (try it!). Even though we can deduce from Program 1 that bill and tom both like baseball, Turbo Prolog does not allow us to express the fact in this way once the *likes* relation has been defined to take just two arguments.

To further illustrate how domains can be used, consider the following program example:

```
        /* Program 2 */

domains
    brand, color  = symbol
    age, price    = integer
    mileage       = real

predicates
    car(brand,mileage,age,color,price)

clauses
    car(chrysler,130000,3,red,12000).
    car(ford,90000,4,gray,25000).
    car(datsun,8000,1,red,30000).
```

Here, the predicate *car* (which is the blueprint for all the *car* relations) has objects that belong to the *age* and *price* domains, which are of integer type, i.e., they must be numbers between −32,768 and +32,767. Similarly, the domain *mileage* is of real type, i.e., numbers outside the range of integers and possibly containing a decimal point.

Erase the program about who likes whom using the method described in Chapter 2. Type in Program 2 and try each of the following goals in turn:

```
car(renault,13,3.5,red,12000).
car(ford,90000,gray,4,25000).
car(1,red,30000,80000,datsun).
```

Each of them produces a domain error. In the first case, for example, it's because *age* must be an integer. Hence, Turbo Prolog can easily detect if someone types in this goal and has reversed the *mileage* and *age* objects in predicate *car*.

By way of contrast, try the goal:

```
car(Make, Odometer, Years_on_road, Body, 25000).
```

which attempts to find a car in the database costing $25000. Turbo Prolog replies

Compound Goals

The last goal above is slightly unnatural, since we'd rather ask a question like:

```
is there a car in the database costing less than $25000?
```

We can get Turbo Prolog to search for a solution to such a query by setting the *compound goal*

```
car(Make,Odometer,Years_on_road,Body,Cost) and Cost < 25000.
```

To fulfill this compound goal, Turbo Prolog will try to solve the subgoal

```
car(Make,Odometer,Years_on_road,Body,Cost)
```

and the subgoal

```
Cost < 25000
```

with the variable *Cost* referring to the same value. Try it out now.

The subgoal

```
Cost < 25000
```

involves the relation < (less than) which is already built into the Turbo Prolog system. In effect, it is no different from any other relation involving two numeric objects, but it is more natural to put the < between the two objects rather than in the strange looking form

```
< (Cost,25000).
```

which more closely resembles relations similar to

```
likes(tom,tennis).
```

Compound goals may also be disjunctions; for example:

```
is there a car in the datbase costing less than $25000
or is there a truck costing less than $20000?
```

To get Turbo Prolog to search for the solution, we can set the compound goal

```
car(Make,Odometer,Years_on_road, Body,Cost)and
cost < 25000 or
truck(Make,Odometer,Years_on_road,Body,Cost)and
cost < 20000
```

To fulfill this compound goal, Turbo Prolog will try to solve the subgoal

```
car(Make,Odometer,Years_on_road,Body,Cost)
```

and the subgoal

```
cost < 25000
```

If a car is found, the goal will succeed; if not, Turbo Prolog will try to fulfill the following compound goal

```
truck(Make,Odometer,Years_on_road,Body,Cost)
```

and the subgoal

```
cost < 20000
```

Anonymous Variables

For some people, cost and age are the two most important factors to consider when buying a car. It's unnecessary, then, to give names to the variables corresponding to brand, mileage, and color in a goal, the settings of which we don't really care about. But according to its definition in Program 2, the predicate *car* must involve five objects, so we must have five variables. Fortunately, we don't have to bother giving them all names. We can use the *anonymous variable* which is written as a single underline symbol ("_"). Try out the goal

```
car(_,_,Age,_,Cost) and Cost < 27000.
```

Turbo Prolog replies

```
Age = 3, Cost = 12000
Age = 4, Cost = 25000
2 Solutions
Goal :_
```

The anonymous variable can be used where any other variable could be used, but it never really gets set to a particular value. For example, in the goal above, Turbo Prolog realizes that "_", in each of its three uses in the goal, signifies a variable in which we're not interested. In this case, it finds two cars costing less than $27000; one three years old, the other four years old.

Anonymous variables can also be used in facts. Thus, the Turbo Prolog facts

```
owns(_,shirt).
washes(_).
```

could be used to express the English statements

everyone owns a shirt
everyone washes

Finding Solutions in Compound Goals—Backtracking

Consider Program 3, which contains facts about the names and ages of some of the pupils in a class.

```
                /* Program 3 */

domains
    child = symbol
    age   = integer

predicates
    pupil(child,age)

clauses
    pupil(peter,9).
    pupil(paul,10).
    pupil(chris,9).
    pupil(susan,9).
```

Delete Program 2 and type in Program 3. We'll use Turbo Prolog to arrange a ping-pong tournament between the nine-year-olds in the class (two games for each pair).

Our aim is to find all possible pairs of students who are nine years old. This can be achieved with the compound goal

```
pupil(Person1,9)  and
pupil(Person2,9)  and
Person1 <> Person2.
```

(In English: Find *Person1* aged 9 and *Person2* aged 9 so that *Person1* and *Person2* are different).

Turbo Prolog will try to find a solution to the first subgoal and continue to the next subgoal only after the first subgoal is reached. The first subgoal is satisfied by taking *Person1* to be *peter*. Now Turbo Prolog can satisfy

```
pupil(Person2,9)
```

by also taking *Person2* to be *peter*. Now we come to the third and final subgoal

```
Person1 <> Person2
```

Since *Person1* and *Person2* are both *peter*, this subgoal fails, so Turbo Prolog *backtracks* to the previous subgoal. It then searches for another solution to the second subgoal

```
pupil(Person2,9)
```

which is fulfilled by taking *Person2* to be *chris*. Now, the third subgoal

```
Person1 <> Person2
```

is satisfied, since *peter* and *chris* are different, and hence the entire goal is satisfied. However, since Turbo Prolog must find all possible solutions to a goal, once again it backtracks to the previous goal hoping to succeed again. Since

```
pupil(Person2,9)
```

can also be satisfied by taking Person2 to be *susan*, Turbo Prolog tries the third subgoal once again. It succeeds since *peter* and *susan* are different, so another solution to the entire goal has been found.

Searching for more solutions, Turbo Prolog once again backtracks to the second subgoal. But all possibilities have been exhausted for this subgoal now, so backtracking continues to the first subgoal. This can be satisfied afresh by taking *Person1* to be *chris*. The second subgoal now succeeds by taking *Person2* to be *peter*, so the third subgoal is satisfied, fulfilling the entire goal.

The final solution is with *Person1* and *Person2* as *susan*. Since this causes the final subgoal to fail, Turbo Prolog must backtrack to the second subgoal, but there are no new possibilities. Hence, Turbo Prolog backtracks to the first subgoal. But the possibilities for *Person1* have also been exhausted and execution terminates.

Type in the above compound goal for Program 3 and verify that Turbo Prolog responds with

```
Person1=peter, Person2=chris
Person1=peter, Person2=susan
Person1=chris, Person2=peter
Person1=chris, Person2=susan
Person1=susan, Person2=peter
Person1=susan, Person2=chris
6 Solutions
Goal :_
```

Figure 3-1 illustrates how Turbo Prolog backtracks to satisfy a goal.

```
pupil(Person1,9) and pupil(Person(2,9) and Person1<>Person2
        |                    |                |        |
      peter                peter            peter    peter   FAILS

pupil(peter,9)     pupil(peter,9)
pupil(paul,10)     pupil(paul,10)
pupil(chris,9)     pupil(chris,9)
pupil(susan,9)     pupil(susan,9)
                                        No (more) possible choices here so
                                        BACKTRACK

pupil(Person1,9) and pupil(Person2,9) and Person1<>Person2
        |                    |               |        |
      peter                chris           peter    chris    SUCCEEDS

pupil(peter,9)     pupil(peter,9)
pupil(paul,10)     pupil(paul,10)
pupil(chris,9)     pupil(chris,9)
pupil(susan,9)     pupil(susan,9)
                                        No (more) possible choices here so
                                        BACKTRACK

pupil(Person1,9) and pupil(Person2,9) and Person1<>Person2
        |                    |               |        |
      peter                susan           peter    susan    SUCCEEDS

pupil(peter,9)     pupil(peter,9)
pupil(paul,10)     pupil(paul,10)
pupil(chris,9)     pupil(chris,9)
pupil(susan,9)     pupil(susan,9)
                                        No (more) possible choices here so
                                        BACKTRACK
                    No (more) possible choices here so
                   BACKTRACK

pupil(Person1,9) and pupil(Person2,9) and Person1<>Person2
        |                    |               |        |
      chris                peter           chris    peter    SUCCEEDS

pupil(peter,9)     pupil(peter,9)
pupil(paul,10)     pupil(paul,10)
pupil(chris,9)     pupil(chris,9)
pupil(susan,9)     pupil(susan,9)
                                        No (more) possible choices here so
                                        BACKTRACK
```

Figure 3-1 Backtracking

Exercise Decide what Turbo Prolog's reply to the goal

```
pupil(Person1,9) and pupil(Person2,10).
```

will be, then check your answer by typing in the exercise.

Turbo Prolog the Matchmaker: Using `Not`

Suppose we want to write a small-scale computer dating program containing a list of registered males, a list of who smokes, and the rule that sophie is looking for a man who is either a non-smoker or a vegetarian. The occurrence of `or` in sophie's selection rule indicates that we can use more than one Turbo Prolog rule to express it:

```
sophie could date(X) if male(X) and not(smoker(X)).
sophie could date(X) if male(X) and vegetarian(X).
```

These rules are used in Program 4, which you should now type into your computer.

```
            /* Program 4 */
domains
    person = symbol

predicates
    male(person)
    smoker(person)
    vegetarian(person)
    sophie_could_date(person)

goal
    sophie_could_date(X) and
    write("a possible date for sophie is ",X) and nl.

clauses
    male(joshua).
    male(bill).
    male(tom).
    smoker(guiseppe).
    smoker(tom).
    vegetarian(joshua).
    vegetarian(tom).
    sophie_could_date(X) if male(X) and not(smoker(X)).
    sophie_could_date(X) if male(X) and vegetarian(X).
```

Apart from the use of two rules (Turbo Prolog lets you use as many as you please), there are several other novel features in this example. First, notice the use of `not` as in

```
not(smoker(X))
```

Turbo Prolog will evaluate this as true if it is unable to prove smoker(X) is true. Using `not` in this way is straightforward, but it must be remembered that Turbo Prolog cannot, for example, assume automatically that someone is either a smoker or a non-smoker. This sort of information must be explicitly built into our facts and rules. Thus, in Program 4, the first clause for *sophie_could_date* assumes that any male not known to be a smoker is a non-smoker.

Second, notice the incorporation of a goal within the program. Every time we execute our mini computer-dating program, it will be with the same goal in mind—to find a list of possible dates for sophie—so Turbo Prolog allows us to include this goal within the program. However, we must then include the standard predicate

```
write(..........)
```

so that the settings (if any) of the variable X which satisfy the goal are displayed on the screen. We must also include the standard predicate

```
nl
```

which simply causes a new line to be printed.

Standard predicates are predicates that are built into the Turbo Prolog system. Generally, they make functions available that cannot be achieved with normal Turbo Prolog clauses, and are often used just for their side-effects (like reading keyboard input or screen displays) rather than for their truth value.

Execute Program 4 and verify that Turbo Prolog displays

```
a possible date for sophie is joshua
```

Surprisingly, even though tom (being male and a vegetarian), would be eligible for a date, if we include a goal in the program, only the *first* solution is found. To find all solutions, try deleting the goal from the program, then give the goal in response to Turbo Prolog's prompt during execution (as we did earlier). This time all possible dates will be displayed. Even if the goal is internal (i.e., written into the program), it is possible for all solutions to be displayed; see Chapter 5.

Comments

It is good programming style to include comments that explain different aspects of the program. This makes your program easy to understand for both you and others. If you choose good names for variables, predicates, and domains, you'll be able to get away with fewer comments, since your program will be more self-explanatory.

Comments in Turbo Prolog must begin with the characters /* (slash, asterisk) and end with the characters */. Whatever is written in between is ignored by the Turbo Prolog compiler. If you forget to close with */, a section of your program will be unintentionally considered as a comment. Turbo Prolog will give you an error message if you forget to close a comment.

```
/* This is an example of a comment */

/***********************************/
/* and so are these three lines    */
/***********************************/
```

A More Substantial Program Example

Program 5 is a family relationships database that has been heavily commented.

```
              /* Program 5 */
domains
    person = symbol

predicates
```

```
    male(person)
    female(person)
    father(person,person)
    mother(person,person)
    parent(person,person)
    sister(person,person)
    brother(person,person)
    uncle(person,person)
    grandfather(person,person)

clauses
    male(alan).
    male(charles).
    male(bob).
    male(ivan).

    female(beverly).
    female(fay).
    female(marilyn).
    female(sally).

    mother(marilyn,beverly).
    mother(alan,sally).

    father(alan,bob)
    father(beverly,charles).
    father(fay,bob).
    father(marilyn,alan).

    parent(X,Y) if mother(X,Y).
    parent(X,Y) if father(X,Y).

    brother(X,Y) if         /*The brother of X is Y if  */
        male(Y) and         /*Y is a male and           */
        parent(X,P) and     /*the parent of X is P and  */
        parent(Y,P) and     /*the parent of Y is P and  */
        X <> Y.             /* X and Y are not the same */

    sister(X,Y) if          /*The sister of X is Y if   */
        female(Y) and       /*Y is female and           */
        parent(X,P) and     /*the parent of X is P and  */
        parent(Y,P) and     /*the parent of Y is P and  */
        X <> Y.             /*X and Y are not the same  */

    uncle(X,U) if           /*The uncle of X is U if    */
        mother(X,P) and     /*the mother of X is P and  */
        brother(P,U).       /*the brother of P is U.    */
    uncle(X,U) if           /*The uncle of X is U if    */
        father(X,P) and     /*the father of X is P and  */
        brother(P,U).       /*the brother of P is U     */

    grandfather(X,G) if     /*The grandfather of X is G */
        father(P,G) and     /*if the father of P is G   */
        mother(X,P).        /*and the mother of X is P. */
    grandfather(X,G) if     /*The grandfather of X is G */
        father(X,P) and     /*if the father of X is P   */
        father(P,G).        /*and the father of P is G  */
```

Type and execute this program and, by formulating appropriate goals, use Turbo Prolog to answer the following questions:

1. Is alan ivan's brother?
2. Who is marilyn's grandfather?
3. Who is fay's sister?
4. What is the relationship (if any) between marilyn and beverly?

The relations *uncle* and *grandfather* are both described by two clauses, though only one is necessary. Try to rewrite *uncle* and *grandfather* using one clause for each.

Summary

A Turbo Prolog program has the following basic structure:

```
domains
        /*... domain statements     ... */

predicates
        /*... predicate statements ... */

goal
        /*... subgoal_1, subgoal_2, etc. */

clauses
        /*... clauses (rules and facts) ... */
```

If you don't include a goal in the program, Turbo Prolog will ask for a goal when the program is executed.

Facts have the general form:

```
relation(object,object,...,object)
```

Rules have the general form

```
relation(object,object,...,object) if
relation(object,...,object) and
.
.
relation(object,...,object).
```

To be consistent with other versions of Prolog, `if` can be replaced by the symbol `:-`, and a comma (,) can be used instead of `and`, and a semicolon (;) can be used instead of `or`.

Thus

```
is_older(Person1,Person2) if
            age(Person1,Age1) and
            age(Person2,Age2) and
            Age1 > Age2.
```

and

```
is_older(Person1,Person2) :-
            age(Person1,Age1),
```

```
            age(Person2,Age2),
            Age1 > Age2.
```

are exactly equivalent.

A *predicate* consists of one or more *clauses*. Clauses that belong to the same predicate must follow one another.

Exercise Use Turbo Prolog to construct a small thesaurus. You should store facts like

```
similar_meaning(big,gigantic).
similar_meaning(big,enormous).
similar_meaning(big,tall).
similar_meaning(big,huge).
similar_meaning(happy,cheerful).
similar_meaning(happy,gay).
similar_meaning(happy,contented).
```

so that a goal of the form

```
similar_meaning(big,X)
```

would cause Turbo Prolog to display a list of alternative words for *big*.

Exercise Given the following facts and rules about a murder mystery, can you use Turbo Prolog to find who dunnit?

```
        person( allan,   25, m, football_player).
        person( allan,   25, m, butcher        ).
        person( barbara,22, f, hairdresser     ).
        person( bert,    55, m, carpenter      ).
        person( john,    25, m, pickpocket     ).

        had_affair( barbara, john ).
        had_affair( barbara, bert ).
        had_affair( susan,   john ).

        killed_with( susan, club ).

        motive( money ).
        motive( jealousy ).

        smeared_in( catherine, blood ).
        smeared_in( allan, mud       ).

        owns( bert, wooden_leg ).
        owns( john, pistol     ).

/* Background-knowledge */
        operates_identically( wooden_leg,        club ).
        operates_identically( bar,               club ).
        operates_identically( pair_of_scissors, knife).
        operates identically( football_boot, club ).

        owns_probably(X,football_boot) if
             person(X,_,_,football_player).
        owns_probably(X,pair_of_scissors) if
             person(X,_,_,hairdresser).
        owns_probably(X,Object) if
             owns(X,Object).
```

```
/*  Suspect all those who own a weapon with which susan could
    possibly have been killed */
        suspect(X) if
                        killed_with(susan,Weapon) and
                        operates_identically(Object,Weapon) and
                        owns_probably(X,Object).

/* Suspect men that have had an affair with susan */
        suspect(X) if
                        motive(jealousy) and
                        person(X,_,m,_) and
                        had_affair(susan,X).

/* Suspect females who have had an affair with a man susan knew*/
        suspect(X) if
                        motive(jealousy) and
                        person(X,_,f,_) and
                        had_affair(X,Man) and
                        had_affair(susan,Man).

/* Suspect pickpockets whose motive could be money*/
        suspect(X) if
                        motive(money) and person(X,_,_,pickpocket).
```

4 Tutorial II: A Closer Look at Domains, Objects and Lists

This chapter will familiarize you with many of the Turbo Prolog features you'll be using the most. We introduce the concepts of free and bound variables, standard domain types, and compound objects. You'll learn how to use recursion in your programs, and see how to take advantage of Turbo Prolog's extensive list-handling facilities.

If a Turbo Prolog variable has a known value, we say it is *bound* to that value and that otherwise it is *free*. This chapter begins by considering the bindings of variables during the evaluation of a goal.

Bound variables have values from a domain which is either itself of standard type or is a user-defined domain built up from one or more such domains. In the second part of this chapter, we study domains in some detail and learn how to build compound domains including those which allow lists of objects to be regarded as a single entity.

Just as lists are one of Turbo Prolog's most important data structures, the most important Prolog programming technique is *recursion*; in particular, recursion allows us to process the elements of a list. This chapter concludes with several examples showing the use of recursion.

FREE AND BOUND VARIABLES

Turbo Prolog distinguishes between two types of variables:

- *Free* variable—Turbo Prolog does not know its value
- *Bound* variable—a known value

Look at Program 6, and consider how Turbo Prolog will solve the following compound goal:

```
likes(X,reading) and likes(X,swimming).
```

```
                          /* Program 6 */
domains
        person, hobby = symbol
predicates
        likes(person,hobby)
clauses
        likes(ellen,reading).
        likes(john,computers).
        likes(john,badminton).
        likes(leonard,badminton).
        likes(eric,swimming).
        likes(eric,reading).
```

Turbo Prolog searches from left to right. In the first subgoal

```
likes(X,reading)
```

the variable X is *free* (its value is unknown before Turbo Prolog attempts to satisfy the subgoal) but, on the other hand, the second argument, *reading*, is known. Turbo Prolog will now search for a fact that can fulfill the demands in the subgoal.

The first fact is a match, so the free variable X will be bound to the relevant value in the first fact, *ellen*.

```
likes(ellen,reading).
```

At the same time, Turbo Prolog places a *pointer* in the database indicating how far down the search procedure has reached.

Next, the second subgoal must be fulfilled. Since X is now bound to *ellen*, Turbo Prolog has to search for the "fact"

```
likes(ellen,swimming).
```

Turbo Prolog searches from the beginning of the database, but in vain. Thus, the second subgoal is false when X is *ellen*.

Turbo Prolog now attempts another solution of the first subgoal with X free once again. The search for a second fact that can fulfill the first subgoal starts from the place last marked (provided there are more untested possibilities).

The skill to bind variables and set them free again when backtracking and the use of pointers to mark backtracking points are substantial elements in Prolog's search strategies. Now let's take a closer look at the most fundamental element in a program—the object—and the different forms it can take.

TURBO PROLOG'S STANDARD DOMAIN TYPES

Turbo Prolog can deal with six standard domain types, as shown in Table 4-1.

Table 4-1 Standard Domain Types

char	character enclosed between two single quotation marks (e.g. 'a').
integer	integers from −32,768 to 32,767.
real	numbers with an optional sign followed by some digits; then (optionally) a decimal point (.) followed by some digits for the fractional part; and finally an optional exponential part—for example, an e followed by an optional sign and an exponent. Following are examples of real numbers: 42705 −9999 86.72 −9111.929437 −521e238 64e−94 −79.83e+21 The permitted number range is ±1e−307 to ±1e+308. Integers are automatically converted to real numbers when necessary.
string	Any sequence of characters written between a pair of double quotation marks, e.g. `"jonathan mark's book"`
symbol	Two formats are permitted for symbols: (1) a sequence of letters, numbers and underscores, provided the first character is lowercase; or (2) a character sequence surrounded by a pair of double quotation marks (this is used in the case of symbols containing spaces, or if a symbol does not start with a lowercase letter). Following are examples of strings: telephone_number "railway_ticket" "Dorid_Inc" Symbols and strings can be used interchangeably, but they are handled differently internally. Symbols are kept in a lookup table, which results in a very quick matching procedure during a search. The disadvantage is that the symbol table takes up room and the insertion takes time. You must determine which domain will offer the best performance in a given program.
file	The file domain type is described in Chapter 9, "The Turbo Prolog File System."
dbasedom	Any database atom (see Chapter 11, "Dynamic Databases in Turbo Prolog").

Let's look at some more examples of objects that belong to domains of standard type.

Table 4-2 Simple Objects

swift, abc, kenneth, "animal lover"	(symbol)
−1 , 3, 5, 0	(integer)
3.45 , 0.01 , −30.5, 123.4e+5	(real)
'a', 'b', 'c' , '/', '&'	(char)
"One two", "name number 5", "&&"	(string)

Objects belonging to character and string domains, and that contain a \ (backslash) have a special meaning:

\Number	a character with the ASCII value *Number*
\n	Newline character
\t	Tabulate character

Thus, the three objects below

```
write('\10')
write('\n')
nl
```

will cause a newline to be displayed.

We will now work out some predicate declarations using these standard domains. If standard domains are the only domains in the predicate declarations, the program need not have a `domains` section. For example, suppose we wish to define a predicate so that a goal similar to

```
alphabet_position(A_character,N)
```

will be true if A_character is the Nth letter in the alphabet. Clauses for this predicate would look like

```
alphabet_position('a',1).
alphabet_position('b',2).
alphabet_position('c',3).
alphabet_position('z',25).
```

The predicate can be declared as follows:

```
predicates
        alphabet_position(char, integer)
```

and there is no need for a `domains` section.

As another example, suppose we wish to declare a predicate that can be used in connection with addition. Thus, we need a predicate such that in the following goal

```
add(X,Y,Z).
```

the arguments are the two numbers to be added and the number that represents the total, corresponding to the equation

```
X + Y = Z
```

Consequently, the `predicates` declaration must stipulate that *add* needs three numeric arguments, and it must describe the types of domain to which they belong:

```
add(integer,integer,integer)
```

or

```
add(real,real,real)
```

If both predicate declarations are used, the predicate *add* can be used for both integers and real numbers. This is due to the fact that Turbo Prolog permits *multiple predicate declarations*. In multiple declarations of the same predicate, the declarations must be given one after the other and they must all have the same number of arguments.

Program 7 is a complete Turbo Prolog program that functions as a mini telephone directory that uses the standard predicates *readln* and *write*. The `domains` section has been omitted, since only standard domains are used. The program asks for a name to be typed in. When the name is entered, the corresponding telephone number is found from the database and displayed on the screen.

```
              /* Program 7 */
predicates
        reference(symbol,symbol)
goal
        write("Please type a name :"),
        readln(The_Name),
        reference(The_Name,Phone_No),
        write("The phone number is ",Phone_No),nl.
clauses
        reference("Albert",  "01-123456").
        reference("Betty",   "01-569767").
        reference("Carol",   "01-267400").
        reference("Dorothy","01-191051").
```

Exercise Type in Program 7 and leave out the goal, then try each of these goals in turn.

```
(1)    reference("Carol",Y).
(2)    reference(X,"01-191951").
(3)    reference("Mavis",Y).
(4)    reference(X,Y).
```

Kim shares a flat with Dorothy and so has the same phone number. Add this information to the clauses for the predicate *reference* and try the goal

```
reference(X,"01-191051").
```

to check your addition.

Finally, to illustrate the char domain type, Program 8 defines *isletter* which, when given the goals

```
isletter('%').
isletter('Q').
```

will return false and true respectively.

```
              /* Program 8 */
predicates
        isletter(char)
clauses
        isletter(Ch) if Ch <= 'z' and 'a' <= Ch.
        isletter(Ch) if Ch <= 'Z' and 'A' <= Ch.
```

Type Program 8 and try each of these goals in turn.

```
(1)    isletter('x').
(2)    isletter('2').
(3)    isletter("hello").
(4)    isletter(a).
(5)    isletter(X).
```

(3) and (4) will result in a TYPE ERROR message. (5) will return an UNBOUND VARIABLE message.

COMPOUND OBJECTS CAN SIMPLIFY YOUR CLAUSES!

Turbo Prolog allows you to make objects that contain other objects. These are called *compound objects*. Compound objects can be regarded and treated as a single object, which greatly simplifies programming.

Consider, for example, the fact

```
owns(john,book("From Here to Eternity","James Jones")).
```

in which we state that john owns the book *From Here to Eternity*, which was written by *James Jones*. Likewise, we could write

```
owns(john,horse(blacky)).
```

which can be interpreted as: john owns a horse by the name of blacky. The compound objects in these two examples are

```
book("From Here to Eternity","James Jones")
```

and

```
horse(blacky)
```

If we had instead written two facts

```
owns( john, "From Here to Eternity").
owns( john, blacky ).
```

we would not have been able to decide whether *blacky* was the title of a book or the name of a horse. On the other hand, the first component of a compound object, the *functor*, is used to distinguish between different objects. In the example above, we made use of the functors *book* and *horse* to indicate the difference.

Compound objects consist of a functor and the sub-objects belonging to it:

```
functor(object1,object2, ... objectN)
```

A functor without objects is written as

```
functor()
```

or just

```
functor
```

Domain Declaration of Compound Objects

We will now look at how domains for compound objects are defined. In the subgoal

```
owns(john,X)
```

the variable *X* can be bound to different types of objects, either a book, a horse, or perhaps other types of objects. Because of this, we can no longer employ the old definition of the *owns* predicate

```
owns(symbol,symbol)
```

where the second argument has to refer to objects belonging to a domain of symbol type. Instead, we use a new formulation of the predicate declaration:

```
owns(name,articles)
```

The articles can then be described with the domain declarations

```
domains
        articles = book(title,author) ; horse(name)
        title, author, name = symbol
```

The semicolon can be read as `or`. In this case, two alternatives are possible: a *book* can be identified by its *title* and *author*, and a *horse* can be identified by a *name*. The domains *title*, *author*, and *name* are all of symbol type.

More alternatives can easily be added to the domain declaration: *articles* could also include a *boat* or a *bankbook*, for example.

For *boat* we can make do with an object with a functor which has no objects. On the other hand, we wish to give the bank balance as a figure within *bankbook*. The **domains** declaration of *articles* is therefore extended to

```
articles=book(title,author);horse(name);boat;bankbook(integer)
```

Here are some examples of how compound objects from the domain *articles* can be used in some facts which define the predicate *owns*:

```
owns(john,book("A friend of the family","Irwin Shaw")).
owns(john,horse(blacky)).
owns(john,boat).
owns(john,bankbook(1000)).
```

With the goal

```
owns(john,Thing).
```

we will now receive the answers:

```
Thing = book("A friend of the family", "Irwin Shaw")
Thing = horse(blacky)
Thing = boat
Thing = bankbook(1000)
```

How domain declarations are written—a summary.

```
domain = alternative1(D,D,...); alternative2(D,D,...) ; ...
```

Here, *alternative1* and *alternative2* are arbitrary (but different) functors. The notation (D,D,...) represents a list of domain names that are either declared elsewhere, or are one of the standard domains symbol, integer, real, string, file, or char.

Notice:

1. The alternatives are separated by semicolons.
2. Every alternative consists of a functor, and possibly a list of domains for the corresponding objects.

Program 9 uses functors to move the cursor around the screen as a "side-effect" of the evaluation of goals. For example

```
move_cursor(4,9,up(2)).
```

moves the cursor up two lines from its starting position of row 4 and column 9 of the screen. It uses the built-in predicate

```
cursor(row,column)
```

to position the cursor at the specified row and column.

```
              /* Program 9 */
domains
       row, column, step = integer
       movement = up(step); down(step);
                  left(step) ; right(step)
predicates
       move_cursor(row,column,movement)
clauses
       move_cursor(R,C,up(Step)):-
                  cursor(R,C),R1=R-Step,cursor(R1,C).
       move_cursor(R,C,down(Step)):-
                  cursor(R,C),R1=R+Step,cursor(R1,C).
       move_cursor(R,C,left(step)):-
                  cursor(R,C),C1=C-Step,cursor(R,C1).
       move_cursor(R,C,right(step)):-
                  cursor(R,C),C1=C+Step,cursor(R,C1).
```

If we added the alternative *no*, a movement could also include "no step" as in move_cursor (R,C,no). Note that the functor *no* is sufficient to represent "no movement." No sub-objects are required.

Going Down a Level

Turbo Prolog allows you to construct compound objects on several levels. For example, in

```
book("The Ugly Duckling", "Andersen")
```

instead of using the author's surname, we could use a new structure that describes the author in more detail, including both the author's first name and surname. Calling the functor for the resulting new compound object *author*, the description of the book is changed to

```
book("The Ugly Duckling",author("Hans Christian","Andersen"))
```

In the old domain declaration

```
book(title,author)
```

we see that the second argument in the *book* functor is *author*. But the old declaration

```
author = symbol
```

can only include a single name which is therefore no longer sufficient. We must now specify that an *author* is also a compound object comprising the author's first name and surname. This is achieved with the domain statement:

```
author = author(firstname,surname)
```

which leads us to the following declarations:

```
domains
        articles = book(title,author) ; ...
        author   = author(firstname,surname)
        title, firstname, surname = symbol
```

When we use compound objects on different levels in this way, it is often helpful to draw a "tree":

```
          book
        /     \
title         author
             /      \
    firstname      surname
```

A domain statement describes only one level of the tree at a time and not the whole tree. For instance, a book cannot be defined with the following domain statement:

```
book = book(title,author(name,surname))
```

As another example, consider how to represent the grammatical structure of the sentence

"ellen owns the book"

using a compound object.

The most simple sentence structure consists of a *noun* and a *verbphrase*:

```
sentence = sentence(noun,verbphrase)
```

A *noun* is just a simple word:

```
noun = noun(word)
```

A *verbphrase* consists of either a *verb* and a *nounphrase* or a single *verb*.

```
verbphrase = verbphrase(verb,noun) ; verb(word)
verb       = verb(word)
```

Using these domain declarations (*sentence, noun, verbphrase* and *verb*), the sentence "ellen owns the book" becomes:

```
sentence(noun(ellen),verbphrase(verb(owns),noun(book)))
```

The corresponding tree is:

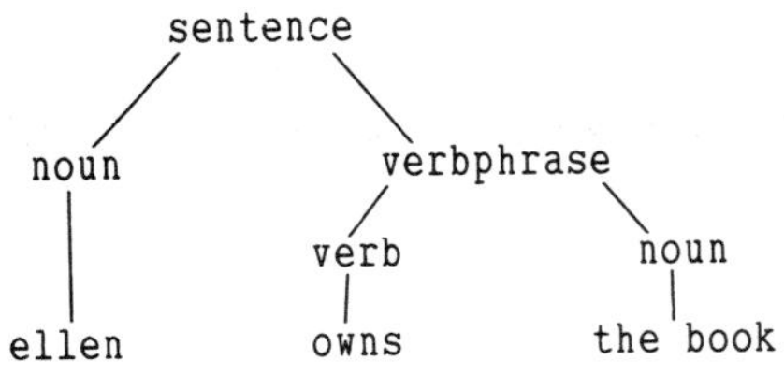

Exercise Write a suitable `domains` declaration using compound objects that could be used in a Turbo Prolog catalog of musical shows. A typical entry in the catalog might be:

Show: West Side Story
Lyrics: Stephen Sondheim
Music: Leonard Bernstein

Exercise Using compound objects wherever possible, write a Turbo Prolog program to keep a database of the current Top Ten hit records. Entries should include the name of the song, the name of the singer or group, its position in the Top Ten chart, and the number of weeks in the charts.

Recursion

Program 10 illustrates an important Turbo Prolog programming technique called *recursion*. Recursion is usually used in two situations:

- when relations are described with the help of the relations themselves
- when compound objects are a part of other compound objects (i.e., they are recursive objects)

The first situation occurs in Program 10. It gives a fact and a rule for the single predicate *factorial* which, when used in a goal like

```
factorial(N,F)
```

will return true if *F* is equal to *N*! i.e., if

```
F = N*(N-1)*(N-2)*...*3*2*1
```

Before we discuss how *factorial* works, type the program in and try out the following goals:

```
factorial(1,Answer).  /* goal 1 */
factorial(2,Answer).  /* goal 2 */
factorial(3,Answer).  /* goal 3 */
factorial(4,Answer).  /* goal 4 */
factorial(5,Answer).  /* goal 5 */
factorial(6,720).     /* goal 6 */
factorial(10,2000). /* goal 7 */
```

```
            /* Program 10 */
domains
      n = real
      f = real      /* REAL number used for answer so answers
                       greater than 32767 can be returned      */
predicates
      factorial(n,f)
clauses
      factorial(1,1).
      factorial(N,Res) if
            N > 1 and
            N1 = N-1 and
            factorial(N1,FacN1) and
            Res = N*FacN1.
```

In the program, N1=N−1 should be regarded as a more readable form of the clause:

```
=(N1,-(N,1))
```

where − is a functor. Thus N1=N−1 evaluates to true provided N1 is bound to the value of N−1.

Let's investigate how *factorial* works when satisfying the goal

```
factorial(2,Answer)
```

Using the rule, we have

```
factorial(2,Res) if
2>1,N1=2-1,factorial(N1,FacN1),Res=2*FacN1.
```

So we must evaluate the goal

```
factorial(1,FacN1).
```

Using the fact

```
factorial(1,1).
```

the goal is satisfied by binding *FacN1* to 1. In turn, we now need to evaluate

```
Res=2*FacN1
```

which is solved with *Res* bound to 2*1, so the initial goal is satisfied with *Answer* bound to 2.

For a more complicated evaluation like

```
factorial(4,Answer)
```

we have the evaluation sequence

```
factorial(4,Res) if
     4>1,N1=4-1,factorial(4-1,FacN1),Res=4*FacN1

factorial(3,FacN1) if
     3>1,N11=3-1,factorial(3-1,FacN11),Res=3*FacN11

factorial(2,FacN11) if
     2>1,N111=2-1,factorial(2-1,FacN111),Res=2*FacN111

factorial(2-1,FacN111) succeeds with FacN111 bound to 1

factorial(3-1,FacN11) succeeds with FacN11 bound to 2

factorial(4-1,FacN1) succeeds with FacN1 bound to 6

factorial(4,Res) succeeds with Res bound to 24
```

Hence, *factorial(4,Answer)* succeeds with *Answer* bound to 24.

```
goal : factorial(4,Answer)

calls: factorial(4,Res)

calls: factorial(4-1,FacN1), 4*FacN1

calls: factorial(4-1-1,FacN11),(4-1)*FacN11

calls: factorial(4-1-1-1,FacN111),(4-1-1)*FacN111

calls: factorial(1,1)
```

Figure 4-1 Evaluation of Factorial(4,Answer)

Exercise Add `domains` and `predicates` declarations to the following facts and rules:

```
factorial(X,Y) if newfactorial(0,1,X,Y).

newfactorial(X,Y,X,Y):-!.
newfactorial(U,V,X,Y) if
        U1=U+1,
        U1V=U1*V,
        newfactorial(U1,U1V,X,Y).
```

and try out the resulting program with the following goals:

```
1. factorial(3,Answer).
2. factorial(4,Answer).
3. factorial(5,Answer).
```

Using pencil and paper, trace the execution of the first goal.

Recursive Objects

Recursion can also be used to describe objects where the number of elements is not known in advance. Consider this problem: Which object can describe the names of all pupils in a school class, without us knowing the number of pupils in advance?

To solve this problem, let's formulate a corresponding `domains` declaration for the domain *classlist*, step by step. We start by describing an empty class with no students:

```
classlist = empty
```

Next, we formulate the recursive definition

```
classlist = class(name,classlist)
```

Thus, a typical object would be

```
class(peter,X)
```

which symbolizes a *classlist* with *peter* as the first member. *X* symbolizes a smaller *classlist* (without *peter*). Hence, a class consisting of two students could be described by

```
class(peter,class(james,empty))
```

and a class consisting of three students by

```
class(andrew,class(peter,class(james,empty)))
```

Note that

```
class(name,classlist)
```

is a compound object where the functor is *class*, *name* is one student in the class, and *classlist* contains the other students. The final, complete **domains** declaration consists of the two alternative definitions

```
classlist=class(name,classlist) ; empty
```

Likewise a series of numbers could, for instance, be defined by

```
integerlist = list(integer,integerlist) ; empty
```

Exercise Write the compound Turbo Prolog terms that describe the following list of numbers:

```
1,3,6,0,3
```

and draw the corresponding tree.

Exercise For the purposes of our Turbo Prolog programs, we wish to treat arithmetic expressions, such as 1+2−3, as objects. Much of this is accomplished by the **domains** declaration:

```
expr=plus(expr,expr) ; number(integer)
```

which gives such object possibilities as

```
plus(number(4),number(5))
```

corresponding to the arithmetic expression 4+5. The expression 1+2+3 could similarly be written as:

```
plus(number(1),plus(number(2),number(3)))
```

or

```
plus(plus(number(1),number(2)),number(3))
```

Append new alternatives to the above **domains** declaration so that objects that describe 2−4 or 2+3−log(5) are also permitted.

THE FASCINATING WORLDS OF LISTS AND RECURSION

Lists are the basic data structure in Turbo Prolog programs, corresponding roughly to Pascal's use of arrays. Because lists are so common, Turbo Prolog provides an easier way to represent them than as compound objects. A list that consists of the numbers 1, 2, and 3 can be written as

```
[ 1,2,3 ].
```

The elements of a list are separated by commas and enclosed by [and]. Here are some examples:

```
[dog,cat,canary]
["valerie ann","jonathan","michael"]
```

To declare a domain for lists of integers, we use a declaration such as

```
domains
      integerlist = integer*
```

where the asterisk indicates that there are 0 or more elements in a list.

The objects in a list can be anything, including other lists. However, all elements in a list must *belong to the same domain* and there must be a `domains` declaration for the objects that follow this form:

```
domains
      objectlist = objects*
      objects    = ....
```

Turbo Prolog processes a list by dividing it into two parts: the *head* and the *tail*. The head of the list [1,2,3] is the element 1. The tail of [1,2,3] is the list you get when you remove the head, namely [2,3].

Table 4-3 List Processing

List	Head	Tail
['a','b','c']	'a'	['b','c']
[1]	1	[] (an empty list)
[ ]	undefined	undefined
[[1,2,3],[2,3,4],[]]	[1,2,3]	[[2,3,4],[]]

Turbo Prolog uses a vertical bar (`|`) to separate the head and tail of a list. Hence, a list with head *X* and tail *Y* is written

```
[ X | Y ]
```

If Turbo Prolog tries to satisfy the goal

```
scores([X|Y])
```

and finds the fact

```
scores([0,1,0,2,6,0,0,1,2,3])
```

the variable *X* will be bound to the head of the list, i.e., to the integer 0, and *Y* will be bound to the tail of the list, i.e., the list

```
[1,0,2,6,0,0,1,2,3].
```

Table 4-4 gives several examples of list matching. Free variables are bound in the same way as *X* and *Y* in the previous example.

Table 4-4 List Matching

List 1	List 2	Variable Binding
[X,Y,Z]	[egbert,eats,icecream]	X=egbert,Y=eats,Z=icecream
[7]	[X | Y]	X=7, Y=[]
[1,2,3,4]	[X, Y | Z]	X=1, Y=2, Z=[3,4]
[1,2]	[3 | X]	The comparison fails, since the heads of the two lists differ.

Using Lists

In this and the following two sections, we'll examine some typical Turbo Prolog list-processing predicates.

List Membership

Suppose we have a list with the names

```
[john, leonard, eric, frank]
```

and would like to use Turbo Prolog to investigate if a given name is in the list. In other words, we must express the relation *member* between two objects—a name and a list of names—corresponding to the predicate statement

```
member(name,namelist).
```

In Program 11, the first clause investigates the head of the list. If the head is equal to the *Name* we are searching for, we can conclude that *Name* is a *member* of the list. Since the tail of the list is of no interest, it is indicated by "_". Thanks to this first clause, the goal

```
member(john,[john,leonard,eric,frank])
```

is satisfied.

```
              /* Program 11 */
domains
       namelist = name*
       name = symbol
predicates
       member(name,namelist)
clauses
       member(Name,[Name|_]).
       member(Name,[_|Tail]) if member(Name,Tail).
```

If the head of the list is different from *Name*, we need to investigate whether *Name* can be found in the tail of the list. In English:

"Name is a member of the list if Name is member of the tail"

and in Turbo Prolog:

```
member(Name,[_|Tail]) if member(Name,Tail).
```

Exercise Type in the above program and try the following goal:

```
member(susan,[ian,susan,john])
```

Add domain and predicate statements so that the *member* predicate can also be used to investigate if a number is a member of a list of numbers. Try several goals to test your resulting new program, including

```
member(X,[1,2,3,4]).
```

Exercise Does the order of the two clauses for the *member* predicate have any significance? Test the behavior of the program when the two rules are swapped. The difference appears if the goal

```
member(X,[1,2,3,4,5])
```

is tested in both situations.

Writing Elements of a List

Now we'll define a predicate that writes out elements of a list on separate lines. Again, we need to think recursively.

```
write_a_list([]).
write_a_list([Head|Tail]) if
    write(Head),nl,write_a_list(Tail).
```

The first clause says: Stop when there are no further elements in the list (the list is empty); the second says: Write the head of the list, write a newline, and then deal with the tail.

Exercise Complete the *write_a_list* program above and test the following goal:

```
write_a_list([2,4,6,8,10])
```

Appending One List to Another: Declarative and Procedural Programming

As given, the *member* predicate of Program 11 works in two ways. Consider its clauses once again:

```
member(Name, [Name|_]).
member(Name, [_|Tail]) if member (Name,Tail).
```

We can think of these clauses from two different points of view. From a *declarative* viewpoint they say that, given a list, *Name* is a member of that list if its head is *Name*; if not, *Name* is a member of the list if it is a member of its tail. From a *procedural* viewpoint the two clauses could be interpreted: to find a member of a list, find its head, otherwise find a member of its tail.

These two points of view correspond to the goals

```
member(2,[1,2,3,4]).
```

and

```
member(X,[1,2,3,4]).
```

since, in effect, the first goal asks Turbo Prolog to check that something is true, whereas the second asks Turbo Prolog to find all members of the list [1,2,3,4].

The beauty of Turbo Prolog lies in the fact that, often, if we construct the clauses for a predicate from one point of view, they'll work for the other. As an example of this, we'll now construct a predicate to append one list to another. For example, let's append the lists [1,2,3] and [4,5] to form the list [1,2,3,4,5]. We'll define the predicate *append* with three arguments:

```
append(List1, List2, List3)
```

This combines *List1* and *List2* to form *List3*. Once again we are using recursion (from a procedural point of view).

If *List1* is empty, the result of appending List1 and List2 will be the same as *List2*. In Turbo Prolog:

```
append([], List2, List2).
```

Otherwise, we can combine *List1* and *List2* to form *List3* by making the head of *List1* the head of *List3*. (Below, the variable X is used as the head of both *List1* and *List3*). The rest of *List3* (its tail) is obtained by putting together the rest of *List1* and the whole of *List2*. (The tail of *List3* is *L3*, which is composed of the rest of *List1* (namely, *L1*) and the whole of *List2*. In Turbo Prolog:

```
append([X|L1], List2, [X|L3]) if
append(L1,List2,L3).
```

The *append* predicate thus operates as follows: While *List1* is not empty, the recursive rule transfers one element at a time to *List3*. When *List1* is empty, the first clause ensures that *List2* hooks onto the back of *List3*.

Exercise The two predicates *append* and *writelist* are defined in the Turbo Prolog program below. Type in the program and run it with the following goal:

```
append([1,2,3],[5,6],L) and writelist(L).
```

Now try this goal:

```
append([1,2],[3],L),append(L,L,LL),writelist(LL).
```

```
              /* Program 12 */
domains
       integerlist = integer*
predicates
       append(integerlist,integerlist,integerlist)
       writelist(integerlist)
clauses
       append([],List,List).
       append([X|L1], List2, [X|L3]) if
                 append(L1,List2,L3).
       writelist([]).
       writelist([Head|Tail]) if
                 write(Head,"")writelist(Tail).
```

One Predicate Can Have Several Applications

Looking at *append* from a declarative point of view, we have defined a relation between three lists. This relation also holds if *List1* and *List3* are known but *List2* isn't *and* if only *List3* is known. For example, to find which two lists could be appended to form a known list, we could use a goal of the form

```
append(L1,L2,[1,2,4]).
```

for which Turbo Prolog will find the solutions

```
L1 = [], L2 = [1,2,4]
L1 = [1], L2 = [2,4]
L1 = [1,2], L2 = [4]
L1 = [1,2,4], L2 = []
4 solutions
```

We can also use *append* to find which list could be appended to [3,4] to form the list [1,2,3,4] by giving the goal

```
append(L1,[3,4],[1,2,3,4]).
```

Turbo Prolog finds the solution L1 = [1,2].

append has defined a relation between an input set and an output set in such a manner that the relation applies both ways. We can therefore ask

"Which output corresponds to this given input?"

or

"Which input corresponds to this given output?"

Exercise By amending the clauses given for *member* in Program 11, construct clauses for a predicate *evenmember* which would be solved given a goal

```
evenmember(2,[1,2,3,4,5,6]).
```

and which, given the goal

```
evenmember(X,[1,2,3,4,5,6]).
```

would display

```
X=2
X=4
X=6
3 solutions
```

5 Tutorial III: Turbo Prolog's Relentless Search for Solutions

This chapter falls into two main parts. In the first, we examine in detail the process Turbo Prolog uses when trying to match a goal with a clause. This process is called *unification* and corresponds to parameter passing in other programming languages.

In the second part, you'll learn how to control Turbo Prolog's search for solutions of goals. This will include techniques that make it possible for a program to carry out a task which would otherwise be impossible, either because the search would take too long or (less likely with Turbo Prolog) because the system would run out of free memory.

MATCHING THINGS UP: THE UNIFICATION OF TERMS

Consider Program 13 in terms of the (external) goal

```
written_by(X,Y).
```

```
               /* Program 13 */

domains
    title,author = symbol
    pages        = integer
    publication  = book(title,pages)
predicates
    written_by(author,publication)
    long_novel(publication)
clauses
    written_by(fleming,book("DR NO",210)).
    written_by(melville,book("MOBY DICK",600)).
    long_novel(book(Title,Length)):-written_by(_,book(Title,Length)),
                       Length > 300.
```

When Turbo Prolog tries to fulfill the goal, it must try each of the clauses for the predicate *written_by* in turn, trying to get a match between the parameters X and Y and the parameters in each clause for written_by. This term matching operation is called *unification*.

Since *X* and *Y* are free variables in this goal, and a free variable can be unified with any other term, the very first *written_by* clause unifies with the goal clause

```
written_by(   X         ,         Y       )
              !                   !
written_by(fleming,book("DR NO",210))
```

Thus *X* becomes bound to *fleming* and *Y* becomes bound to *book("DR NO",210)* so Turbo Prolog displays

```
X = fleming, Y = book("DR NO",210)
X = melville, Y = book("MOBY DICK",600)
2 Solutions
```

If, on the other hand, we give Program 13 the goal

```
written_by(X,book("MOBY DICK",Y)).
```

then again unification is attempted with the first clause for *written_by*:

```
written_by(   X    ,book("MOBY DICK", Y )).
              !                 !
written_by(fleming,book("DR NO"     ,210)).
```

This fails because MOBY DICK and DR NO don't match, and Turbo Prolog tries the next fact

```
written_by(melville,book("MOBY DICK",600))
```

This will unify and *X* will be bound to Melville and *Y* to 600.

A compound term can unify with another compound term provided they both involve the same functor and the same number of arguments, and all the subterms unify pairwise. In this case, the functor is the same (*book*) and the number of subterms is two in each case. However, the constant *MOBY DICK* can unify only with itself or with a free variable. Thus, no match is possible between *MOBY DICK* and *DR NO* and unification fails.

Turbo Prolog now attempts a match between

```
written_by(   X    ,book("MOBY DICK", Y ))
```

and

```
written_by(melville,book("MOBY DICK",600))
```

The free variable *X* unifies (and becomes bound with) the constant *melville*. The compound terms

```
book("MOBY DICK", Y )
```

and

```
book("MOBY DICK",600)
```

unify, since they both involve the same functor *book*; they have the same number of arguments; the constant *MOBY DICK* unifies with itself; and the constant *600* can be unified with the free variable *Y*. Thus the goal succeeds and Turbo Prolog responds

```
X = melville, Y = 600
1 Solution
```

Finally, consider execution of the goal

```
long_novel (X).
```

When Turbo Prolog tries to fulfill a goal, it investigates whether or not there is a matching fact or left side of a rule. In this case, the match is with the left side of a rule

```
long_novel( X )

long_novel(book(Title,Length)):-
     written_by(_,book(Title,Length)),Length>300.
```

since the free variable *X* can be unified with any other term and, in particular, another free variable. Next, Turbo Prolog makes the first clause on the right side of this rule the current sub-goal, and unification is achieved with the first fact for *written_by* as follows:

```
written_by(_,book(Title,Length))
written_by(fleming,book("DR NO",  210 ))
```

in which *Length* has become bound to 210, and the title is bound to *DR NO*.

Now the second clause on the right side of the *long_novel* rule becomes the current sub-goal

```
Length > 300
```

the comparison is made—and, of course, returns false. Turbo Prolog now attempts a different unification of

```
written_by(Name,book(Title,Length))
```

(see the next section) and binds *Title* to *"MOBY DICK"* and *Length* to 600. Now

```
Length > 300
```

unifies with *Length* replaced by 600 (the value to which it is bound) and indeed succeeds, so that *long_novel* also succeeds with *Title* bound to "MOBY DICK". Turbo Prolog displays

```
X = book("MOBY DICK",600)
1 Solution
```

Summary of Turbo Prolog's Unification Algorithm

- A free variable can be unified with any term. The variable is then bound to the other term.
- A constant (an integer, for example) can unify with itself or with a free variable.
- A compound term can unify with another compound term, provided they both involve the same functor and have the same number of arguments. Further, all the subterms must unify pairwise. (Lists are treated as a special kind of compound term).

Bound variables are replaced with the value to which they were bound prior to unification.

Thus, unification takes care of:

- Assigning values to variables (i.e., parameter passing).
- Accessing data structures via a general pattern-matching mechanism.
- Certain kinds of tests for equality.

CONTROLLING THE SEARCH FOR SOLUTIONS

In this section we'll look at some techniques we can use to control Turbo Prolog's search for solutions of our goals.

Let's start by looking at Program 14 in light of this goal, which consists of two subgoals:

```
likes(X,wine) and likes(X,books)
```

```
        /* Program 14 */
domains
        name, thing = symbol
predicates
        likes(name,thing)
        reads(name)
        is_inquisitive(name)
clauses
        likes(john,wine).
        likes(lance,skiing).
        likes(Z,books) if
                    reads(Z) and
                    is_inquisitive(Z).
        likes(lance,books).
        likes(lance,films).
        reads(john).
        is_inquisitive(john).
```

When evaluating the goal, Turbo Prolog notes which subgoals have been satisfied and which have not. This search can be represented by a *goal tree*:

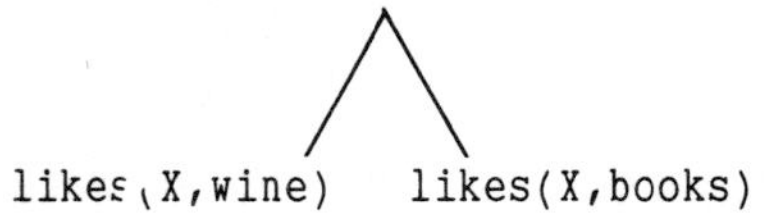

Before goal evaluation begins, the goal tree consists of two unsatisfied subgoals. In what follows, subgoals already satisfied in a goal tree are underlined with a dotted line, and the corresponding satisfying clause head is shown underneath.

In our example, the goal tree shows that two subgoals must be satisfied. To do so, Turbo Prolog follows the *first basic principle*:

Subgoals must be satisfied from left to right.

The clause Turbo Prolog chooses to satisfy the first subgoal is determined by the *second basic principle*:

Predicate clauses must be tested in the order they appear in the program.

When executing Program 14, Turbo Prolog finds a suitable clause in the first fact. Let's look at the goal tree again:

```
                  /\
                 /  \
likes(X,wine)  /      likes(X,books)
---------------
likes(john,wine)
```

The subgoal

```
likes(X,wine)
```

matches the fact:

```
likes(john,wine).
```

by binding X to the value *john*. Turbo Prolog next tries to satisfy the next subgoal to the right.

The satisfaction of the second subgoal starts a completely new search procedure, with X = *john*. The first clause

```
likes(john,wine)
```

does not match the subgoal

```
likes(X,books)
```

since *wine* is not the same as *books*. Turbo Prolog must therefore try the next clause, but *lance* does not match the value of X (*john*), so the search continues with the third clause

```
likes(Z,books) if reads(Z) and is_inquisitive(Z).
```

The parameter Z is a variable and so matches with X, and the second parameters agree. When X matches Z, Turbo Prolog demands that Z also be bound to the value *john*.

We know now that the subgoal matches the left side of a rule. Continued searching is determined by the *third basic principle*:

When a subgoal matches the left side of a rule, the right side of that rule must be satisfied next. The right side constitutes the new set of subgoals.

From this we get the following goal tree:

```
                 /\
 likes(X,wine)  /  \likes(X,books)
---------------    --------------
likes(john,wine)  likes(Z,books)
                      /      \
          reads(Z)  is_inquisitive(Z)
```

The goal tree now includes the subgoals

```
reads(Z) and is_inquisitive(Z)
```

where *Z* has the value *john*. Turbo Prolog will now search for facts that match both subgoals. The resulting final goal tree is shown below:

```
                   /\
                  /  \
 likes(X,wine)   /    likes(X,books)
---------------       --------------
likes(john,wine)      likes(Z,books)
                           /\
                          /  \
 reads(Z)       is_inquisitive(Z)
----------      -------------------
reads(john)     is_inquisitive(john)
```

According to the *fourth basic principle*:

> *A goal has been satisfied when a matching fact is found for all the extremities (leaves) of the goal tree,*

so we know now that our initial goal is satisfied.

Turbo Prolog uses the result of the search procedure in different ways, depending on how it was initiated. If the goal is a subgoal in a rule, Turbo Prolog keeps trying to satisfy the next subgoal in the rule. If the goal is a question from the user, Turbo Prolog replies directly:

```
X = john
1 solution
Goal :_
```

As we saw in Chapter 3, having once satisfied an external goal, Turbo Prolog backtracks to find alternative solutions. It will also backtrack if a subgoal fails, hoping to resatisfy a previous subgoal in such a way that the failed subgoal is satisfied with new variable values.

To fulfill a subgoal, Turbo Prolog begins a search with the first clause in a predicate. Two things can happen:

1. A matching clause head is found. The following then happens:
   a. If there is another clause that can possibly resatisfy the subgoal, the first such clause is marked with a pointer to indicate a backtracking point.
   b. All free variables in the subgoal that match values in the clause head are assigned these values (the variables become bound).
   c. If the matching clause is the left side of a rule, that rule must be satisfied. This is done by treating the right side of the rule as a new goal.
2. A matching clause head cannot be found and the goal fails. Turbo Prolog backtracks as it attempts to resatisfy a previous subgoal. All variables that were free before the subgoal was previously satisfied are made free again.

   Turbo Prolog first searches the clause indicated by the pointer. If the search is unsuccessful, it backtracks again. If backtracking exhausts all clauses for all subgoals, the goal fails.

Use of Fail

Turbo Prolog contains a standard predicate that forces backtracking—*fail*. The effect of *fail* corresponds to the effect of 2=3. We'll use Program 15 to illustrate the use of this predicate.

```
              /* Program 15 */
domains
      name = symbol
predicates
      father(name,name)
      everybody
clauses
      father(leonard,katherine).
      father(carl,jason).
      father(carl,marilyn).
      everybody if
              father(X,Y) and
              write(X," is ",Y,"'s father\n") and
              fail.
```

The goal *father(X,Y)* could be used in two different situations:

- As an inquiry to the Turbo Prolog system (an *external goal*)
- On the right side of a rule (an *internal goal*), as in:

```
grandfather(X,B) if father(X,Y) and father(Y,B).
```

With *father(X,Y)* as an external goal, Turbo Prolog will write out all possible solutions in the usual way:

```
X= .... , Y= ....
X= .... , Y= ....
.... solutions
```

With *father(X,Y)* as an internal goal, Turbo Prolog will continue with the next subgoal once it has been satisfied and will display only one solution. However, the predicate *everybody* in Program 15 uses the *fail* predicate to disturb the usual mechanism.

The object of the predicate *everybody* is to produce neater responses from program runs. Compare the answers to the two goals

```
Goal: father(X,Y)
X=leonard, Y = katherine
X=carl, Y=jason
X=carl, Y=marilyn
3 solutions

Goal: everybody
leonard is katherine's father
carl is jason's father
carl is marilyn's father
False
```

The predicate *everybody* makes use of backtracking to generate more solutions for *father(X,Y)* by trying to satisfy the right side of *everybody*:

```
father(X,Y) and write(X," is ",Y,"'s father\n") and fail.
```

These subgoals must be satisfied from left to right. The first

```
father(X,Y)
```

can be satisfied with X = *leonard* and Y = *katherine*, so that Turbo Prolog continues to the next subgoal, the standard predicate *write*. It fulfills its task by writing some values, and then continues to the last subgoal, the standard predicate *fail*.

Fail can never be satisfied, so Turbo Prolog is forced to backtrack. *write* cannot be resatisfied (offer new solutions), so Turbo Prolog must backtrack again to the first subgoal.

A new solution, namely X = *carl* and Y = *marilyn*, is found. Turbo Prolog can now continue to the next subgoal, where the values are written out, and finally reaches the last subgoal—*fail*—which once again initiates backtracking, and so on.

Exercise Type in Program 15 and evaluate the following goals:

```
father(X,Y).
```

and

```
everybody.
```

Why are the solutions to *everybody* terminated by *False*? For a clue, append:

```
everybody.
```

as a second clause to the definition of predicate *everybody* and reevaluate the goal.

PREVENTING BACKTRACKING: THE CUT ELEMENT

Turbo Prolog contains an element that prevents backtracking under certain circumstances. The element is called the *cut* and is written as an exclamation mark (**!**). Its effect is simple:

It is impossible to backtrack past a cut

There are two main uses of the cut:

- When you know in advance that certain possibilities will never give rise to meaningful solutions, so it is a waste of time and storage space to backtrack over them. By using a cut in this situation, the resulting program will run quicker and use less memory.
- When the logic of a program demands the cut.

In the following examples, we will use several schematic Turbo Prolog rules *r1*, *r2*, *r3* which all describe the same predicate *r*, plus several subgoals *a*,*b*,*c*, etc.

Using the Cut to Prevent Backtracking to a Previous Subgoal in a Rule

```
r1 if a and b and ! and c.
```

This is a way of telling Turbo Prolog that we are satisfied with the first solution of subgoals *a* and *b*. As a concrete example, consider Program 16. It is based on the idea that two people might like one another if they have at least one interest in common.

```
                 /* Program 16 */
domains
    name,sex,interest = symbol
    interests = interest*

predicates
    findpairs
    person(name,sex,interests)
    member(interest,interests)
    common_interest(interests,interests,interest)
clauses
    findpairs if person(Man, m, ILIST1 ) and
          person( Woman, f, ILIST2 ) and
          common_interest( ILIST1, ILIST2, _ ) and

          write( Man, " might like  ",Woman ) and nl and
          fail.
     findpairs:- write ("-----------end of the List---").

     common_interest( IL1, IL2, X ) if
           member(X, IL1 ) and member(X, IL2) and !.

     person(tom,m,[travel,books,baseball]).
     person(mary,f,[wine,books,swimming,travel]).

     member( X, [X|_] ).
     member( X, [_|L] ) if member( X, L ).
```

The use of the *cut* in the predicate *common_interest* is the reason the predicate finds only one common interest. If the *cut* were not employed, the same names would be written many times if the *persons* had many interests in common.

Using the Cut to Prevent Backtracking to the Next Clause

This is a way to tell Turbo Prolog that it has chosen the correct clause for this predicate. For example, given

```
r1 if ! and a and b and c.
r2 if ! and d.
r3 if c.
```

the two cuts ensure that only one of the following clauses *r1*, *r2* or *r3* will be used. (Remember, *r1*, *r2*, *r3* are clauses for the same predicate *r*).

Our example in this case is based on Program 10 (Chapter 4), which defined the factorial predicate without the use of the *cut*:

```
factorial(1,1).
factorial(N,Res) if
        N>1 and
        N1=N-1 and
        factorial(N1,Temp) and
        Res=N*Temp.
```

The condition $N>1$ was necessary, since the second clause could be satisfied with $N=1$. Without this condition the first argument in *factorial* could become negative and the program would loop forever (or until memory was exhausted).

With the use of the *cut*, however, we can adopt the new clauses

```
factorial(1,1) if !.
factorial(N,Res) if
        N1=N-1 and factorial(N1,Between) and Res=N*Between.
```

where the *cut* indicates that, for $N=1$, the second clause should not be tested.

Determinism and the Cut

The *member* predicate (defined in Chapter 4) is an example of a predicate having *non-deterministic* clauses, i.e., clauses capable of generating multiple solutions through backtracking. In many implementations of Prolog, special care must be taken with non-deterministic clauses because of the attendant demands made on memory resources at run time. In Turbo Prolog, however, internal checks are made for non-deterministic clauses and these are dealt with in a special way, thus reducing the burden upon the programmer.

However, for debugging (and other) purposes, it can still sometimes be necessary for the programmer to intercede and the *check_determ* compiler directive is provided for this reason. If *check_determ* is inserted at the very beginning of a program, a warning will be displayed if any non-deterministic clauses are encountered during the evaluation of a goal. Pressing F10 causes the warning to be ignored, while pressing any other key aborts evaluation of the goal.

Non-deterministic clauses can be made deterministic by inserting cuts. Thus, *verify_member* with clauses

```
verify_member (X,[X|_]):-!.
verify_member (X,[_|Y]):-verify_member(X,Y).
```

is a deterministic version of *member*, the only difference between the two being the *cut* to stop backtracking in the first clause.

verify_member can be used to check that an element is a member of a given list, but cannot be used in a goal like

```
verify_member (X,[1,2,3,4,5]).
```

to successively bind X to the members of [1,2,3,4,5], since the goal succeeds with X bound to 1 and no backtracking takes place.

Exercise Suppose an average taxpayer in the USA is a US citizen, a married person with two children, and earns no less than $500 a month and no more than $2,000 per month. Define a Turbo Prolog predicate *special_taxpayer* which, with this goal

```
special_taxpayer(fred).
```

will succeed only if *fred* fails one of the conditions for an average taxpayer. Use the *cut* to ensure that there is no unnecessary backtracking.

Exercise Players in a certain squash club are divided into three leagues, and players may only challenge members in their own league or the league below (if there is one). Write a Turbo Prolog program that will display all possible matches between club players in the form:

```
tom versus bill
marjory versus annette
```

Use the *cut* to ensure, for example, that

```
tom versus bill
```

and

```
bill versus tom
```

are not both displayed.

6 Tutorial IV: Arithmetic, Simple Input and Output, and Debugging

Turbo Prolog's arithmetic capabilities are similar to those provided in programming languages such as BASIC, C and Pascal. It includes a full range of arithmetic functions and standard predicates as diverse as the arctangent function, and a family of predicates for bitwise logical operations. These are described in the first part of this chapter, along with standard predicates for basic input and output of numeric and non-numeric values.

The final part of this chapter resumes the discussion of debugging at the point where Chapter 2 left off. As programs become larger and more complex, you'll require more control over the amount of information produced by the various trace facilities, and this section tells how to gain that control.

PROLOG CAN DO ARITHMETIC TOO!

We have already seen some simple examples of Turbo Prolog's arithmetic capabilities. Turbo Prolog can perform all four basic arithmetic operations (addition, subtraction, multiplication and division) between integer and real values, the type of the result being determined according to Table 6-1.

Table 6-1 Arithmetic Operations

Operand 1	Operator	Operand 2	Result
integer	+, −, *	integer	integer
real	+, −, *	integer	real
integer	+, −, *	real	real
real	+, −, *	real	real
integer or real	/	integer or real	real

The Order of Evaluation of Arithmetic Expressions

Arithmetic expressions, such as the one on the right side of the = predicate in

```
A = 1 + 6 / (11 + 3 ) * Z
```

may include operands (numbers and variables), operators +, −, *, /, and parentheses "("and")". Hexadecimal numbers are identified by a preceding dollar sign. The value of an expression can only be calculated if *all variables are bound* at the time of evaluation. This calculation must then be made in a certain order, determined by the priority of the arithmetic operators; operators with the highest priority are evaluated first. Thus, evaluation of arithmetic expressions proceeds as follows:

- If the expression contains subexpressions in parentheses, the subexpressions are evaluated first.
- If the expression contains * (multiplication) or / (division), these operations are carried out next, working from left to right through the expression.
- Finally + (addition) and − (subtraction) are carried out, again working from left to right.

Returning to our example expression, since variables must be bound before evaluation, assume that *Z* has the value 4. The value of (11 +3) is the first subexpression to be evaluated, and it evaluates to 14. Now 6/14 can be evaluated to give 0.428571 and then 0.428571 *4 gives 1.714285. Finally, evaluating 1 + 1.714285 gives the value of the expression as 2.714285. If *A* belongs to a domain of real type, *A* will be bound to 2.714285, but if *A* belongs to a domain of integer type, *A* will be bound to 2.

Table 6-2 Operator Priority

Operator	Priority
+ −	1
* /	2
mod div	3
− + (unary)	4

Comparisons

In the following statement:

```
X+4 < 9 - Y
```

(which is the Turbo Prolog equivalent of: The total of X and 4 is less than 9 minus *Y*), the relational operator < (less than) indicates the relation between the two expressions, X+4 and 9−Y. If *Value1* and *Value2* represent the values of the two expressions, we could write this relation in a "normal" Turbo Prolog statement format as

```
less_than(Value1,Value2)
```

We could also write the Turbo Prolog sentences

```
plus(X,4,Value1)
minus(9,Y,Value2)
```

Table 6-3 Relational Operators

<	less than
<=	less than or equal to
=	equal
>	greater than
>=	greater than or equal to
<> or ><	different from

to describe how $X+4$ and $9-Y$ are evaluated to *Value1* and *Value2*, respectively. The entire comparison $X+4 < 9-Y$ could thus be formulated as:

```
plus(X,4,Value1) and
minus(9,Y,Value2) and
less_than(Value1,Value2)
```

Turbo Prolog allows the more familiar formulation we began with, but be aware that a single comparison such as $X+4<9-Y$ (this is called *infix* notation) corresponds to as many Turbo Prolog statements as there are operators in the original sentence.

The complete range of relational operators allowed in Turbo Prolog is shown in Table 6-3.

Besides numeric expressions, it is also possible to compare single characters, strings and symbols. Consider the following comparisons:

```
'a' < 'b'
peter > sally
"antony" > "antonia"
```

Turbo Prolog converts the comparison 'a' < 'b' to the equivalent arithmetic expression 97 < 98 using the corresponding ASCII code value for each character. With two string or symbol values, the outcome depends on a character-by-character comparison of corresponding positions. The result will be the same as from a comparison of their initial characters, unless these two characters are the same. If they are, Turbo Prolog will compare the next corresponding pair of characters and return that result, unless these are also equal, in which case a third pair will be examined, and so on.

Hence, the second expression above is false—as is determined by comparing the ASCII values for the characters that make up *peter* and *sally*, respectively. The character *p* comes before *s* in the alphabet, so *p* has the lowest ASCII value and the expression is false. (The ASCII values for the entire character set can be found in Appendix B). Similarly, the third comparison is true, since the two symbols first differ at the position where one contains the letter *y* and the other the letter *i*.

Compound objects, however, must be compared for equality using an *equal* predicate, as shown in Program 17:

```
                  /* Program  17*/
domains
  d = pair(integer,integer) ; single(integer) ; none
predicates
     equal(d,d)
clauses
     equal(X,X).
```

Type in Program 17 and try out these goals:

```
equal(single(4),pair(3,4)).
equal(pair(2,1),pair(2,1)).
equal(none,none).
```

Try also

```
equal(5,4).
```

which will result in a *domain error*. Now append a new predicate declaration of *equal*.

```
equal(integer,integer)
```

and retry the goal

```
equal(5,4).
```

Special Conditions for Equality

In Turbo Prolog, statements like $N=N1-2$ indicate a relation between the three objects: *N*, *N1* and 2; or a relation between two objects: *N* and the value of $N1-2$. If *N* is still free, the statement can be satisfied by binding *N*. This corresponds to what other programming languages call an *assignment statement*; in Turbo Prolog, it is a logical statement. On the other hand, *N1* must always be bound to a value since it is part of an expression.

When using the *equal* predicate to compare real values, care must be taken to ensure that the necessarily approximate representation of real numbers does not lead to unexpected results. Thus the goal

```
4.99999999999=5.00000000000
```

will fail, indicating that when comparing two real values for equality, it is better to check that the two are within a certain range of one another.

Program 18 illustrates how to use the *equal* predicate and tries to find solutions for the quadratic equation

```
A * X*X + B * X + C = 0
```

where the existence of solutions depends on the value of the discriminant

```
D = B*B-4*A*C.
```

D>0 implies that there are two solutions, D = 0 implies there is one solution only, and D<0 implies that there are no solutions if *X* is to take a real value.

```
                     /* Program 18 */
predicates
     solve(real,real,real)
     reply(real,real,real)
     mysqrt(real,real,real)
     equal(real,real)
clauses
     solve(A,B,C) :-
                D = B*B-4*A*C, reply(A,B,D), nl.
```

```
reply(_,_,D) :- D < 0, write("No solution"), !.
reply(A,B,D) :-
        D = 0, X=-B/(2*A), write("x=",X), !.
reply(A,B,D) :-
        mysqrt(D,D,SqrtD),
        X1 = (-B + SqrtD)/(2*A),
        X2 = (-B - SqrtD)/(2*A),
        write("x1 = ",X1," and x2 = ",X2).

mysqrt(X,Guess,Root) :-
        NewGuess = Guess-(Guess*Guess-X)/2/Guess,
        not(equal(NewGuess,Guess)),!,
        mysqrt(X,NewGuess,Root).
mysqrt(_,Guess,Guess).

equal(X,Y) :-
        X/Y > 0.99999   , X/Y < 1.00001.
```

The program calculates square roots by an iterative formula where a better guess (*NewGuess*) for the square root of X can be obtained from the previous guess (*Guess*):

```
NewGuess =  ( Guess - (Guess * Guess - X)   ) /2
```

Each iteration brings us a little closer to the square root of X. Once the condition *equal* is satisfied, no further progress can be made and the calculation terminates.

Exercise Type in Program 18 and try the following goals:

```
solve(1,2,1).
solve(1,1,4).
solve(1,-3,2).
```

The solutions should be

```
x = -1
No solution
x1 = 2 and x2 = 1
```

respectively.

Exercise The object of this exercise is to experiment with the *mysqrt* predicate in Program 18. We can ensure that temporary calculations can be monitored by adding the following as the first subgoal in the first *mysqrt* clause:

```
write(Guess).
```

To see the effect of this amendment, try this goal

```
mysqrt(8,1,Result).
```

Next, replace the *equal* clause with this fact

```
equal(X,X).
```

and retry the goal. Experiment a little more with the properties of *equal*. Try, for instance

```
equal(X,Y) :- X/Y < 1.1 , X/Y > 0.9.
```

Exercise Turbo Prolog has a built-in square root function *sqrt*. Thus,

```
X = sqrt(D)
```

will bind X to the square root of the value to which D is bound. Rewrite Program 18 using *sqrt* and compare the answers with those from the original version.

ARITHMETIC FUNCTIONS AND PREDICATES

Unlike other versions of Prolog, Turbo Prolog has a full range of built-in mathematical functions and predicates that operate on integer and real values. The complete list is given in Table 6-4.

Table 6-4 Turbo Prolog Arithmetic Predicates and Functions

Functional Predicate	Description
bitand(X,Y,Z) *bitor(X,Y,Z)* *bitnot(X,Z)* *bitxor(X,Y,Z)*	If X and Y are bound to integer values, Z will be bound to an integer which is the result of (1) representing the values of X and Y as signed 16-bit numbers and (2) performing the corresponding logical operation AND, OR, NOT, XOR on those numbers.
bitleft(X,N,Y) *bitright(X,N,Y)*	If X and N are bound to integer values, Y is bound to the integer which is the result of representing X as a signed 16-bit number and shifting left or right the number of places specified by N.
X mod Y	Returns the remainder of X divided by Y.
X div Y	Returns the quotient of X divided by Y.
abs(X)	If X is bound to a positive value *v*, *abs(X)* returns that value; otherwise it returns *− 1 *v*.
cos(X), sin(X), tan(X)	The trigonometric functions require that X be bound to a value representing an angle in radians.
arctan(X)	Returns the *arctan* of the real value to which X is bound.
exp(X)	e raised to the value to which X is bound.
ln(X)	Logarithm to base e.
log(X)	Logarithm to base 10.
sqrt(X)	Square root.
random(X)	Binds X to a random real when 0<=X<1.
round(X)	Returns the rouded value of X.

Thus

```
test1(Xreal,AnswerReal):-
        AnswerReal = ln(exp(sin(sqrt(XReal*XReal))))
```

and

```
test2(X,AnswerInt):-
     bitand(X,X,Y1),bitnot(Y1,Y2),bitor(Y2,X,AnswerInt).
```

could be used as clauses for predicates *test1* and *test2* in a test program. In particular, the goal

```
test1(4,A).
```

will return

```
A= -0.756802
```

and

```
test2(4,B).
```

will return

```
B=-1
```

since − 1 is the signed 16-bit integer equivalent of 1111111111111111 in binary.

Exercise Use the trigonometric functions in Turbo Prolog to display a table of sine, cosine and tangent values on the screen. The left column of the table should contain angle values in degrees, starting at 0 degrees and continuing to 360 degrees in steps of 15 degrees.

Exercise Write a Turbo Prolog program to test the theory that

```
myxor(A,B,Result):-
        bitnot(B,NotB),bitand(A,NotB,AandNotB),
        bitnot(A,NotA),bitand(NotA,B,NotAandB),
        bitor(AandNotB,NotAandB,Result).
```

behaves like

```
bitxor(A,B,Result)
```

SIMPLE INPUT AND OUTPUT

Writing

The predicate *write* can be called with an optional number of arguments:

```
write( Arg1, Arg2, Arg3, ....... )
```

These arguments can either be constants (from domains of standard type) or variables, but variables must be bound beforehand.

The standard predicate *nl* is often used in conjunction with *write* and causes printing on the display screen to continue from a new line. Thus

```
pupil(PUPIL,CL),
write(PUPIL," is in the ",CL," class"),
nl,
write("----------------------------------").
```

might result in the display:

```
Helen Smith is in the fourth class
----------------------------------;
```

whereas

```
....,
write( "List1= ", L1, ", List2= ", L2 ).
```

could give

```
List1= [cow,pig,rooster], List2= [1,2,3]
```

Also, if in,

```
domains
        sentence      = sentence( subject, sentence_verb )
        subject       = subject( symbol ) ; ......
        sentence_verb = sentence_verb( verb ) ; ......
        verb          = symbol
clauses
        .... write( " SENTENCE= ", My_sentence ).
```

My_sentence is bound to

```
sentence(subject(john),sentence_verb(sleeps))
```

we might obtain this display:

```
SENTENCE= sentence(subject(john),sentence_verb(sleeps))
```

Often *write* does not, by itself, give you as much control as you'd like over the printing of compound objects like lists, but it's easy to use it in programs that give better control. To conclude this section, we'll give you four small examples to illustrate the possibilities. The first, Program 19, prints out lists without the opening and closing brackets, [and].

```
                 /* Program 19 */
domains
       integerlist = integer*
       namelist    = symbol*
predicates
       writelist(integerlist)
       writelist(namelist).
clauses
       writelist([]).
       writelist([H|T]) :- write(H," "), writelist(T).
```

Try typing in the program and evaluating this goal:

```
writelist([1,2,3,4]).
```

Our next example, Program 20, writes out the values in a list, with at most five elements per line.

```
                 /* Program  20  */

domains
    integerlist = integer*
predicates
    writelist(integerlist)
    write5(integerlist,integer)
clauses
    writelist( NL )   :- nl, write5( NL, 0 ), nl.

    write5( TL, 5 )   :-!, nl, write5( TL, _).
    write5( [H|T], N ) :- write(H," "),N1=N+1,write5(T,N1).
    write5( [], _ ).
```

If Program 20 is given this goal

```
writelist([2,4,6,8,10,12,14,16,18,20,22]).
```

Turbo Prolog responds with

```
2 4 6 8 10
12 14 16 18 20
22
```

Frequently, you may want a predicate that displays compound objects in a more readable form. Program 21 displays a compound object like

```
plus(mult(x,number(99)),mult(number(3),x))
```

in the form

```
x*99+3*x
```

```
          /* Program 21 */
domains
     expr = number(integer) ; x ; log(expr) ;
            plus(expr,expr) ; mult(expr,expr)
predicates
     writeExp(expr)
clauses
     writeExp(x)            :- write('x').
     writeExp(number(No)) :- write(No).
     writeExp(log(Expr))   :-
            write("log("),writeExp(Expr),write(')').
     writeExp(plus(U1,U2)):-
             writeExp(U1), write('+'), writeExp(U2).
     writeExp(mult(U1,U2)):-
             writeExp(U1), write('*'), writeExp(U2).
```

Program 22 is another, similar example. Try it with the goal

```
write_sentence(sentence(name(bill),verb(jumps))).
```

```
                  /* Program 22 */
domains
    sentence   = sentence(nounphrase,verbphrase)
    nounphrase = nounp(article,noun) ; name(name)
    verbphrase = verb(verb) ; verbphrase(verb,nounphrase)
    article,noun,name,verb = symbol
predicates
    write_sentence(sentence)
    write_nounphrase(nounphrase)
    write_verbphrase(verbphrase)
clauses
    write_sentence(sentence(S,V)) if
             write_nounphrase(S) and write_verbphrase(V).

    write_nounphrase(nounp(A,N)) if write(A,' ',N,' ').
    write_nounphrase(name(N) if write(N,' ')).

    write_verbphrase(verb(V)) if write(V,' ').
      write_verbphrase(verbphrase(V,N)) if
           write(V,' ') and write_nounphrase(N).
```

Exercise Write a Turbo Prolog program that, given a list of addresses contained in the program as clauses of the form

```
address("Sylvia Dickson","14 Railway Boulevard","Any Town",27240).
```

displays the addresses in a form suitable for mailing labels such as:

Sylvia Dickson
14 Railway Boulevard
Any Town
27240

Reading

Turbo Prolog includes standard predicates for reading:

- whole lines of characters
- integer, real, and character values from the keyboard
- from a disk file

By themselves, these predicates cannot be used to read compound objects or lists directly (but see *readterm* in Chapter 11). The construction of compound objects or lists from users' input is the programmer's responsibility. Table 6-5 contains a list of available predicates.

Program 23 illustrates both the use of *readln* and the extraction of compound objects from input lines.

```
                /* Program 23 */
domains
    person       = p(name,age,telno,job)
    age          = integer
    telno,name,job = string
predicates
    readperson(person)
    run
goal
    run.
clauses
    readperson(p(Name,Age,Telno,Job)):-
        write("Which name ? "),readln(Name),
        write("Job ?"),readln(Job),
        write("Age ?"),readint(Age),
        write("Telephone no ?"),readln(Telno).
    run:-
        readperson(P),nl,write(P),nl,nl,
        write("Is this compound object OK (y/n)"),
        readchar(Ch),Ch='y'.
    run:-
        nl,nl,write("Alright, try again"),nl,nl,run.
```

The final example in this section uses *readint* to read a list of integers. One integer per line is read until *readint* fails.

```
                /* Program 24 */
domains
    list = integer*
predicates
    readlist(list)
goal
    write("Write a list of integers"),readlist(L),
    write("\nThe Turbo Prolog list is ",L).
```

```
clauses
    readlist([H|T]):- readint(H),!,readlist(T).
    readlist([]).
```

Exercise Write and test clauses for a predicate *readbin* which in the call

```
readbin(IntVar)
```

would convert a user-input 16-bit binary number to a corresponding Turbo Prolog integer value to which *IntVar* is bound. Check your work by writing a program that contains *readbin*.

Table 6-5 Standard Reading Predicates

`readln(Line)`	The domain for the variable *Line* must be of either string or symbol type. The variable *Line* must be free prior to the *readln* invocation. *readln* reads up to 150 characters for a symbol, up to 64K for strings, and up to the limit from other devices (see Chapter 8). The string entered must be terminated by a carriage return.
`readint(X)`	The domain for the variable X must be of integer type, and X must be free prior to the call. When the line read will be converted to an integer, *readint* will read characters from the current input device (probably the keyboard, but see Chapter 9) until the ↵ key is pressed. If the line does not correspond to the usual syntax for integers, *readint* fails and Turbo Prolog's backtracking mechanism is invoked.
`readreal(X)`	The domain for the variable X must be of real type, and X must be free prior to the call. *readreal* reads characters from the current input device until the ↵ key is pressed. This input is then converted to a real number. If the input does not correspond to the usual syntax for a real number, *readreal* fails.
`file_str(Filename,X)`	The domains for *Filename* and X must be of symbol or string type (preferably string, since long texts slow down symbol-table lookup). The variable X must be free prior to the invocation of *file_str*. *file_str* reads characters from the file until an end-of-file character (normally a Ctrl Z) terminates the process. The contents of the file *Filename* are transferred to the variable X so that, for example `file_str("t.dat",My_text)` binds *My_text* to the contents of the file *t.dat*. In this way, the string can contain carriage return characters. Files that are read from a disk will automatically contain an end-of-file character as the last character. The file read must not exceed 64K bytes in length.
`readchar(CharParam)`	*CharParam* must be a free variable prior to invocation of readchar and belong to a domain of char type. The predicate then reads a single character from the current input device. *readchar* returns as soon as a single character is typed.

DEBUGGING AND TRACING

Before a program is executed, it is first checked to see that it conforms with Turbo Prolog syntax and to verify that values from different domain types have not been mixed up. As we saw in Chapter 2, if any error is found, the system returns control to the editor and places the cursor where the error was detected.

Once a program has been verified to be syntactically correct, Turbo Prolog provides unique debugging and tracing facilities for efficient program development. When a program has successfully compiled and Turbo Prolog is waiting for an external goal, the next stage in debugging is to choose goals carefully so that predicates can be tested for a representative sample of all possible values. If unexpected behavior occurs, the *trace* compiler directive introduced in Chapter 2 can be used to obtain a step-by-step trace of execution in the trace, edit and dialog windows.

Turbo Prolog uses a good deal of optimization to increase execution speed. One important optimizing technique is *tail recursion elimination* (see Chapter 11). Using the *trace* compiler directive, the trace contains all RETURNs that are logically part of program execution. To trace execution using these optimizations, use the *shorttrace* directive instead.

shorttrace also results in less trace output in the trace window. When tracing a fairly large program section, this may be an advantage in itself. It may be, however, that use of either directive generates too much tracing information, in which case you can use the *shorttrace* predicate to dramatically reduce trace display.

The *trace* predicate always succeeds, and works only when one of the compiler directives *trace* or *shorttrace* appears at the top of a program. Subsequently, if your program contains

```
trace(off)
```

trace will be turned off until the command

```
trace(on)
```

is reached, which will turn trace back on. Thus, if the clauses for the predicate *works_already* were known to behave as expected, the clause for the predicate *test* defined by

```
test(X):-works_already(X,Z),....
```

might be more effectively traced by temporarily redefining it as

```
test(X):-trace(off),
         works_already(X,Z),
         trace(on),
         ...
```

When you press Alt T with the *trace* compiler option present in you program, you are presented with a small window of three options: Status, Trace window, Editor window. Use the cursor to select an option and press F10 to continue.

The Status line determines if *trace* will remain on or be turned off. To change the status of *trace*, press ↵ to toggle between on and off. (Note that with all toggles set to on, *trace* is the same as in version 1.0)

The Trace window line determines if output normally sent to the Trace window will remain there. With Trace window toggled off, Turbo Prolog will glide through the source code from call to call without sending any messages to the Trace window.

The Editor window line determines if each step of execution will be shown in the Editor window. With Editor window toggled off, only those steps that result in output sent to Trace window will be shown.

Another way of controlling the information supplied by the tracing facilities is to use *trace* or *shorttrace* in the form

```
trace p1,p2,p3,...
```

or

```
shorttrace p1,p2,p3,...
```

which result only in calls to and returns from the named predicates *p1,p2,p3,...* occurring in the trace.

Some Predicates are Special

You may have noticed that *write* is not traced in the same way as other predicates (its CALL and RETURN are not marked). This is because *write* is implemented in a rather special way so that it is allowed to have an arbitrary number of parameters.

Several other predicates are specially treated in a trace for similar reasons. These include: all comparison operators (=,< etc), *not, findall, free, bound, asserta, assertz, retract, writef,* and *readterm.* (Several of these have yet to be introduced in the tutorial, but all are described in Chapter 12).

An Exercise in Tracing

Type in Program 25, which seeks to define the predicate *intersect* so that it serves two purposes. With this assumption, a goal

```
intersect(X,List1,List2).
```

would succeed if X is bound to the list of integers which *List1* and *List2* have in common, so that

```
intersect(X,[1,2,3],[2,3,4,5])
```

succeeds with X bound to [2,3] and

```
intersect([2,3],X,[2,3,4,5])
```

succeeds with X bound to [2,3,4,5]. Use the Turbo Prolog *trace* facilities to discover why the program doesn't work as intended.

```
                /* Program 25 */
domains
    list = integer*
```

```
predicates
    member(integer,list)
    intersect(list,list,list)
clauses
    member(X,[X|_]).
    member(X,[_|Y]):- member(X,Y).

    intersect([],[],_).
    intersect([X|Y],[X|L1],L2):-
        member(X,L2),intersect(Y,L1,L2)./* Try to place cut (!) at */
    intersect(Y,[_|L1],L2):-            /* the end of this clause. */
        intersect(Y,L1,L2).
```

7 Tutorial V: Seeing Through Turbo Prolog's Windows

Turbo Prolog allows you to incorporate windows in your programs (in full color if you have the necessary hardware) and have full access to DOS. Before introducing Turbo Prolog's first-class windowing capabilities, this chapter describes how to determine the screen attribute values that will be used in window commands to determine the colors both inside a given window and for the window frame (if there is one).

The chapter concludes with two exciting illustrations of the potential of Turbo Prolog's windowing features (an arcade style "shoot-em-up" game and a word guessing game) and then gives a few simple examples of how to interface your Turbo Prolog programs with DOS.

SETTING THE SCREEN DISPLAY ATTRIBUTES

Turbo Prolog allows you to control such screen display characteristics as inverse video, underlining and colors. This information is passed to standard predicates via an *attribute* value which, among other things, determines the color of the characters (the foreground) and the color behind the characters (the background). It is possible to give attributes for single characters or for a whole screen area.

If your computer has a Monochrome Display Adapter, display attribute values are calculated as follows:

- Choose the integer representing the desired foreground and background combination from Table 7-1.
- Add 1 if you want characters to be underlined in the foreground color.
- Add 8 if you want the white part of the display to be in high intensity.
- Add 128 if you want the character to blink.

Table 7-1 Monochrome Display Adapter Atribute Values

Black characters on a black background (i.e. blank)	0
White characters on a black background (normal video)	7
Black characters on a white background (inverse video)	112

To calculate the values of screen attributes for a Color/Graphics display, follow this procedure:

- Choose one foreground color and one background color.
- Add the corresponding integer values from Table 7-2.
- Add 128 if you want whatever is displayed with this attribute to blink.

Table 7-2 Color/Graphics Adapter Attribute Values

Foreground colors		Background colors	
Black	0	Black	0
Gray	8	Blue	16
Blue	1	Green	32
Light Blue	9	Cyan	48
Green	2	Red	64
Light Green	10	Magenta	80
Cyan	3	Brown	96
Light Cyan	11	White	112
Red	4		
Light Red	12		
Magenta	5		
Light Magenta	13		
Brown	6		
Yellow	14		
White	7		
White (High Intensity)	15		

Thus, for black and white display on a color monitor, the corresponding screen attribute is 0+7=7, whereas for red foreground on a yellow background the attribute value is 4+104=108.

WINDOWS IN YOUR PROGRAMS

Turbo Prolog provides eight standard predicates that allow your programs to handle *windows*, i.e., to define areas of the screen and direct output to these areas. These predicates are:

```
gotowindow(...)
makewindow(...)
shiftwindow(...)
```

```
removewindow(...)
clearwindow(...)
window_str(...)
window_attr(...)
scroll(...)
```

Also useful in this connection is the cursor positioning standard predicate

```
cursor(...)
```

We'll now consider each predicate, starting with *makewindow*.

```
makewindow(WNo,ScrAttr,FrameAttr,Header,Row,Col,Height,Width)
```

The predicate *makewindow* defines an area of the screen as a window. All parameters except *Header* must be integers. *Header* must be a string or symbol, and it is used as a title in the upper frame line. Windows are identified by a number (*WNo*) which is used to select which on-screen window is active. If *FrameAttr* is greater or less than zero, a border is drawn around the defined area (i.e., the window is framed) in the color specified by that attribute. Once defined, the window is "cleared" to the background color and the cursor is moved to its topmost left corner.

The row and column positions of the top left corner of the window—relative to the whole screen—are specified by parameters *Row* and *Col* respectively, and *Height* and *Width* give the dimensions of the window. *Row*, *Col*, *Height* and *Width* should correspond to the size of the display. Typically, display size is 25 rows of 80 characters, but this can be changed with the *graphics* standard predicate (see Chapter 8). Here's an example use of *makewindow*:

```
makewindow(1,7,135,"My first window",1,20,4,34)
```

Here, *makewindow* specifies window number 1, with a black and white display. A border will be drawn (*FrameAttr* is 135) with the header "My first window" and the window itself will be 4 rows high, 34 columns wide and be positioned with the top left corner at row 1, column 20 of the screen (note that rows and columns are numbered from 0 onwards).

On the other hand

```
makewindow(2,7,135,"count the rows",8,20,19,34)
```

will result in the error message

```
the parameters in makewindow are illegal
```

since a window with height 19 is impossible if positioned starting from row 8 ($8+19 > 25$!). Notice also that if *Height* and *Width* are bound to 10 and 20 respectively, the actual display area of the window will be 8 rows and 18 columns if the window is framed (i.e., *FrameAttr* is bound to a non-zero value), since the frame will then occupy a total of two rows and two columns.

The unbuffered window predicate allows very fast window shifts between two windows that do not overlap. It also allows a window to stay on the screen while shifting to a window behind it. *Gotowindow* makes another window the current window without saving the contents of the old window or refreshing the contents of the new window from its buffer.

The *scroll* predicate indicates the number of lines to scroll in the active window.

Read and Write With Windows

The standard predicates *readln*, *readint*, *readchar*, *write* and *nl* automatically affect the most recently made window. Thus, in Program 26, the messages will be written in the appropriate window (first window 1, then window 2) and the first call to *readint* will echo digits typed in window 2. Once the ↵ key has been pressed, window 2 will be removed by the *removewindow* predicate. *removewindow* removes the currently active window and the screen returns to the display prior to the "making" of that window. Then *readint* will echo digits typed in window 1 until ↵ is pressed, when window 1 will be removed (being the currently active window). Hence the final *readint* will echo to the bottom of the screen as usual.

```
                /* Program 26 */
predicates
    run
clauses
    run :-
      makewindow(1,20,7,"A blue window",2,5,10,50),
      write("The characters are red"),nl,
      makewindow(2,176,7,"A light cyan window",14,25,10,40),
      write("This window is light cyan and the "),
        write("letters are black and blink."),nl,
        write("Please type an integer to exit."),nl,
        readint(_),
        removewindow,
        write("Please type an integer to exit."),nl,
        readint(_),
        removewindow.
```

Windows can overlap. To see this, replace the *makewindow* commands in Program 26 with

```
makewindow(1,20,7,"First",1,3,20,30)
```

and

```
makewindow(2,184,7,"Second",6,18,18,50)
```

respectively.

If the text is too big to fit in a window, the text will scroll, just as it would on the full display screen. To see this, replace the *makewindow* commands in Program 26 with

```
makewindow(1,20,7,"First",1,3,20,15)
```

and

```
makewindow(2,184,7,"Second",6,18,18,30)
```

Output to the screen is re-routed to window *WindowNo* by the standard predicate

```
shiftwindow(WindowNo)
```

and that window becomes the currently active window. (Turbo Prolog remembers any previously active window.) The cursor returns to where it was when window *WindowNo* was last active. If window *WindowNo* does not exist, a runtime error occurs.

You can change the attribute of the currently active window with the

```
window_attr(Attr)
```

standard predicate. *window_attr* causes the entire active window to receive the attribute *Attr.*

The *cursor* standard predicate also gives more control over screen display. If *Row* and *Col* are bound to positive integer values, then

```
cursor(Row,Col)
```

moves the cursor to the indicated position in the currently active window. (*Row* and *Col* denote row and column values *within* the window, where the top left corner inside the window is at row 0, column 0). If *Row* and *Col* are free, *cursor(Row,Col)* binds *Row* and *Col* to the current cursor position.

Program 27 uses the window standard predicates to turn your computer into a simple adding machine that repeatedly adds two integers and displays the result. Both operands and the sum are displayed in windows.

Note the redefinition of window 2 in the program. The new window definition is referred to by the same number; the latest definition is always used. *clearwindow* clears the currently active window by filling that window with the selected background color. To run the program, give the goal *start.*

```
                 /* Program 27 */
predicates
    start
    run(integer)
    do_sums
    set_up_windows
    clear_windows
clauses
  start :-
         set_up_windows,do_sums.
  set_up_windows :-
       makewindow(1,7,7,"",0,0,25,80),
       makewindow(1,7,7,"Left operand",2,5,5,25),
       makewindow(2,7,7,"",2,35,5,10),
       nl,write(" PLUS"),
       makewindow(2,7,7,"Right operand",2,50,5,25),
       makewindow(3,7,7,"Gives", 10,27,5,25),
       makewindow(4,7,7,"",17,22,5,35).
  do_sums :-
         run(_),clear_windows,do_sums.
  run(Z)  :-
       shiftwindow(1),
       cursor(2,1),readint(X),
       shiftwindow(2),
       cursor(2,10),readint(Y),
       shiftwindow(3),Z=X+Y,cursor(2,10),write(Z),
       shiftwindow(4),
       write("  Please press the space bar"),
       readchar(_).
  clear_windows :-
       shiftwindow(1),clearwindow,
       shiftwindow(2),clearwindow,
       shiftwindow(3),clearwindow,
       shiftwindow(4),clearwindow.
```

SCREEN-BASED INPUT AND OUTPUT

The basic *read* and *write* family of standard predicates is not adequate for more sophisticated uses of Turbo Prolog's screen and window display facilities. There are some other specially designed standard predicates that make full screen and window handling easier. In this section, we'll first describe the facilities available and then use some of them to construct a simple program which could be the basis of a "shoot-em-up" computer game.

The entire screen or a window can be accessed and manipulated on three levels:

- One character at a time.
- One field at a time. (A field is any contiguous sequence of character display positions occurring on the same row.)
- One window at a time.

On the character level, the important predicates for screen and window handling are *scr_char* and *scr_attr*. The predicate *scr_char* takes the form

```
scr_char(Row,Column,Character)
```

and is used both to read and write a character. With all three parameters bound, the *Character* will be written in the indicated position. With *Row* and *Column* bound and *Character* free, a character is read from the indicated position. If *Row* or *Column* refers to a position outside the borders of the active window, a runtime error occurs.

scr_attr is used analogously to *scr_char* and takes the form

```
scr_attr(Row,Column,Attr)
```

The attribute of the character position (*Row,Column*) is assigned or read depending on whether *Attr* is bound or free.

On the field level, *field_str* takes the form

```
field_str(Row,Column,Length,String)
```

and works similarly. It can be used to read text from, or write text to a field on the screen or inside a window. The position of the field is indicated by variables *Row*, *Column* and *Length*, which must refer to a position within the borders of the currently active window. If *field_str* refers to positions outside the screen or currently active window, the program will stop with a runtime error. If *String* is bound to a value containing more characters than *Length* indicates, only the first *Length* characters are used. If *String* is shorter than *Length*, the rest of the field will be filled with blank spaces.

All the positions in a selected field can be assigned an attribute value with a single call of the standard predicate *field_attr*, which takes the form

```
field_attr(Row,Column,Length,Attr)
```

All parameters must be bound, although if *field_attr* is called with *Row*, *Column* and *Length* bound and *Attr* free, *Attr* will be bound to the current attribute setting of the specified field (which will be determined by the attribute of the first character in the field).

The *window_str* predicate takes the form:

```
window_str(StringParam)
```

If *StringParam* is free when *window_str* is called, *StringParam* will be bound to the string currently displayed in the active window and thus have the same number of lines as are in the active window. The length of every line in the string is determined by the last non-blank character in that line.

If, on the other hand, *StringParam* is bound to a string value, that string is written in the window according to the following algorithm:

- If there are more lines in the string than there are lines in the window, lines will be written until the window space is exhausted.
- If there are fewer lines in the string than in the window, the remaining lines in the window will be filled out with blank spaces.
- If there are more characters in a string line than are available on a window line, the string line will be truncated to fit.
- If there are fewer characters in a line than there are columns in the window, the line will be filled out with blank spaces.

A SIMPLE ARCADE GAME

To illustrate the power of Turbo Prolog's window handling facilities, we'll now use *scr_char* to construct a very simple arcade game program. When the program is run, monsters will appear at the top of the screen and gradually make their way down towards the player who is stationed at the bottom. The player must direct the fire from the *zapGun* using the Z and X keys. The object of the game is to zap the monsters before they zap you.

Since Turbo Prolog works so fast, we need to slow it down to give the screen display a chance to catch up. Otherwise the whole game would be played so quickly that we wouldn't see a thing. Thus, we define the predicate *delay*, whose sole purpose is to waste an amount of time indicated by its single integer parameter. Its clauses are:

```
delay(N) :-  N>0,!,N1=N-1,delay(N1).
delay(_).
```

Now, we can define the predicate *zapGun* which when called in the form

```
zapGun(24,Column)
```

will simulate the firing of a laser beam from the bottom of the screen straight up the given *Column*. We do this by repeatedly drawing and erasing the "^" character.

```
zapGun(N,C):- N>0,!,scr_char(N,C,'^'),delay(150),
              scr_char(N,C,' '),N1=N-1,zapGun(N1,C).
zapGun(_,_).
```

The attacking monsters are represented by a list of integers denoting the numbers of the columns down which they will descend. We want to be able to draw the monsters (represented by the ASCII character '\1') and to erase them (to simulate movement). Predicate *showThem* takes three parameters: a list of columns occupied by monsters; the row on which they are to be displayed; and a character which will be displayed in every monster position.

```
showThem([],_,_) :-!.
showThem([Monster|TheRest],Row,Char) :-
        scr_char(Row,Monster,Char),
        showThem(TheRest,Row,Char).
```

At different points in the game, we'll check to see which monsters still "live" and which row they have reached:

```
testresult([],_):-
       write("\nWell done champion zapper !"),
       delay(32000),exit.
testresult(_,Row):-   Row<24,!.
testresult(_,_):-
        write("\nToo late, YOU have been zapped!"),
        delay(32000),exit.
```

Once a monster has been zapped, it is deleted from the list of live monsters by the *delete* predicate:

```
delete(_,[],[]).
delete(X,[X|R],R) :-!.
delete(X,[Y|R],[Y,R2]) :-  !,delete(X,R,R2).
```

There are a few other details to consider. We must prevent the zap gun from going off the sides of the screen, move it one column to the left if Z is pressed, or one column to the right if X is pressed. Pressing any other key has no effect. Here's the relevant code:

```
test('z',0,0):-!.
test('x',79,79):-!.
test('z',OldCol,NewCol):-!,NewCol=OldCol-1.
test('x',OldCol,NewCol):-!,NewCol=OldCol+1.
test(_,C,C).
```

The internal goal for the program is

```
doit(56,[42,45,50,55,56,59],0)
```

which starts the game with the zap gun in column 56, monsters in columns 42,45,50,55,56 and 59, and all monsters at row 0. The defining clause for *doit* is

```
doit(Initial,Monsters,Row):-
        testresult(Monsters,Row),
        showThem(Monsters,Row,'\1'),
        readchar(Ch),test(Ch,Initial,Final),
        zapGun(24,Final),
        delete(Final,Monsters,LiveMonsters),
        NewRow=Row+1,
        cursor(24,Final),
        showThem(Monsters,Row,' '),
        doit(Final,MovedMonsters,NewRow).
```

Program 28 shows the entire program.

```
                          /* Program 28 */
domains
      monsters=integer*
predicates
     delay(integer)
     zapGun(integer,integer)
     delete(integer,monsters,monsters)
     testresult(monsters,integer)
     test(char,integer,integer)
     doit(integer,monsters,integer)
     showThem(monsters,integer,char)
goal
     makewindow(1,7,0,"",0,0,25,80),
     doit(56,[4,22,45,50,5,56,59,62],0).
clauses
     doit(Initial,Monsters,Row):-
          testresult(Monsters,Row),
          showThem(Monsters,Row,'\1'),
          readchar(Ch),
          test(Ch,Initial,Final),
          zapGun(24,Final),
          delete(Final,Monsters,LiveMonsters),
          NewRow=Row+1,
          cursor(24,Final),
          showThem(Monsters,Row,' '),
          doit(Final,LiveMonsters,NewRow).
     testresult([],_):-
          write("\nWell done champion zapper !"),
          delay(32000),exit.
     testresult(_,Row) :-  Row<24,!.
     testresult(_,_) :-
          write("\nToo late, YOU have been zapped !"),
          delay(32000),exit.

     showThem([],_,_) :-!.
     showThem([Monster|TheRest],Row,Char) :-
            scr_char(Row,Monster,Char),
            showThem(TheRest,Row,Char).

     zapGun(N,C):-
            N>0,!,scr_char(N,C,'^'),delay(150),
            scr_char(N,C,' '),N1=N-1,zapGun(N1,C).
     zapGun(_,_).

     test('z',0,0):-!.
     test('x',79,79):-!.
     test('z',OldCol,NewCol):-!,NewCol=OldCol-1.
     test('x',OldCol,NewCol):-!,NewCol=OldCol+1.
     test(_,C,C).

     delete(_,[],[]).
     delete(X,[X|R],R):-!.
     delete(X,[Y|R],[Y|R2]) :- !,delete(X,R,R2).

     delay(N):-N>0,!,N1=N-1,delay(N1).
     delay(0).
```

A WORD GUESSING GAME USING WINDOWS

Program 29 uses Turbo Prolog's window facilities to produce a word guessing game. To keep it fairly short, the operation of the program is quite primitive, but the windows make its on-screen presentation impressive nevertheless.

The player must guess a total of three words in turn. First, s/he is asked to type in a letter. If that letter is in the word, it is put in the YES window. If not, the letter goes into the NO window. After each guess at a letter, the player is asked to guess the whole word, which must then be typed in letter-by-letter, and the ↵ key pressed after every letter. A record is kept of the total number of guesses.

```
                /* Program 29 */
domains
    list=symbol*
    scores=integer
predicates
    member(symbol,list)
    run
    continue(list,scores)
    yes_no_count(symbol,list)
    guessword(scores,list)
    word(list,integer)
    read_as_list(list,integer)
goal
    makewindow(1,7,0,"",0,0,25,80),
    makewindow(2,7,135,"Counting",1,20,4,34),
    makewindow(3,112,112,"YES",5,5,7,30),
    makewindow(4,112,112,"NO",5,40,7,30),
    makewindow(5,7,7,"",14,20,10,34),
    run.
clauses
    run:- word(W,L),
          shiftwindow(1),clearwindow,
          write("The word has ",L," letters"),
          shiftwindow(2),clearwindow,
          shiftwindow(3),clearwindow,
          shiftwindow(4),continue(W,0),fail.
    continue(L,R):-
          shiftwindow(5),clearwindow,
          write("Guess a letter :"),
          Total=R+1,readln(T),yes_no_count(T,L),
          shiftwindow(5),clearwindow,
          guessword(Total,L),continue(L,Total).
    yes_no_count(X,List):-
          member(X,List),shiftwindow(3),write(X),
          shiftwindow(2),write(x),!.
    yes_no_count(X,_):-
          shiftwindow(4),write(x),
          shiftwindow(2),write(X).
```

```
guessword(Count,Word):-
      write("Know the word yet? Press y or n"),
      readchar(A),A='y',cursor(0,0),
      write("Type it in one letter per line \n"),
      word(Word,L),read_as_list(G,L),
      G=Word,clearwindow,window_attr(112),
      write("Right! You used ",Count," guess(es)"),
readchar(_),window_attr(7),!,fail.
      guessword(_,_).
      word([b,i,r,d],4). word([p,r,o,l,o,g],6).
      word([f,u,t,u,r,e],6).
      member(X,[X|_]):-!.
      member(X,[_|T]):-member(X,T).
      read_as_list([],0) :-!.
      read_as_list([Ch|Rest],L) :-
       readln(Ch),L1=L-1,read_as_list(Rest,L1).
```

A WINDOW TO DOS

Turbo Prolog programs can provide access to DOS via the *system* predicate, which takes the form

```
system("Any DOS command or the name of an executable file")
```

If the argument is an empty string (""), DOS will be called, as long as the DOS file COMMAND.COM is accessible from the current DOS directory (see Chapter 12, "Setup"). You can then give commands to DOS. To return to Turbo Prolog, type

```
EXIT
```

(Evaluation of the related standard predicate *exit* will stop the execution of a Turbo Prolog program and return control to Turbo Prolog).

For example, to copy the file B:ORIGINAL.FIL to a file A:ACOPY.FIL from within the Turbo Prolog system, you could give the goal

```
system("").
```

and then copy the file using the usual DOS command

```
>copy b:original.fil a:acopy.fil
```

and then return to Turbo Prolog

```
A>EXIT
```

after which Turbo Prolog replies

```
Goal :_
```

Program 30 displays directories for the disk in drive A (left window) and drive B (right window), and returns to Turbo Prolog when the space bar is pressed.

```
                 /* Program 30 */
goal
     makewindow(1,7,7,"Directory for disk A",0,0,20,35),
     dir("a:","*.*",_),
     makewindow(2,7,7,"Directory for disk B",0,40,20,35),
     dir("b:","*.*",_),
     makewindow(3,7,7,"",21,25,3,30).
```

Program 31 illustrates a file copy utility with a very elegant, window-driven user interface. In this design, the user needn't remember whether it is the name of the copy or the name of the file *to be copied* that comes first in the DOS *copy* command (a point of confusion for many novice computer users). Program 31 uses the standard predicate *concat* (see Chapter 9) which takes the form

```
concat(X,Y,Z)
```

and is true if *Z* is bound to the concatenated strings to which *X* and *Y* are bound. Thus

```
concat("hello"," mother",X)
```

will succeed and binds *X* to "hello mother" and

```
concat("valerie","ann","valerie-ann")
```

fails (because of the extra hyphen in "valerie-ann").

```
                 /* Program 31 */
goal
        makewindow(1,7,7,"Source",0,0,20,35),
        write("Which file do you want to copy ?"),
        cursor(3,8),readln(X),
        makewindow(2,7,7,"Destination",0,40,20,35),
        write("What is the name of the new copy ?"),
        cursor(3,8),readln(Y),
        concat(X," ",X1),concat(X1,Y,Z),
        concat("copy ",Z,W),
        makewindow(3,7,7,"Process",14,15,8,50),
        write(" Copying ",X," to ",Y),cursor(2,3),
        system(W).
```

Date and Time

There are two other DOS-related standard predicates that are handy to use: *date* and *time*. They can each be used in two ways, depending on whether all their parameters are free or bound on entry. If all variables in

```
time(Hours,Minutes,Seconds,Hundredths)
```

are bound, *time* will reset the internal system time clock. If all variables are free, they will be bound to the current values of the internal clock.

Date, which also relies on the internal system clock, operates in the same way, and takes the form

```
date(Year,Month,Day)
```

Program 32 uses *time* to display the time elapsed during a listing of the directory in drive A.

```
                  /* Program 32 */
goal
     makewindow(1,7,7,"Timer",8,10,12,60),
     time(0,0,0,0),dir("a:\\","*.*",_),
     time(H,M,S,Hundredths),
     write(H," hours  "),
     write(M," minutes  "),
     write(S," seconds  "),
     write(Hundredths," hundredths of a second"),nl,nl.
```

For a more sophisticated example of the use of *time*, see Program 60 in Chapter 10.

8 Tutorial VI: Graphics and Sound

Apart from windows, the other way to brighten up your programs is to use graphics and sound. Turbo Prolog offers a choice of point- and line-based graphics or a full set of Turtle Graphics commands. Complex shapes are easy to draw with Turtle Graphics—all you have to do is guide a little pen-carrying turtle around the screen. This chapter describes these facilities in detail, gives some attractive example programs and concludes with two applications of the *sound* standard predicate, one of which turns your computer into a piano!

TURBO PROLOG'S GRAPHICS

Before using Turbo Prolog's graphics commands, you must set up the screen in an appropriate way using the standard predicate *graphics*. When you've finished with graphics, the standard predicate *text* can be used to clear the screen and return to text mode.

The *graphics* predicate takes the form

```
graphics(ModeParam,Palette,Background)
```

and initializes the screen in medium, high or extra-high resolution graphics. The possible values for *ModeParam* and the resulting screen formats are shown in Table 8-1. The standard IBM Color/Graphics Adapter supports modes 1 and 2; and modes 3, 4, and 5 are supported by the Enhanced Graphics Adapter. In all cases, *graphics* clears the screen and positions the cursor at the upper left corner.

In mode 1 four colors can be used (colors 0, 1, 2, and 3), as shown in Table 8-2. Color 0 is the current background color. Colors are determined by one of two palettes, selected according to whether *Palette* is bound to 0 or 1. Modes 3 and 4 offer 16 colors, and mode 5 offers 13.

Background (also an integer value) selects one of the background colors shown in Table 8-3.

Table 8-1 Graphics Resolution Choices

ModeParam	Number of Cols	Number of Rows	Description
1	320	200	Medium resolution, 4 colors.
2	640	200	High resolution black and white.
3	320	200	Medium resolution, 16 colors.
4	640	200	High resolution, 16 colors.
5	640	350	Enhanced resolution, 13 colors.

Table 8-2 Palette Choices in Medium Resolution

Palette	Color 1	Color 2	Color 3
0	green	red	yellow
1	cyan	magenta	white

Table 8-3 Background Colors

0	black	8	gray
1	blue	9	light blue
2	green	10	light green
3	cyan	11	light cyan
4	red	12	light red
5	magenta	13	light magenta
6	brown	14	yellow
7	white	15	high intensity white

The two fundamental graphics standard predicates are *dot* and *line*. The call

```
dot(Row,Column,Color)
```

places a dot at the point determined by the values of *Row* and *Column*, in the specified *Color*. *Row* and *Column* are integers from 0 to 31999 and are independent of the current screen mode. (*Dot* returns the color value if the variable *Color* is free prior to the call). Similarly,

```
line(Row1,Col1,Row2,Col2,Color)
```

draws a line between the points (*Row1*, *Col1*) and (*Row2*, *Col2*) in the specified *Color*. Program 33 shows a typical sequence of standard graphics predicate calls.

```
                /* Program 33 */
goal
   write("Before graphics"),readchar(_),
   graphics(1,1,4),
   line(4000,4000,10000,20000,2),
   write("ordinary write during graphics mode"),
   readchar(_),
   text,
   write("After graphics").
```

Program 34 uses standard graphics predicates to construct a "doodle pad." A border is drawn around the screen, and you can draw by pressing the U (for Up), D (for Down), L (for Left), and R (for Right) keys. Try the program out before examining the code. Keys other than U, D, L and R are ignored, except that pressing * exits the program.

```
                /* Program 34 */
predicates
   move(char,integer,integer,integer,integer)
   start
   changestate(integer,integer)
goal
   start.
clauses
   start:-
       graphics(1,1,4),
       line(1000,1000,1000,31000,2),
       line(1000,31000,31000,31000,2),
       line(31000,31000,31000,1000,2),
       line(31000,1000,1000,1000,2),
       changestate(15000,15000).
   changestate(X,Y):-
        readchar(Z),move(Z,X,Y,X1,Y1),changestate(X1,Y1).
   move('r',X,31000,X,31000):- !.
   move('r',X,Yold,X,Ynew):- !,Ynew=Yold+100,dot(X,Yold,3).
   move('l',X,1000,X,1000):- !.
   move('l',X,Yold,X,Ynew):- !,Ynew=Yold-100,dot(X,Yold,3).
   move('u',1000,Y,1000,Y):- !.
   move('u',Xold,Y,Xnew,Y):- !,Xnew=Xold-100,dot(Xold,Y,3).
   move('d',31000,Y,31000,Y):- !.
   move('d',Xold,Y,Xnew,Y):- !,Xnew=Xold+100,dot(Xold,Y,3).
   move('*',X,Y,X,Y):- !,exit.
   move(_,X,Y,X,Y).
```

Turtle Graphics Commands

Standard predicates that produce effects similar to Program 34 are built into Turbo Prolog—the Turtle Graphics commands.

The effect of these predicates depends on

- The position of the turtle
- The direction of the turtle
- Whether the "pen" is drawing (activated) or not
- The color of the pen

The standard predicate *pendown* activates the pen and *penup* deactivates it. Immediately after a call to *graphics*, the pen is activated. The color of the trail left by the pen is determined by the parameter *Color* in *pencolor(Color)* according to the colors in Table 7-1.

The movement of the turtle is controlled by four standard predicates: *forward*, *back*, *right*, and *left*. Thus

```
forward(Step)
```

indicates how many steps the turtle is to move from its current position along its current direction (the size of the step depends on the graphics mode). *forward* fails if the movement leads to a position outside the screen; there are 32000 horizontal steps and 32000 vertical steps. The current position of the turtle is updated only if *forward* is successful.

The predicate

```
back(Step)
```

does the opposite of *forward*: *back(X)* corresponds to *forward(−X)*.

To make the turtle turn right, use the predicate

```
right(Angle)
```

If *Angle* is bound, the turtle will turn through the indicated angle in degrees to the right. If *Angle* is free prior to calling *right*, it is bound to the current direction of the turtle.

The predicate

```
left(Angle)
```

works the same for left turns.

Thus, the following sequence would draw a triangle on the screen and end up with the turtle facing in its original direction:

```
pendown,
forward(5000),right(120),
forward(5000),right(120),
forward(5000),right(120).
```

Program 35 draws a star in a similar way.

```
                  /* Program 35 */
goal
   graphics(1,1,0),
   forward(5000),right(144),forward(5000),right(144),
   forward(5000),right(144),forward(5000),right(144),
   forward(5000),right(144),forward(5000).
```

Here are some more examples of what you can do with Turtle Graphics: Programs 36 and 37 draw spirals, Program 38 draws a pattern, and Program 39 a circle.

```
                  /* Program 36 */
predicates
    polyspiral(integer)
goal
    graphics(1,1,0),polyspiral(500).
clauses
    polyspiral(X):-!,X<15000,
         forward(X),right(62),Y=X+100,polyspiral(Y).


                  /* Program 37 */
predicates
    inspiral(integer)
goal
```

```
    graphics(1,1,0),
    inspiral(70).
clauses
    inspiral(X):-
        X<330,!,forward(5000),right(X),Y=X+1,inspiral(Y).
```

```
            /* Program 38 */
predicates
    square(integer)
    fillsquare(integer)
goal
    graphics(1,1,0),
    penpos(0,0,90).
    fillsquare(5000).
clauses
    square(X):-
        forward(X),right(90),forward(X),right(90),
        forward(X),right(90),forward(X),right(90).
    fillsquare(X):-X>10000,!.
    fillsquare(X):-square(X),Y=X+500,fillsquare(Y).
```

```
            /* Program 39 */

predicates      circle(integer)
goal            graphics(1,1,0),circle(0).
clauses         circle(X):-
                  !,360>X,forward(100),right(1),Y=X+1,circle(Y).
```

Turbo Prolog's graphics can also be used within windows, as illustrated in Program 40. A window is drawn and a "spotlight" effect (several lines drawn from a fixed point to fifteen other points) is repeated at five different positions. Another overlapping window is drawn and five more "spotlights" appear. Finally, a text window is drawn, which contains an invitation for the user to press the space bar. Each time the space bar is pressed, one of the windows is removed and the invitation reappears.

Note that text and graphics can be used simultaneously both inside a window and on the full screen.

```
              /* Program 40 */
domains
    list=integer*
predicates
    spotlight(integer,integer,integer)
    xy(list)
    undo
goal
    graphics(2,0,1),
    makewindow(1,7,7,"First",1,1,18,70),
    xy([0,0,0,6000,4000,20500,20000,24000,16100,1000]),
    xy([0,0,0,9000,3000,26500,20100,24400,20100,1000]),
```

```
     makewindow(2,7,7,"Second",10,20,14,60),
     xy([0,1000,0,9000,0,20000,15000,20000,15000,1000]),
     makewindow(3,7,7,"Text",15,0,6,35),
     write(""),nl,
     write("Turbo Prolog window & graphics."),
     undo,undo,undo.
clauses
     xy([X,Y|Rest]):-
         spotlight(15,X,Y),!,xy(Rest).
     xy(_).
      spotlight(0,_,_):-!.
      spotlight(N,R,C):-
         X=N*1200,line(R,C,9000,X,1),N1=N-1,
         spotlight(N1,R,C).
      undo:-
         write("\n\nPress the space bar"),
         readchar(_),removewindow.
```

LET'S HEAR TURBO PROLOG

Turbo Prolog has two standard predicates for making noises. The simplest takes the form

```
beep
```

and makes the computer beep. The other can be used to make more imaginative noises, and takes the form

```
sound(Duration,Frequency)
```

A note of the indicated *Frequency* is played for *Duration* hundredths of a second. Using the *sound* predicate, we can turn the computer into a miniature piano, given the frequencies of various notes. In Program 41 we have done just that, using the frequencies shown in Table 8-4 and using the keys

```
    W   E       T   Y   U
  A   S   D   F   G   H   J   K
```

to mimic the normal piano keyboard layout. For example, pressing ASDFGHJK (in that order) would produce a C major scale. Keys not on our pretend piano keyboard produce a high-pitched peep thanks to the clause

```
tone(_,5000).
```

and thus only Ctrl Break interrupts the execution.

Table 8-4 The Computer as Piano

Note	Frequency	Keyboard Character
C (low)	131	A
C sharp	139	W
D	147	S
D sharp	156	E
E	165	D
F	175	F
F sharp	185	T
G	196	G
G sharp	208	Y
A	220	H
A sharp	233	U
B	247	J
C (middle)	262	K

```
                /* Program 41 */
predicates
    piano
    tone(char,integer)
goal
    piano.
clauses
    piano:-
        readchar(Note),tone(Note,Freq),sound(5,Freq),piano.

    tone('a',131).  tone('w',139).  tone('s',147).
    tone('d',165).  tone('e',156).  tone('f',175).
    tone('t',185).  tone('g',196).  tone('y',208).
    tone('h',220).  tone('u',233).  tone('j',247).
    tone('k',262).
    tone(_,5000). /*all other keys squeak */
```

Program 42 runs up and down a musical scale.

```
                /* Program 42 */
domains
    direction=up;down
predicates
      jack_and_jill(direction,integer)
goal
      jack_and_jill(up,500).
clauses
      jack_and_jill(up,F):-
          F<5000,!,sound(1,F),F1=F+200,jack_and_jill(up,F1).
      jack_and_jill(up,F):-
          jack_and_jill(down,F).
      jack_and_jill(down,F):-
          F>500,!,sound(1,F),F1=F-200,jack_and_jill(down,F1).
      jack_and_jill(down,F):-
          jack_and_jill(up,F).
```

9 Tutorial VII: Files and Strings

Turbo Prolog is extremely rich in file- and string-handling facilities. Rather than giving a long list of standard predicates that might seem daunting at first sight, this chapter gives the standard predicates in related families. Each family of predicates is followed by some example programs which illustrate the use of predicates in that family. A complete classified (and alphabetized) list of standard predicates can be found in Chapter 12.

The chapter concludes with a description of the very important standard predicate *findall* (which is used to collect the values of a variable that satisfy a given clause into a list) and of the random number generator *random*.

THE TURBO PROLOG FILE SYSTEM

In this section, we'll take a look at the Turbo Prolog file system and the standard read and write predicates that are relevant to files. The standard predicates for reading and writing are elegant and efficient. With just a single command, output can, for instance, be routed to a file instead of being displayed on the screen.

In fact, Turbo Prolog makes use of a *current_read_device*, from which input is read, and a *current_write_device*, to which output is sent. Normally, the keyboard is the current read device and the screen is the current write device, but you can specify other devices. For instance, input could be read from a file that is stored externally (on disk perhaps), and output could be sent to a printer. Moreover, it is possible to reassign the current input and output devices while a program is running.

Regardless of what read and write devices are used, reading and writing are handled identically within a Turbo Prolog program.

To access a file, it must first be opened. A file can be opened in four ways:

- For reading
- For writing
- For appending to the file
- For modification

A file opened for any activity other than reading must be closed when that activity is finished or the changes to the file will be lost. Several files may be open simultaneously, and input and output can be quickly redirected between open files. In contrast, it takes longer to open and close a file than to redirect data between files.

When a file is opened, Turbo Prolog connects a symbolic name to the actual name of the file used by DOS. This symbolic name is used by Turbo Prolog when input and output are redirected. Symbolic file names must start with a lowercase letter and must be declared in the file domain declaration:

```
file = file1 ; source ; auxiliary
```

Only one file domain is allowed in any program, and the four symbols

```
printer   keyboard
screen    com1
```

are automatically defined in advance in the file domain and must *not* appear in the file declaration. *printer* refers to the parallel printer port and *com1* refers to the serial communication port.

Following are the standard predicates for opening and closing files.

openread(SymbolicFileName,DosFileName)

The file *DosFileName* is opened for reading. The file is then referred to by the symbolic name *SymbolicFileName*. If the file is not found, the predicate fails. If *DosFileName* is illegal, an error message is displayed.

openwrite(SymbolicFileName,DosFileName)

The file *DosFileName* is opened for writing. If the file already exists, it is deleted. Otherwise, the file is created and an entry made in the appropriate DOS directory.

openappend(SymbolicFileName,DosFileName)

The file *DosFileName* is opened for appending. If the file is not found, an error message is displayed and execution halted.

openmodify(SymbolicFileName,DosFileName)

The file *DosFileName* is opened for both reading and writing. *openmodify* can be used in conjunction with the *filepos* standard predicate (see page 102) to update a random access file.

filemode(SymbolicFileName,FileMode)

The file *FileMode* is opened to speciy text mode: 0 or binary mode: 1. *Filemode* can be used to access binary files.

`closefile(SymbolicFileName)`

The indicated file is closed. This predicate is successful even if the file has not been opened.

`readdevice(SymbolicFileName)`

Reassigns the current read device provided *SymbolicFileName* is bound and has been opened for reading. If *SymbolicFileName* is free, the call will bind it to the name of the current active read device.

`writedevice(SymbolicFileName)`

Reassigns the current write device provided the indicated file has been opened either for writing or appending.

For example: The following sequence opens the file MYDATA.FIL for writing and directs all output produced by clauses between the two occurrences of *writedevice* to that file. In the following code excerpt, the file is associated with the symbolic file name *destination* appearing in a `domains` declaration of the file domain:

```
domains
    file = destination
goal
    openwrite(destination,"mydata.fil"),
    writedevice(destination),
            :
            :
    writedevice(screen),
```

As another example, the following sequence will redirect all output produced by clauses between the two occurrences of *writedevice* to the *printer* device. (The *printer* need not be "opened," since this is handled by the system. **Caution:** If no printer is connected, the system will "hang" if such a sequence is executed; Ctrl Break can be used to allow Turbo Prolog to regain control).

```
writedevice(printer),
        :
        :
writedevice(screen),
```

Also, the *com1* device is opened automatically. If your computer has no serial card, there will be a runtime error if *com1* is used in *writedevice* or *readdevice*.

In Program 43, we have used some standard read and write predicates to construct a program that stores characters typed at the keyboard in the DOS file TRYFILE.ONE on the current default disk. Characters typed are not echoed on the display screen; it would be a good exercise for you to change the program so that characters are echoed. The file is closed when the # key is pressed.

During text entry, each ASCII code for a carriage return received from the keyboard is sent to the file as two ASCII codes, carriage return and line feed. This is because the DOS TYPE command requires both characters to be present in order to produce a proper listing of the contents of the file.

```
                    /* Program 43 */
domains
    file = myfile
predicates
    start
    readin(char)
goal
    start.
clauses
    start:-
        write("this program reads your input and writes it to"),
        write(" tryfile.one\n"),
        openwrite(myfile,"tryfile.one"),
        writedevice(myfile),
        readchar(X),
        readin(X),
        closefile(myfile),
        writedevice(screen),
        write("Your input has been transferred a file").
    readin( '#' ):-!.
    readin('\13'):-!,write("\13\10"),readchar(X),readin(X).
    readin(  X  ):- write(X),readchar(Y),readin(Y).
```

The position where reading or writing takes place in a file can be controlled by the *filepos* predicate, which takes the form

```
filepos(SymbolicFileName,FilePosition,Mode)
```

This predicate can change the read and write position for a file identified by *SymbolicFileName*, which has been opened via *openmodify*, or it can return the current file position if called with *Fileposition* free and *Mode* bound to 0. *Fileposition* is a real value (any fractional part is disregarded). *Mode* is an integer and specifies how the value of *Fileposition* is to be interpreted, as shown in Table 9-1.

Thus the sequence

```
Text="A text to be written in the file",
openmodify(myfile,"some.fil")
writedevice(myfile),
filepos(myfile,100,0),
write(Text).
```

will write the value of *Text* in the file starting at position 100 (relative to the beginning of the file).

Using *filepos*, the contents of a file can be inspected position by position, and this is precisely what Program 44 allows you to do. The program requests a filename and then displays the contents of positions in the file as their position numbers are entered at the keyboard.

Table 9-1 Mode and Fileposition

Mode	Fileposition
0	Relative to the beginning of the file
1	Relative to current position
2	Relative to the end of the file i.e., the end of the file counts as position 0.

```
                    /* Program 44 */

domains
    file = input
predicates
    start
    inspect_positions
goal
    start.
clauses
    start:-
        write("Which file do you want to work with ?"),
        readln(FileName),
        openread(input,FileName),
        inspect_positions.
    inspect_positions:-
        readdevice(keyboard),nl,write("Position No?"),
        readreal(X),
        readdevice(input),filepos(input,X,0),readchar(Y),
        write(Y),inspect_positions.
```

In a similar vein, Program 45 dumps the contents of a file onto the display screen in (decimal) ASCII codes. It uses the *eof* predicate, which has the form

```
eof(SymbolicFileName)
```

eof can check whether the file position during a read operation is at the end of the file, in which case *eof* succeeds; otherwise, it fails.

```
                    /* Program 45 */
domains
    file = input
predicates
    start
    print_contents
goal
    start.
clauses
    start:-
        write("Which file do you want to work with ?"),
        readln(FileName),
        openread(input,FileName),
        readdevice(input),
        print_contents.
    print_contents:-
        not(eof(input)),!,readchar(Y),char_int(Y,T),
        write(T," "),print_contents.
    print_contents:-
        nl,readdevice(keyboard),
        write("\nPlease press the space bar"),readchar(_).
```

Following are the remaining file-handling standard predicates.

`flush(SymbolicFileName)`

Forces the contents of the internal buffer to be written to the named file. *flush* is useful when the output is directed to a serial port and it may be necessary to send data to the port before the buffer is full. During normal disk file operations, the buffer is *flush*ed automatically.

existfile(DosFileName)

This predicate succeeds if *DosFileName* is found in the DOS directory in the current default disk drive. The predicate fails if the name does not appear in the directory or if the name is an invalid file name or includes wildcards, e.g. *.*. The sequence

```
open(File,Name):-
      existfile(Name),!,openread(File,Name).
open(_,Name):-
      write("Error: the file ",Name," is not found").
```

can be used to verify that a file exists before attempting to open it.

deletefile(DosFileName)

DosFileName is deleted. *DeleteFile* always succeeds if the file name is a valid DOS file name; otherwise, a runtime error will occur.

renamefile(OldDosFileName,NewDosFileName)

The file *OldDosFileName* is renamed *NewDosFileName* provided a file called *NewDos-FileName* doesn't already exist and both names are valid file names. The predicate fails otherwise.

STRING PROCESSING

The following special characters are understood by Turbo Prolog when used in strings:

Character(s)	Meaning
"\n"	new line
"\t"	tab
"\b"	back space
"\\"	\

The backslash is a control character in Turbo Prolog. To print the backslash character, type two backslashes. For example, to designate a DOS path name, enter

```
"A:\\myfile.pro"
```

The predicates described in this section are used to divide strings either into a list of their individual characters or into a list of corresponding symbols. The predicate

```
frontchar(String1,CharParam,String2)
```

operates as if it were defined by the equation

```
String1 = (the concatenation of CharParam and String2).
```

If *String1* is empty, the predicate will fail. In Program 46, *frontchar* is used to define a predicate that changes a string to a list of characters. Try the goal

```
string_chlist("ABC",Z)
```

This goal will return *Z* bound to ['A','B','C'].

```
                 /* Program 46 */
domains
    charlist=char*
predicates
    string_chlist(string,charlist)
clauses
    string_chlist("",[]).
    string_chlist(S,[H|T]):-
        frontchar(S,H,S1),
        string_chlist(S1,T).
```

Fronttoken can be used to split a string into a list of tokens. It takes the form

```
fronttoken(String1,SymbolParam,Rest)
```

If *fronttoken* is called with *String1* bound, it finds the first token of *String1* which is then returned in *SymbolParam*. The remainder of the string is returned in the third parameter, *Rest*. Preceding blank spaces are ignored.

A sequence of characters is grouped as one *token* when it constitutes one of the following:

- A name according to normal Turbo Prolog syntax.
- A number (a preceding sign is returned as a separate token).
- A non-space character.

The following predicates can be used to determine the nature of the returned token: *isname*, *str_int*, and *str_len*, as demonstrated in Program 48. But first, let's look at an illustration of the division of a sentence into a list of *names*. If Program 47 is given the goal

```
string_namelist("bill fred tom dick harry",X).
```

X will be bound to

```
        [bill,fred,tom,dick,harry]
```

```
                 /* Program 47 */
domains
    namelist = name*
    name   = symbol
predicates
    string_namelist(string,namelist)
clauses
    string_namelist(S,[H|T]):-
        fronttoken(S,H,S1),!,string_namelist(S1,T).
    string_namelist(_,[]).
```

As another example, we'll define the predicate *scanner*, which will transform a string into a list of tokens, this time classified by associating each token with a functor.

```
                /* Program 48 */
domains
    tok = numb(integer);char(char);name(string)
    tokl = tok*
predicates
    scanner(string,tokl)
    maketok(string,tok)
clauses
    scanner("",[]).
    scanner(Str,[Tok|Rest]):-
        fronttoken(Str,Sym,Str1),
        maketok(Sym,Tok),
        scanner(Str1,Rest).
    maketok(S,name(S)):- isname(S).
    maketok(S,numb(N)):- str_int(S,N).
    maketok(S,char(C)):- str_char(S,C).
```

We conclude this section with a short summary of other useful string-handling standard predicates.

concat(String1,String2,String3)

concat states that *String3* is the string obtained by concatenating *String1* and *String2*. At least two of the parameters must be bound prior to invoking *concat*, which means that *concat* always gives only one solution (i.e., is deterministic). Thus

```
concat("croco","dile",Animal)
```

binds *Animal* to "*crocodile*".

frontstr(NumberOfChars,String1,StartStr,String2)

String1 is split into two parts. *StartStr* will contain the first *NumberOfChars* characters in *String1* and *String2* will contain the rest. Before *fronstr* is called, the first two parameters must be bound and the last two must be free.

str_len(StringParam,IntegerLength)

The predicate *str_len* returns the length of *StringParam* or tests if *StringParam* has the given *IntegerLength*.

isname(String)

Tests the *String* to verify whether it is a name according to normal Turbo Prolog syntax, i.e., whether it starts with a letter of the alphabet followed by any number of letters, digits and underscore characters. Preceding and succeeding spaces are ignored.

TYPE CONVERSION STANDARD PREDICATES

Following is a summary of the available type conversion standard predicates. Full details can be found in Chapter 12.

The standard predicates convert between a character and its ASCII value, a string and a character, a string and an integer, a string and a real, and uppercase and lowercase characters. The predicates are:

```
char_int(ACharacter,AnInteger)
str_char(OneCharInAString,OneCharacter)
str_int(AString,AnInteger)
str_real(AString,AReal)
upper_lower(UpperCaseStr,LowerCaseStr)
```

Conversions between the domain types symbol and string and between integer and real are handled automatically when using standard predicates and during evaluation of arithmetic expressions. This automatic conversion is necessarily performed when a predicate is called, as in the following example:

```
predicates
     p(integer)
clauses
     p(X):-write("The integer value is _",X),nl.
```

in which case the two goals

```
X=1.234,p(X).
X=1,p(X).
```

have the same effect.

As another example, we define two predicates which explicitly describe the conversions (the conversions are actually performed by the standard predicate =).

```
predicates
        int_real(integer,real)
        str_symbol(string,symbol)
clauses
        int_real(X,Y):- X=Y.
        str_symbol(X,Y):- X=Y.
```

FINDALL AND RANDOM

findall is used to collect values obtained from backtracking into a list. It takes the form

```
findall(VarName,mypredicate(...),ListParam)
```

findall is called with three parameters: the first parameter specifies which variable in that predicate designates the values to be collected in a list; the second is a predicate that gives multiple values by backtracking; and the third parameter is a variable that holds the list of values from backtracking. (There must be a user-defined domain to which the values of *ListParam* belong). Program 49 uses *findall* to print the average age of some *persons*.

```
                /* Program 49 */
domains
    name,address = string
    age = integer
    list = age*
predicates
    person(name,address,age)
    sumlist(list,age,integer)
```

```
goal
    findall(Age,person(_,_,Age),L),sumlist(L,Sum,N),
    Ave = Sum/N,
    write("Average =",Ave),nl.
clauses
    sumlist([],0,0).
    sumlist([H|T],Sum,N) :-
        sumlist(T,S1,N1),Sum=H+S1,N=1+N1.
    person("Sherlock Holmes","22B Baker Street",42).
    person("Pete Spiers","Flat 22, 21st Street",36).
    person("Mary Darrow","Flat 2, Omega Home",51).
```

The standard predicate

```
random(RealNumber)
```

returns a real number X satisfying

```
0 <= X < 1
```

Program 50 uses *random* to select three names from five at random.

```
                    /* Program 50 */
predicates
    person(integer,symbol)
    rand_int_1_5(integer)
    rand_person(integer)
goal
    rand_person(3).
clauses
    person(1,fred).
    person(2,tom).
    person(3,mary).
    person(4,dick).
    person(5,george).

    rand_int_1_5(X):-random(Y),X=Y*4+1.

    rand_person(0):-!.
    rand_person(Count):-
        rand_int_1_5(N),person(N,Name),write(Name),nl,
        NewCount=Count-1,rand_person(NewCount).
```

10 Tutorial VIII: Spreading Your Wings

In this final section of the tutorial, we present some example programs intended to stimulate your own ideas and to provide further illustration of the topics covered in the earlier tutorial chapters. Nearly all of the examples offer plenty of room for expansion; your own ideas can grow into full-blown programs using one of our programs as a basis. For complete information about the Turbo Prolog system, see Chapters 11 and 12.

BUILDING A SMALL EXPERT SYSTEM

We shall use Turbo Prolog to construct a small expert system that will figure out which of seven animals (if any) the user has in mind. It will do so by asking questions and then making deductions from the replies given. A typical user dialogue with our expert system might be:

```
Goal :_run.
has it hair ?
yes
does it eat meat ?
yes
has it a fawn color ?
yes
has it dark spots ?
yes
Your animal may be a (an) cheetah !
```

Turbo Prolog's ability to check facts and rules will provide our program with the reasoning capabilities germane to an expert system. Our first step is to provide the knowledge with which to reason, shown in Program 51.

```
        /* Program 51*/
predicates
    animal_is(symbol)
    it_is(symbol)
    positive(symbol,symbol)
    negative(symbol,symbol)
clauses
    animal_is(cheetah) if
          it_is(mammal) and
          it_is(carnivore) and
          positive(has,tawny_color) and
          positive(has,dark_spots).

    animal_is(tiger) if
          it_is(mammal) and
          it_is(carnivore) and
          positive(has,tawny_color) and
          positive(has,black_stripes).

    animal_is(giraffe) if
          it_is(ungulate) and
          positive(has,long_neck) and
          positive(has,long_legs) and
          positive(has,dark_spots).

    animal_is(zebra) if
          it_is(ungulate) and
          positive(has,black_stripes).

    animal_is(ostrich) if
          it_is(bird) and
          negative(does,fly) and
          positive(has,long_neck) and
          positive(has,long_legs) and
          positive(has,black_and_white_color).

    animal_is(penguin) if
          it_is(bird) and
          negative(does,fly) and
          positive(does,swim) and
          positive(has,black_and_white_color).

    animal_is(albatross) if
          it_is(bird) and
          positive(does,fly_well).

    it_is(mammal) if
          positive(has,hair).
    it_is(mammal) if
          positive(does,give_milk).

    it_is(bird) if
          positive(has,feathers).
    it_is(bird) if
          positive(does,fly) and
          positive(does,lay_eggs).
```

```
it_is(carnivore) if
      positive(does,eat_meat).
it_is(carnivore) if
      positive(has,pointed_teeth) and
      positive(has,claws) and
      positive(has,forward_eyes).

it_is(ungulate) if
      it_is(mammal) and
      positive(has,hooves).
it_is(ungulate) if
      it_is(mammal) and
      positive(does,chew_cud).
```

We can ask questions like

```
does it have hair?
```

We want to add corresponding clauses to Turbo Prolog's database so it can reason with the new clauses. We can add facts to the Turbo Prolog database via the `asserta` standard predicate. Thus

```
asserta(xpositive(has,black_stripes))
```

will cause

```
xpositive(has,black_stripes).
```

to be added to the Turbo Prolog database, provided *xpositive* has been declared in a `database` declaration at the top of the program:

```
domains
        .......
database
        xpositive(symbol,symbol)
predicates
        .......
clauses
        .......
```

Clauses for a predicate declared in a `database` declaration must not contain any rules—only facts. For a more detailed discussion of database predicates, see Chapter 11, "Dynamic Databases."

Our `database` declaration will be as follows:

```
database
        xpositive(symbol,symbol)
        xnegative(symbol,symbol)
```

The relationship between *xpositive* and *positive* is contained in the first of two rules for *positive*:

```
positive(X,Y) if xpositive(X,Y),!.
```

In other words, *xpositive* is the database equivalent of *positive*. We have a similar rule for negative:

```
negative(X,Y) if xnegative(X,Y),!.
```

The other rule for *positive* will ask the user for information if nothing is already known which contradicts a certain fact:

```
positive(X,Y) if
        not(xnegative(X,Y)) and ask(X,Y,yes).
```

The second rule for *negative* is similar:

```
negative(X,Y) if
        not(xpositive(X,Y)) and
        ask(X,Y,no).
```

Predicate *ask* asks the questions and organizes the remembered replies. If a reply starts with *y*, Turbo Prolog assumes the answer is *yes*; if it starts with *n*, the answer is *no*.

```
ask(X,Y,yes):-
        write(X," it ",Y,"\n"),
        readln(Reply),
        frontchar(Reply,'y',_),!,
        remember(X,Y,yes).
ask(X,Y,no):-
        write(X," it ",Y,"\n"),
        readln(Reply),
        frontchar(Reply,'n',_),!,
        remember(X,Y,no).

remember(X,Y,yes):-
        assertz(xpositive(X,Y)).
remember(X,Y,no):-
        assertz(xnegative(X,Y)).
```

We start the program by giving the goal *run*, with the following clauses:

```
run:-
        animal_is(X),!,
        write("\nYour animal may be a (an) ",X),
        nl,nl,clear_facts.
run:-
        write("\nUnable to determine what "),
        write("your animal is. \n\n"),clear_facts.
```

clear_facts removes any extra facts we may have added to the database, so that subsequent goals for the same program are not confused by information added to the database during the execution of previous goals. *Clear_facts* then waits for the user to press the space bar before returning to the Turbo Prolog system:

```
clear_facts:-
        retract(xpositive(_,_)),fail.
clear_facts:-
        retract(xnegative(_,_)),fail.
clear_facts:-
        write("\n\nPlease press the space bar to exit\n"),
        readchar(_).
```

For practice, type in the above "inference engine" and the "knowledge" clauses given earlier. Add appropriate declarations to make a complete program, and then try out the result.

PROTOTYPING: A SIMPLE ROUTING PROBLEM

This program illustrates the properties that make Turbo Prolog especially useful as a prototyping tool. Suppose we want to construct a computer system to help decide the best route between two U.S. cities. We could first use Turbo Prolog to build a miniature version of the system (see Program 52), since it will then become easier to investigate and explore different ways of solving the problems involved. We will use the final system to investigate questions such as:

- Is there a direct road from one particular town to another?
- Which towns are situated less than ten miles from a particular town?

```
            /* Program 52 */
domains
    town     = symbol
    distance = integer
predicates
    road(town,town,distance)
    route(town,town,distance)
clauses
    road(tampa,houston,200).
    road(gordon,tampa,300).
    road(houston,gordon,100)
    road(houston,kansas_city,120).
    road(gordon,kansas_city,130).

    route(Town1,Town2,Distance):-
        road(Town1,Town2,Distance).
    route(Town1,Town2,Distance):-
        road(Town1,X,Dist1),
        route(X,Town2,Dist2),
        Distance=Dist1+Dist2,!.
```

Figure 10-1 shows a simplified map for our prototype.

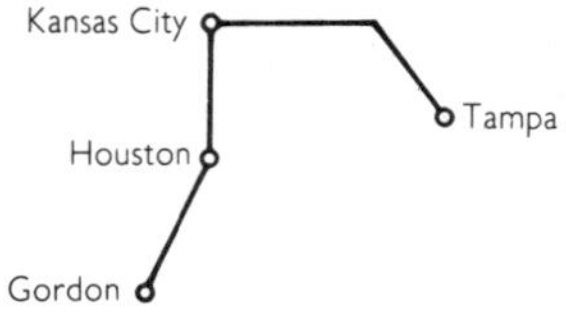

Figure 10-1 Prototype Map

Each clause for the *road* predicate describes a road, with a certain length in miles, that goes from one town to another The *route* predicate's clauses indicate that it is possible to make a route from one town to another over several stretches of road. Following the route, one drives a *distance* given by the third parameter.

The *route* predicate is defined recursively; a route can simply consist of one single stretch of road. In this case, the total distance is merely the length of the road.

Alternatively, it is possible to construct a route from *Town1* to *Town2* by driving from *Town1* to X and afterwards following some other route from X to *Town2*. The total distance is the sum of the distance from *Town1* to X and the distance from X to *Town2*.

Try the program with the goal

```
route(tampa,kansas_city,X).
```

Can the program handle all possible combinations of starting point and destination? If not, can you modify the program to avoid any omissions? The next example will give you ideas about how to get this program to collect names of towns visited enroute into a list. This prevents Turbo Prolog from choosing a route that involves visiting the same town twice, thereby avoiding going around in circles—and ensuring that the Turbo Prolog program doesn't go into an infinite loop. When you've solved problems of this type, you can enlarge the program by adding more cities and roads.

ADVENTURES IN A DANGEROUS CAVE

You are an adventurer who has heard that there is a vast gold treasure hidden inside a cave. Many people before you have tried to find it, but to no avail. The cave is a labyrinth of galleries connecting different rooms in which there are dangerous beings like monsters and robbers. In your favor is the fact that the treasure is all in one room. Which route should you follow to get to the treasure and escape with it unhurt?

Given the following map of the cave

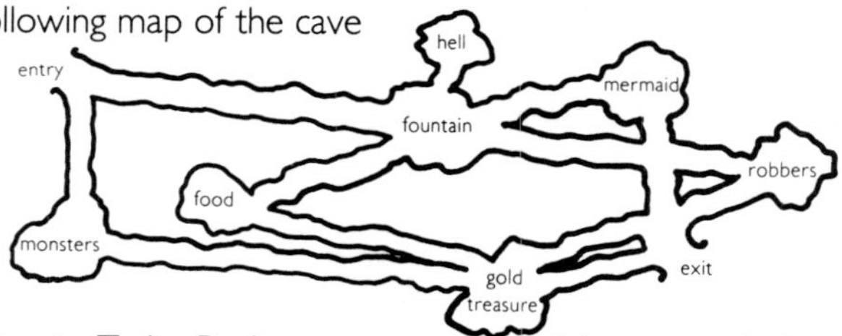

we can construct a Turbo Prolog representation of the map to help us find a safe route. Each gallery is described by a fact. Rules are given by the predicates *go* and *route*. Let's give the program the goal

```
go(entry,exit).
```

The answer will consist of a list of the rooms we should visit to capture the treasure and return with it safely.

An important design feature of this program is that the rooms already visited are collected in a catalog. This happens thanks to the *route* predicate, which is defined recursively; if one is standing in the exit room, the third parameter in the *route* predicate will be a list of the rooms already visited. If the *gold_treasure* room is a member of this list, we will have achieved our aim. Otherwise, the list of rooms visited is enlarged with *Nextroom*, provided *Nextroom* is neither one of the dangerous rooms nor has been visited before.

```
                /* Program 53 */
domains
     room  =  symbol
     roomlist = room*
predicates
    gallery(room,room)  /* There is a gallery between
                           two rooms */
    neighborroom(room,room) /* Necessary because it does
                               not matter which direction
                               we go along a gallery */
    avoid(roomlist)
    go(room,room)
    route(room,room,roomlist) /* This is the route to be
                                 followed. Roomlist consists
                                 of a list of rooms already
                                 visited. */
    member(room,roomlist)
clauses
    gallery(entry,monsters).      gallery(entry,fountain).
    gallery(fountain,hell).       gallery(fountain,food).
    gallery(exit,gold_treasure).  gallery(fountain,mermaid).
    gallery(robbers,gold_treasure).gallery(fountain,robbers).
    gallery(food,gold_treasure).  gallery(mermaid,exit).
    gallery(monsters,gold_treasure).

    neighborroom(X,Y) if gallery(X,Y).
    neighborroom(X,Y) if gallery(Y,X).

    avoid([monsters,robbers]).

    go(Here,There) if route(Here,There,[Here]).
    go(_,_)

    route(Room,Room,VisitedRooms) if
         member(gold_treasure,VisitedRooms) and
         write(VisitedRooms) and nl.
    route(Room,Way_out,VisitedRooms) if
         neighborroom(Room,Nextroom) and
         avoid(DangerousRooms) and
         not(member(NextRoom,DangerousRooms)) and
         not(member(NextRoom,VisitedRooms)) and
         route(NextRoom,Way_out,[NextRoom|VisitedRooms]).

    member(X,[X|_]).
    member(X,[_|H]) if member (X,H).
```

After verifying that the program does find a solution to the goal

```
go(entry,exit).
```

you might want to try adding some more galleries, for example,

```
gallery(mermaid,gold_treasure).
```

and/or extra nasty things to avoid.

Even though there is more than one possible solution to the problem, our program will only come up with one. To obtain all the solutions, we must make Turbo Prolog backtrack as soon as one solution has been found. This can be done by adding the *fail* predicate to the first rule for *route*:

```
route(Room,Room,VisitedRooms) if
                        member(gold_treasure,VisitedRooms) and
                        write(VisitedRooms) and nl and
                        fail.
```

We could use the list writing predicate *write_a_list* to write the list of names, without the containing square brackets [and] or the separating commas. However, the rooms visited are collected in the *VisitedRooms* list in reverse order, i.e., *exit* first and *entry* last. *write_a_list* must therefore be changed so that it first writes the tail of the list and then the head.

HARDWARE SIMULATION

Every logical circuit can be described with a Turbo Prolog predicate, where the predicate indicates the relation between the signals on the input and output terminals of the circuit. The fundamental circuits are described by giving a table of corresponding truth values (see the *and_*, *or_* and *not_* predicates in Program 54).

Fundamental circuits can be described by indicating the relationships between the internal connections as well as the terminals. As an example, let's construct an exclusive OR circuit from *and_*, *or_*, and *not_* circuits, and then check its operation with a Turbo Prolog program. The circuit is shown in Figure 10-2.

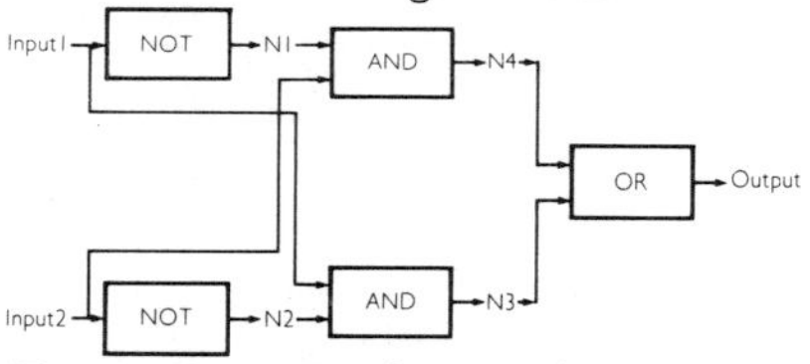

Figure 10-2 Fundamental XOR Circuit

In Program 54, this network is described by the *xor* predicate.

```
                        /* Program 54 */
domains
    d = integer
predicates
    not_(D,D)
    and_(D,D,D)
    or_(D,D,D)
    xor(D,D,D)
clauses
    not_(1,0).    not_(0,1).
    and_(0,0,0). and_(0,1,0). and_(1,0,0).  and_(1,1,1).
    or_(0,0,0).  or_(0,1,1).  or_(1,0,1).   or_(1,1,1).

    xor(Input1,Input2,Output) if
         not_(Input1,N1) and not_(Input2,N2) and
         and_(Input1,N2,N3) and and_(Input2,N1,N4) and
         or_(N3,N4,O).
```

Given the goal

```
xor(Input1,Input2,Output)
```

we obtain this result:

```
Input1 = 0, Input2 = 0, Output = 0
Input1 = 0, Input2 = 1, Output = 1
Input1 = 1, Input2 = 0, Output = 1
Input1 = 1, Input2 = 1, Output = 0
4 solutions
```

which verifies that the above circuit does indeed perform the task expected of it.

TOWERS OF HANOI

The ancient puzzle of the Towers Of Hanoi consists of a number of wooden disks and three poles attached to a baseboard. The disks each have different diameters and a hole in the middle large enough for the poles to pass through. In the beginning all the disks are on the left pole as shown in Figure 10-3.

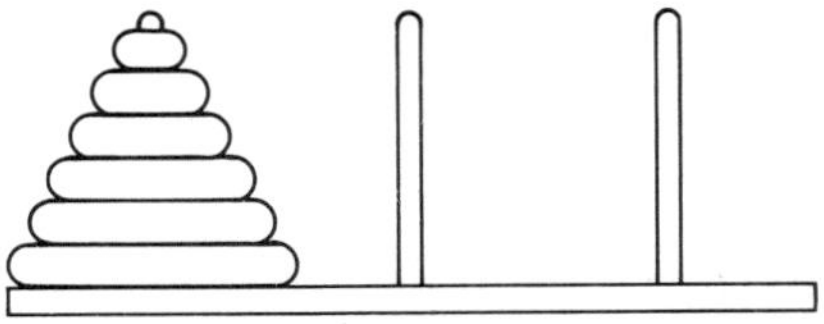

Figure 10-3 The Towers of Hanoi

The object of the puzzle is to move all the disks over to the right pole, one at a time, so that they end up in the original order on that pole. The middle pole may be used as a temporary resting place for disks, but at no time is a larger disk to be on top of a smaller one. Towers Of Hanoi can be easily solved with one or two disks, but becomes more difficult with three or more disks.

A simple strategy for solving the puzzle is:

- A single disk can be moved directly.
- *N* disks can be moved in three steps:
  - Move *N*−1 disks to the middle pole.
  - Move the last disk directly over to the right pole.
  - Move the *N*−1 disks from the middle pole to the right pole.

Our Turbo Prolog program to solve the Towers Of Hanoi puzzle uses three predicates: *hanoi*, with one parameter that indicates just how many disks we are working with; *move*, which describes the moving of *N* disks from one pole to another using the remaining pole as a temporary resting place for disks; and *inform*, which displays what has happened to a particular disk.

```
                        /* Program 55 */
domains
    loc = right ; middle ; left
predicates
    hanoi(integer)
    move(integer,loc,loc,loc)
    inform(loc,loc)
clauses
    hanoi(N) :- move(N,left,middle,right).

    move(1,A,_,C) :- inform(A,C),!.
    move(N,A,B,C) :-
         N1=N-1,move(N1,A,C,B),inform(A,C),move(N1,B,A,C).

    inform(Loc1,Loc2):-
         write("\nMove a disk from ",Loc1," to ",Loc2).
```

To solve Towers Of Hanoi with three disks, we give the goal

```
hanoi(3).
```

The output is:

```
Move a disk from left to right
Move a disk from left to middle
Move a disk from right to middle
Move a disk from left to right
Move a disk from middle to left
Move a disk from middle to right
Move a disk from left to right
```

DIVISION OF WORDS INTO SYLLABLES

A computer program can decide how to divide words into syllables using a very simple algorithm, which involves looking at the sequence of vowels and consonants each word contains. For instance, consider the two sequences below:

1. vowel consonant vowel

   In this case, the word is divided after the first vowel. For example, this rule can be applied to the following words:

   ```
   ruler   >  ru-ler
   prolog   >  pro-log
   ```

2. vowel consonant consonant vowel

   In this case, the word is divided between the two consonants. For example:

   ```
   number   >  num-ber
   anger   >  an-ger
   ```

These two rules work well for most words, but fail with words like *handbook*, which conform to neither pattern. To divide such words, our program would have to use a library containing all words.

Let's write a Turbo Prolog program to divide a word into syllables. First, it will ask for a word to be typed in, and then attempt to split it into syllables using the above two rules. As we have observed, this will not always produce correct results.

First, the program should split the word up into a list of characters. We therefore need the `domains` declarations

```
domains
     letter = symbol
     word   = letter*
```

We must have a predicate that determines the type of letter—vowel or consonant. However, our two rules can also work with the *vocals*, that is, the usual vowels (a, e, i, o, u) plus the letter *y*. The letter *y* sounds like (and is considered) a vowel in many words, for example hyphen, pity, myrrh, and martyr. Hence, we have the clauses

```
vocal(a). vocal(e). vocal(i).
vocal(o). vocal(u). vocal(y).
```

for the predicate *vocal*.

A *consonant* is defined as a letter that is not a *vocal*:

```
consonant(L) if not(vocal(L)).
```

We also need two more predicates. First, we need the *append* predicate (described on page 49).

```
append(word,word,word)
```

Secondly, we need a predicate to convert a string to a list of the characters in that string:

```
string_word(string,word)
```

This predicate will use the *frontchar* standard predicate (described in Chapter 9) as well as the standard predicates *free* and *bound* where

```
free(X)
```

succeeds if *X* is a free variable at the time of calling and

```
bound(Y)
```

succeeds if *Y* is bound.

Now we are ready to attack the main problem: the definition of the predicate *divide* which separates a word into syllables. *divide* has four parameters and is defined recursively. The first and second parameters contain, respectively, the *Start* and the *Remainder* of a given word during the recursion. The last two parameters return, respectively, the first and the last part of the word after the word has been divided into syllables.

The first rule for *divide* is

```
divide(Start,[T1,T2,T3|Rest],D,[T2,T3|Rest]):-
            vocal(T1),consonant(T2),vocal(T3),
            append(Start,[T1],D).
```

where *Start* is a list of the first group of characters in the word to be divided. The next three characters in the word are represented by *T1*, *T2* and *T3*, and *Rest* represents the remaining characters in the word. In the list *D*, the characters *T2* and *T3*, and the list *Rest* represent the complete sequence of letters in the word. The word is divided into syllables at the end of those letters contained in *D*.

This rule can be satisfied by the call

```
divide([p,r],[o,l,o,g],P1,P2)
```

To see how, let's insert the appropriate letters into the clause

```
divide( [p,r],[o,l,o|[g]], [p,r,o], [l,o | [g]]):-
        vocal(o),consonant(l),vocal(o),
        append([p,r],[o],[p,r,o]).
```

append is used to concatenate the first vocal to the start of the word. *P1* becomes bound to [p,r,o], and *P2* is bound to [l,o,g].

Program 56 shows the complete program.

```
                        /* Program 56 */
domains
    letter = symbol
    word = letter*
predicates
    divide(word,word,word,word)
    vocal(letter)
    consonant(letter)
    string_word(string,word)
    append(word,word,word)
goal
    clearwindow,
    repeat,
    write("Write a word: "),readln(S),string_word(S,Word),
    append(First,Second,Word),
    divide(First,Second,Part1,Part2),
    string_word(Syllable1,Part1),
    string_word(Syllable2,Part2),
    write("Division: ",Syllable1,"-",Syllable2),nl,
    fail.
clauses
    divide(Start,[T1,T2,T3|Rest],D1,[T2,T3|Rest]):-
        vocal(T1),consonant(T2),vocal(T3),
        append(Start,[T1],D1).
    divide(Start,[T1,T2,T3,T4|Rest],D1,[T3,T4|Rest]):-
        vocal(T1),consonant(T2),consonant(T3),vocal(T4),
        append(Start,[T1,T2],D1).

    divide(Start,[T1|Rest],D1,D2):-
        append(Start,[T1],S),
        divide(S,Rest,D1,D2).

    vocal(a).vocal(e).vocal(i).vocal(o).vocal(u).vocal(y).

    consonant(B):-not(vocal(B)), B <=z , a <= B.

    string_word("",[]):-!.
    string_word(Str,[H|T]):-
        bound(Str),frontstr(1,Str,H,S),string_word(S,T).
    string_word(Str,[H|T]):-
        free(Str),bound(H),string_word(S,T),concat(H,T,Str).
```

```
append([],L,L):-!.
append([X|L1],L2,[X|L3]) :- append(L1,L2,L3).
```

THE *N* QUEENS PROBLEM

In the *N* Queens problem, we try to place *N* queens on a chessboard in such a way that no two queens can take each other. Thus, no two queens can be placed on the same row, column, or diagonal.

To solve the problem, we'll number the rows and columns of the chessboard from 1 to *N*. To number the diagonals, we divide them into two types, so that a diagonal is uniquely specified by a type and a number calculated from its row and column numbers:

```
Diagonal = N + Column - Row      (type 1)
Diagonal = Row + Column - 1      (type 2)
```

When the chessboard is viewed with row 1 at the top and column 1 on the left side, type 1 diagonals resemble the "\" character in shape and type 2 diagonals resemble the shape of "/". The numbering of type 2 diagonals on a 4*4 board is shown in Figure 10-4.

	1	2	3	4
1	1	2	3	4
2	2	3	4	5
3	3	4	5	6
4	4	5	6	7

Figure 10-4 The *N* Queens Chessboard

To solve the *N* Queens problem with a Turbo Prolog program, we must record which rows, columns and diagonals are free and also make a note of where the queens are placed.

A queen's position is described with a row number and a column number, as in the domain declaration

```
queen = q(integer,integer)
```

to represent the position of one *queen*. To describe more positions, we can make use of a list:

```
queens = queen*
```

Likewise, we need several numerical lists indicating the rows, columns and diagonals that are not occupied by a *queen*. These lists are described by:

```
freelist = integer*
```

We will treat the chessboard as a single object via the `domains` declaration:

```
board = board(queens,freelist,freelist,freelist,freelist)
```

freelist represents the free rows, columns and diagonals of type 1, and the free diagonals of type 2, respectively.

By way of example, let's let *board* represent a 4*4 chessboard in two situations: (1) without queens and (2) with one queen at the top left corner.

(1) board without queens

```
board([],[1,2,3,4],[1,2,3,4],[1,2,3,4,5,6,7],[1,2,3,4,5,6,7])
```

(2) board with one queen

```
board([q(1,1)], [2,3,4],[2,3,4],[1,2,3,5,6,7],[2,3,4,5,6,7])
```

The problem can now be solved by describing the relation between an empty board and a board with *N* queens. We define the predicate

```
placeN(integer,board,board)
```

with the two clauses below. Queens are placed one at a time until every row and column is occupied. This can be seen in the first clause, where the two lists of *freerows* and *freecols* are empty:

```
placeN(_,board(D,[],[],X,Y),board(D,[],[],X,Y)):-!.
placeN(N,Board1,Result) :-
      place_a_queen(N,Board1,Board2),
      placeN(N,Board2,Result).
```

In the second clause, the predicate *place_a_queen* gives the connection between *Board1* and *Board2*. (*Board2* has one more queen than *Board1*). We use the `predicates` declaration

```
place_a_queen(integer,board,board)
```

The core of the *N* Queens problem is in the description of how to add extra queens until all have been successfully placed, starting with an empty board. To solve this problem, we add the new queen to the list of those who are already placed:

```
[q(R,C)|Queens]
```

Among the remaining free rows, *Rows*, we need to find a row *R* where we can place the next queen. At the same time, *R* must be removed from the list of free rows resulting in a new list of free rows, *NewR*. This is formulated as

```
findandremove(R,Rows,NewR)
```

Correspondingly, we must find and remove a vacant column *C*. From *R* and *C*, the numbers of the diagonals can be calculated on which a queen in row *R* and column *C* is placed. Then we can determine if *D1* and *D2* are among the vacant diagonals.

The clause is shown below:

```
place_a_queen(N,board(Queens,Rows,Columns,Diag1,Diag2),
        board([q(R,C)|Queens],NewR,NewS,NewD1,NewD2)):-

        findandremove(R,Rows,NewR),
        findandremove(C,Columns,NewC),
        D1=N+S-R,findandremove(D1,Diag1,NewD1),
        D2=R+S-1,findandremove(D2,Diag2,NewD2).
```

Program 57 is the complete program. It contains a number of smaller additions to define *nqueens*, so we need only give a goal like

```
nqueens(5)
```

to obtain a possible solution (in this case, for placing five queens on a 5*5 board).

```
                    /* Program 57 */
domains
    queen=q(integer,integer)
    queens=queen*
    freelist = integer*
    board=board(queens,freelist,freelist,freelist,freelist)
predicates
    placeN(integer,board,board)
    place_a_queen(integer,board,board)
    nqueens(integer)
    makelist(integer,freelist)
    findandremove(integer,freelist,freelist)
clauses
    nqueens(N):-
        makelist(N,L),Diagonal=N*2-1,makelist(Diagonal,LL),
        placeN(N,board([],L,L,LL,LL),Final),write(Final).

    placeN(_,board(D,[],[],D1,D2),board(D,[],[],D1,D2)):-!.
    placeN(N,Board1,Result):-
        place_a_queen(N,Board1,Board2),
        placeN(N,Board2,Result).

    place_a_queen(N,board(Queens,Rows,Columns,Diag1,Diag2),
            board([q(R,C)|Queens],NewR,NewC,NewD1,NewD2)):-
        findandremove(R,Rows,NewR),
        findandremove(C,Columns,NewC),
        D1=N+C-R,findandremove(D1,Diag1,NewD1),
        D2=R+C-1,findandremove(D2,Diag2,NewD2).

    findandremove(X,[X|Rest],Rest).
    findandremove(X,[Y|Rest],[Y|Tail]):-
        findandremove(X,Rest,Tail).

    makelist(1,[1]).
    makelist(N,[N|Rest]):-
        N1=N-1,makelist(N1,Rest).
```

USING THE KEYBOARD

When using full-screen input/output, our program must be able to read and react to special keys, such as the arrow and function keys. This is often tricky, because these keys are sometimes described by more than one ASCII value and may not have an associated printable image. Thus, the left arrow is represented by a single ASCII value, '\75', and the function key F10 is represented by two ASCII values, '\0' and '\68', but neither key corresponds to any printable character.

Program 58 shows how all keys can be read and recognized. We take advantage of the fact that keys represented by *two* ASCII codes always produce 0 when pressed without the [Shift], [Alt] or [Ctrl] keys. A predicate *readkey* is defined which returns symbolic values for the keys read. Symbolic values are easier to use than sequences of numerical values. The predicates *key_code* and *key_code2* specify the relationship between the symbolic names and the ASCII values.

```
                    /* Program 58 */
domains
    key = cr;esc;break;tab;btab;del;bdel;ins;end;home;
          fkey(integer);up_arrow;down_arrow;left_arrow;right_arrow;
          char(CHAR);other
predicates
    readkey(key)
    key_code(key,char,integer)
    key_code2(key,integer)
goal
    clearwindow,
    write("Keyboard test. Press a key!"),
    readkey(Key),nl,
    write("The ",Key,"-key was pressed").
clauses
    readkey(Key):-
        readchar(T),char_int(T,Val),key_code(Key,T,Val).

    key_code(Key,_,0):-
        readchar(T),char_int(T,Val),key_code2(Key,Val),!.
    key_code(break,_,3):-!.          key_code(bdel,_,8):-!.
    key_code(tab,_,10):-!.           key_code(cr,_,13):-!.
    key_code(esc,_,27):-!.           key_code(char(T),T,_).

    key_code2(btab,15):-!.           key_code2(home,71):-!.
    key_code2(up_arrow,72):-!.       key_code2(left_arrow,75):-!.
    key_code2(right_arrow,77):-!.    key_code2(end,79):-!.
    key_code2(down_arrow,80):-!.     key_code2(ins,82):-!.
    key_code2(del,83):-!.
    key_code2(fkey(N),V):- V>58, V<70, N=V-58, !.
    key_code2(other,_).
```

Program 59 uses the *readkey* predicate to build a simple field editor defined by the predicate *scr*.

When the program is run, the left and right arrow keys are used to move the cursor's position without modifying the contents of the field being edited. In the program, these arrow keys are referred to by the objects *left_arrow* and *right_arrow*, respectively. The [F10] key is used to terminate editing (and, therefore, to accept the amendments made up to that point), while the [Esc] key is used to abandon editing and to ignore any changes made. If a key is pressed that is not recognized by the program, the computer beeps.

Program 59 makes use of the *readkey* predicate from Program 58. If Program 58 has been saved in a disk file called EXAMPL58.PRO, the definition of *readkey* can be easily incorporated into Program 59 using the *include* compiler directive (see Chapter 11). It takes the form

```
include "filename"
```

and causes the contents of the named text file to be inserted into the containing program at the position of the *include* directive. Thus, using

```
include "EXAMPL58.PRO"
```

after compilation, Program 59 will contain the complete text of Program 58. However, since we wish to give a different goal to initiate the field editor from that used to demonstrate *readkey*, it is necessary to save Program 58 on disk *without the goal it contains.*

```
                    /* Program 59 */

include "exampl58.pro"  /*excluding the goal*/
domains
    row,col,length=integer
    field=f(row,col,length)
    position=pos(row,col)
predicates
    scr(field,position,key)
goal
    Row=10,Col=10,Length=30,cursor(Row,Col),
    makewindow(1,23,1,"Example Editor",0,0,25,80),
    write("Edit the text. Use the arrow keys to move"),
    field_attr(Row,Col,Length,112),
    scr(f(Row,Col,Length),pos(Row,Col),home),nl,nl,
    field_str(Row,Col,Length,Contents),
    write("Edited contents: ",Contents).
clauses
    scr(_,_,esc):-!, fail.
    scr(_,_,fkey(10)):-!.
    scr(f(Row,Col,L),pos(R,C),char(Ch)):-
        scr_char(R,C,Ch),C1=C+1,C1<Col+L,cursor(R,C1),
        readkey(Key), scr(f(Row,Col,L),pos(R,C1),Key).
    scr(f(Row,Col,L),pos(R,C),right):-
        C1=C+1,C1<Col+L,cursor(R,C1),readkey(Key),
        scr(f(Row,Col,L),pos(R,C1),Key).
    scr(f(Row,Col,L),pos(R,C),left):-
        C1=C-1,C1>=Col,cursor(R,C1),
        readkey(Key),scr(f(Row,Col,L),pos(R,C1),Key).
    scr(Field,Pos,_):-
        beep,readkey(Key),scr(Field,Pos,Key).
```

As an exercise, add predicates to Program 59 to move a part of the field to the right or the left and thereby add insert and delete functions to the simple field editor.

To conclude this section, we give an example of how to use the *inkey* standard predicate which takes the form

```
inkey(CharParam)
```

If a key has been pressed since the last read operation was performed, *inkey* succeeds by binding the variable *CharParam* to the ASCII character associated with the key pressed. *inkey* fails if no key has been pressed. Thus *inkey*—unlike *readchar*—allows execution to continue even if a key has not been pressed. The example below uses *inkey* and *time* to test a person's reaction time.

```
                    /* Program 60 */
predicates
  wait(char)
  equal(char,char)
  test(string)
goal
  makewindow(3,7,0,"",0,0,25,80),
  makewindow(2,7,7,"Key to press now",2,5,6,70),
  makewindow(1,7,7,"Accepted letters",8,10,10,60),
  Word = "Peter Piper picked a peck of pickled peppers"),
  write("Please type :\n\t",Word,\n\t),
  time(0,0,0,0),test(Word),
  time(_,_,S,H),
  shiftwindow(1),
  write("\nYou took ",S," seconds and ",H," hundredths").
clauses
  wait(X):- inkey(Y),equal(X,Y).
  wait(X):- shiftwindow(2),write(X),wait(X).
  test(W):- frontchar(W,Ch,R),wait(Ch),
            shiftwindow(2),write(Ch),test(R).
  test("").
  equal(X,X):-!.
  equal(_,_):-beep,fail.
```

11 Programmer's Guide

This chapter is intended for the professional programmer (which includes all those who have worked through the tutorial chapters 3 through 10). The first section summarizes the difference between Turbo Prolog and other versions of Prolog, and then gives a detailed summary of Turbo Prolog's syntax.

Like an encyclopedia, this chapter is not intended to be read from beginning to end in one sitting. Sections on memory management (page 134), compiler directives (page 135), flow patterns (page 144) and programming style (page 145) should be read by everyone. Some of the information given in Chapter 12 will only make sense after reading "Control of Input and Output Parameters: Flow Patterns," on page 144. For details about system-level operation—including installation and the specifications of the menu commands—see Chapter 12.

AN OVERVIEW OF THE TURBO PROLOG SYSTEM

Turbo Prolog is a *typed* Prolog *compiler*, which means that while it contains virtually all the features described in *Programming in Prolog* by Clocksin and Mellish (Springer, 1981), it is much faster than interpreted Prolog.

Compiled Turbo Prolog makes Prolog a practical tool for several reasons, some of which are listed below.

1. It is possible to produce stand-alone programs for the IBM PC and compatibles using the full capabilities of the hardware, windows, and full (color) graphics. Any window can contain mixed text and graphics. Turbo Prolog provides easy access to the PC's memory and I/O ports, as well as facilities for including machine code subroutines in Turbo Prolog programs.
2. Unlike the Clocksin and Mellish version of Prolog, Turbo Prolog maintains the programmer's own variable names. This means you can maintain control over your source code, even though the program is compiled. During debugging, the trace facility allows you to watch the execution of your program through a window onto the source text, and to single step through the evaluation of any goal.

3. The unique type system in Turbo Prolog not only offers a more secure program development environment, but also reduces the space requirements of the Prolog language.
4. Turbo Prolog is an integrated, fully modular program development environment. Modules written in Prolog or other languages (such as C and assembly language) can be linked into an executable unit. It is even possible to access the built-in system editor via a standard predicate call, so that a stand-alone program written in Turbo Prolog can include the complete editing subsystem.
5. Standard predicates for file handling allow the use of random access files.
6. Both integer and real arithmetic are built into the system, as are a complete range of mathematical operators and functions. These include all the usual trigonometric functions, as well as predicates defining bit-wise operations for control and robotic applications.
7. Turbo Prolog permits arithmetic expressions written in infix notation (including relational operators, arithmetic functions, and bracketed subexpressions).

There are a few other ways that Turbo Prolog differs from other versions of Prolog:

1. You are not allowed to define your own infix operators; full functorial notation must be used instead.
2. = is both a standard predicate *and* an operator.
3. The result of arithmetic operations (e.g., X/Y) depends on the types of their arguments.

BASIC LANGUAGE ELEMENTS

Names

Names are used to denote symbolic constants, domains, predicates, and variables. A name consists of a letter or underscore followed by any combination of letters, digits, and underscores. Two important restrictions are imposed on names:

- Names of symbolic constants must start with a lowercase letter.
- Names of variables must start with an uppercase letter or an underscore symbol.

Otherwise, you can either use uppercase or lowercase letters in your programs. For instance, you could make a name more readable by using mixed uppercase and lowercase, as in

```
MyLongestVariableNameSoFar
```

or by using underscores, as in

```
pair_who_might_make_a_happy_couple(henry,ann)
```

Reserved Names

The following are reserved words and must not be employed as user-defined names:

and	clauses	findall	if	predicates
asserta	database	free	include	readterm
assertz	domains	global	not	retract
bound	fail	goal	or	

Restricted Names

The following words have a special meaning in Turbo Prolog and should be avoided in user-defined names to prevent confusion:

abs	cursorform	fronttoken	pendown	sqrt
arctan	date	graphics	penup	storage
attribute	deletefile	include	port_byte	str_char
back	diagnostics	inkey	project	str_int
beep	dir	isname	ptr_dword	str_len
bios	disk	left	random	str_real
bitand	display	length	readchar	system
bitleft	div	line	readdevice	tan
bitnot	dot	ln	readint	text
bitor	edit	log	readln	time
bitright	editmsg	makewindow	readreal	trace
bitxor	eof	membyte	reference	trail
char_int	existfile	memword	removewindow	upper_lower
check_cmpio	exit	mod	renamefile	window_attr
check_determ	exp	nl	right	window_str
clearwindow	field_attr	nobreak	save	write
closefile	file_str	nowarnings	scr_attr	writedevice
code	filepos	openappend	scr_char	writef
concat	flush	openmodify	shiftwindow	
consult	forward	openread	shorttrace	
cos	frontchar	openwrite	sin	
cursor	frontstr	pencolor	sound	

Program Sections

A Turbo Prolog program consists of several program sections, each identified with a keyword and given in the sequence shown in Table 11-1.

You need not include all sections in your programs. For example, if you omit the `goal` section, your program will behave more like the Clocksin and Mellish version, in which all goals are given at runtime. Alternatively, a program could consist entirely of a single `goal` section. For example:

```
goal  readint(X),Y=X+3,write("X+3=",Y).
```

Table 11-1 Keyword Contents

`domains`	Zero or more domain declarations.
`global domains`	Zero or more domain declarations.
`database`	Zero or more database predicate declarations.
`predicates`	One or more predicate declarations.
`global predicates`	Zero or more predicate declarations.
`goal`	Goal.
`clauses`	Zero or more clauses (facts or rules).

Usually, a program will require at least `predicates` and `clauses` sections. For large programs, a `domains` section will help you economize on code for the same reason that types are used in Pascal. (This is a system *requirement* if any of the objects in a Turbo Prolog program belong to *domains of a non-standard type*).

For modular programming, the keywords `domains` and `predicates` can be prefixed with the word `global`, indicating that the subsequent domain declarations or predicate declarations affect several program modules globally (modular programming is discussed on page 152).

A program can contain several `domains`, `predicates`, or `clauses` sections, provided the following restrictions are observed:

- A program section must be prefaced with the corresponding keyword (`domains`, `database`, `predicates`, `clauses`, or `goal`).
- Only one goal must be met during compilation.
- All clauses that describe the same predicate must occur one after the other.
- At most, one `global predicates` section may be encountered during compilation, and then only if there have been no ordinary `predicates` declarations earlier.
- Sections containing `database` predicates must occur before all `global` and ordinary `predicates` declarations.

Domain Declarations

A `domains` section contains domain declarations. Four formats are used:

1. `name = d`

   This declaration declares a domain, *name*, which consists of elements from a standard domain type, *d*, which must be either integer, char, real, string, or symbol.

   This declaration is used for objects that are syntactically alike but are semantically different. For instance, *NoOfApples* and *HeightInFeet* could both be represented as integers and thus be mistaken for one another. This can be avoided by declaring two *different* domains of integer type

   ```
   apples,height = integer
   ```

   This allows Turbo Prolog to perform domain checks to ensure that apples and heights are never inadvertently mixed.

2. `mylist = elementDom*`

   This is a convenient notation for declaring a *list* domain. *mylist* is a domain consisting of lists of elements, from the domain *elementDom*. *elementDom* can be either a user-defined domain, or one of the standard types of domain. The asterisk should be read as "list" so that, for example

   ```
   numberlist = integer*
   ```

   declares a domain for lists of integers, such as `[1, -5,2, -6]`.

3. `myCompDom=f1(d11,..,d1N);f2(d21,..,d2M);..;fM(dN1,..,dNK)`

   Domains that consist of compound objects are declared by stating a functor and the domains for all the subcomponents. For example, we could declare a domain of *owners* comprising elements like

   ```
   owns(john,book(wuthering_heights,bronte))
   ```

   with the declaration

   ```
   owners = owns(name,book)
   ```

   where *owns* is the functor of the compound object, and *name* and *book* are domains of the subcomponents.

   The right side of such a `domains` declaration can define several alternatives, separated by a semicolon or the word `or`. Each alternative must contain a unique functor and a description of the domains for the actual subcomponents. For example,

   ```
   owners = owns(name,car);credit_card_purchase(name,car)
   ```

   could be two alternative domain definitions for compound objects in the *owners* domain.

4. `file = name1 ; name2 ; ... ; nameN`

   A file domain must be defined when the user needs to refer to files by symbolic names. A program can have only one domain of this type, which must be called file. Symbolic file names are then given as alternatives for the file domain. For example

   ```
   file = sales ; salaries
   ```

   introduces the two symbolic file names *sales* and *salaries*.

Shortening Domain Declarations

As we saw in the name=d declaration, the left side of a `domain` declaration (except for a file domain) can consist of a list of names

```
mydom1, mydom2, ..mydomN = ...
```

thereby declaring several domains, *mydom1*, ...*mydomN*, at the same time.

Predicate Declarations

Sections that follow the keyword `predicates` contain predicate declarations. A predicate is declared by stating its name and the domains of its arguments

```
predname ( domain1, domain2,...,domainN )
```

where *predname* stands for the new predicate name and *domain1, . . ., domainN* stand for user-defined domains or standard types of domain.

A predicate can consist of a name only, so that, for example, we could have a rule for the predicate *choose_teams* which looks like

```
choose_teams:-
     same_league(X,Y),never_played(X,Y),write(X,Y).
```

Multiple predicate declarations are also allowed. As an example, we can declare that *member* works on both numbers and names by

```
member(name,namelist)
member(number,numberlist)
```

where *name, namelist, number* and *numberlist* are user-defined domains. The alternatives must have the same number of arguments.

Clauses

A clause is either a fact or a rule corresponding to one of the declared predicates. In general, a clause is either an atom or consists of an atom followed by :−, then by a list of atoms separated by commas or semicolons. Also:

- The keyword **if** can be used instead of :− (a colon and hyphen)
- The keyword **and** can be used instead of , (a comma)
- The keyword **or** can be used instead of ; (a semicolon)

(The precise syntax for clauses—as well as the rest of Turbo Prolog—can be found in Chapter 12).

For example, the Turbo Prolog fact

```
same_league(ucla,usc).
```

consists of a single atom (which is itself a name, *same_league*), and a bracketed list of terms (*ucla,usc*).

A *term* is either a (simple) constant, a variable, or a compound term. We'll look at these three syntactic elements in greater detail now.

Simple Constants

Simple constants belong to one of the six standard types of domain:

A *character* belongs to the char domain type (an 8-bit ASCII character enclosed between two single quotation marks). An ASCII character is indicated by the ESCAPE symbol (\) followed by an ASCII code. \n and \t produce a newline and a tabulate character, respectively. \ followed by any other character produces the character itself.

An *integer* belongs to an integer domain type and is a whole number in the range −32,768 to 32,767.

A *real number* belongs to the domain of real type and is a number in the range ±1e−307 to ±1e+308, written with a sign, a mantissa, a decimal point, a fractional part, a sign, an e and an exponent, all without included spaces. The sign, fractional, and exponent parts are optional (though if the fractional part is omitted, so is the decimal point). Integers will be automatically converted to real numbers when necessary.

A *string* belongs to the string domain type (any sequence of characters between a pair of double quotation marks). Strings can contain characters produced by an ESCAPE sequence as mentioned under *character* above.

A *symbolic constant* belongs to the symbol domain type (a name starting with a lowercase letter). Strings are accepted as symbols too, but symbols are kept in a lookup table for quicker matching. The symbol table does take up some storage space, as well as the time required to make an entry in the table.

A *symbolic file name* belongs to the file domain (either a name starting with a lowercase letter and appearing on the right side of the file domain declaration, or one of the predefined symbolic file names: *printer, screen, keyboard,* and *com1*).

Variables

Variables are names starting with an uppercase letter or, to represent the anonymous variable, a single underscore character. The anonymous variable is used when the value of that variable is not of interest. A variable is said to be *free* when it is not yet associated with another term and *bound* when it is instantiated, i.e., when the variable is unified with a term. The predicate *free(X)* determines whether the variable X is free or not. *free* succeeds only if the value of the variable is still unknown when *free* is called. *bound(X)* succeeds only if X is bound to a value.

Compound Terms

A compound term (or structure) is a single object that consists of a collection of other objects (called *components*) and a describing name, the *functor.* The components are enclosed in parentheses and separated by commas. The functor is written just before the left parenthesis. For example, the compound term below consists of the functor *author* and three components:

```
author(emily,bronte,1818)
```

A compound term belongs to a user-defined domain. The `domains` declaration corresponding to the *author* compound term might look like

```
domains
     authors = author(firstname,lastname,year_of_birth)
     firstname,lastname = symbol
     year_of_birth = integer
```

Lists—a Special Kind of Compound Term. Lists are a common data structure in Turbo Prolog; they are actually a form of compound object. A list consists of a sequence of terms enclosed in square brackets and separated by commas. A list of integers would appear as

```
[1,2,3,9,-3,2]
```

Such a list belongs to a user-defined domain, such as

```
domains
     ilist = integer*
```

If the elements in a list are of mixed types, for example, a list containing both characters and integers, this must be stated in a corresponding declaration. Thus the declarations

```
domains
     element = c(char) ; i(integer)
     list = element*
```

would allow lists like

```
[i(12),i(34),i(-567),c('x'),c('y'),c('z'),i(987)]
```

TURBO PROLOG MEMORY MANAGEMENT

From the point of view of the Turbo Prolog system, available memory is divided into the areas shown in Figure 11-1.

Figure 11-1 Memory Partitioning in Turbo Prolog

- The *Stack* is used for parameter transfer, especially in recursive programs where tail recursion cannot be eliminated.
- The area used for the user's program *Source* text.
- The area used for the generated *Code*.
- The area allocated for the *Trail*, which is used to register the binding and unbinding of *reference variables*.
- The area allocated for the *Heap*.

The Heap is used for two different purposes and, depending upon the purpose, spare Heap resources can be released in two ways. Within the Heap, a stack is used for building structures, storing strings, etc., and stack storage is released when predicates fail. Hence, the principles of programming style discussed starting on page 145 (especially rules 3 and 5) should be carefully observed. The Heap is also used when facts are inserted in a database. These areas are automatically released whenever possible to keep Heap demands to a minimum.

Since individual programs vary in their demands on different memory areas, users can control memory partitioning as follows:

Stack. To allow for greater recursion in programs in which tail recursion cannot be eliminated, stack size should be increased. The size of the Stack can be reconfigured using the **M**iscellaneous option of the **S**etup command by specifying the number of paragraphs (1 paragraph is 16 bytes) between 600 and 4000 as required. The configuration via **S**etup must then be saved, then loaded (via **S**etup) so that the new Stack is correctly installed.

Source. The capacity for source text can be increased by using *include* files (see page 137).

Code. By default, 16K bytes are allocated for code. This default can be altered using the compiler directive *code* (see page 136).

Trail. By default, no space is allocated for the trail, because the trail is not normally needed in Turbo Prolog. However, this can be changed via the compiler directive *trail* (see page 139).

Heap. Once the Stack, Source, Code, and Trail areas have been allocated, any remaining memory is used for the Heap.

The standard predicate

```
storage(StackSize,HeapSize,TrailSize)
```

returns the available size of the three runtime memory areas used by the system (Stack, Heap, and Trail, respectively).

COMPILER DIRECTIVES

A number of compiler features are controlled through compiler directives. One or more of the following directives can be introduced as keywords at the beginning of the program text:

```
config, check_cmpio, check_determ, code, diagnostics, nobreak,
nowarnings,  project,  shorttrace, trace,  trail
```

and the *include* directive can appear wherever one of the program section keywords can be used.

config

To let a stand-alone .EXE application read a configuration file that defines default window attributes and code size, place the option `config "ConfigFileName."` into your program. This will read *ConFigFileName* and react the same as the Turbo Prolog system does with PROLOG.SYS.

check_cmpio

When the *check_cmpio* compiler directive is specified, a warning will be given whenever compound flow patterns are used.

If a predicate can be called with a parameter that is partly used for input (that is to say, some subcomponents are *bound*), and with other subcomponents used for output (that is, *free*), then we say that this parameter has a corresponding compound flow pattern or a compound input/output pattern. As an example, consider a list of compound objects:

```
domains
     object = int(integer) ; str(string) ; real(real)
     list = object*
predicates
     member(object,list).
```

A call

```
member(int(X),List)
```

to the *member* predicate with a compound flow pattern could then be used to return all the *ints* in a list.

Compound flow patterns tend to produce more code, so it is sometimes more appropriate to test a parameter on return from the predicate.

check_determ

When *check_determ* is specified, a warning will be given for each program clause that results in a nondeterministic predicate. *check_determ* can be used to guide the setting of cuts (see page 149). Turbo Prolog itself performs extensive tests to decide whether a predicate is deterministic or nondeterministic, so your programs need not be filled with cuts merely to save stack space.

If some predicates are nondeterministic and you wish to overcome the warning messages, it is possible to precede a predicate declaration by the keywords *determ* or *nondeterm*, which state that the predicate is to be deterministic or nondeterministic, respectively:

```
predicates
  nondeterm rep
  determ readname(string)
```

All global predicates are by default treated as nondeterministic because global predicates can be defined in modules other than those in which they are used. *determ* makes it possible to declare a global predicate as deterministic.

code

code is used to specify the size of the internal code array. The default is 16K bytes. For very large programs it may be desirable (or even essential) to specify a larger size. For computers with limited RAM capacity, you may want to specify a smaller size to make more room for stack space, for instance. The format is

```
code = Number_of_paragraphs
```

where *Number_of_paragraphs* represents the number of memory paragraphs (16 bytes each) required in the code array. Thus

```
Code = 1024
```

sets the size of the code array to 16K bytes.

To include code modifications in a stand-alone program, use the *config* compiler directive.

diagnostics

When *diagnostics* is specified, the compiler will display an analysis of the user's program containing the following information:

- The names of the predicates used.
- Whether or not all the clauses for the predicate are facts.
- Whether the predicate is deterministic or nondeterministic.
- The size of the code for each predicate.
- The flow pattern for each predicate.
- The domain types of the parameters.

An example display is shown in Figure 11-2.

```
Predicate Name  Dbase Determ Size  Doml--flow pattern
--------------- ----- ------ ----- --------------------------
goal            NO    YES        0 --
person          YES   NO       168 name,address,age,sex,inter
                                   --outp,outp,outp,inp,outp
list_all        NO    NO       176 --
shared_inter    NO    YES       80 inters,inters--inp,inp
member          NO    NO        72 inter,inters--outp,inp
member          NO    NO        87 inter,inters--inp,inp
--------------- ----- ------ ----- --------------------------
Total size                     583
```

Figure 11-2 Sample Diagnostic Display

include

include is used in programs or modules when the contents of a text file are to be included in a program during compilation. The syntax is

```
include "dos-file-name"
```

`dos-file-name` may include a path name.

Include files can only be used on "natural" boundaries in a program. Thus, the keyword `include` may appear only where one of the keywords `domains`, `predicates`, `goal`, or `clauses` is permitted. An include file may itself contain further *include* directives. However, include files must *not* be used recursively in such a way that the same file is included more than once during compilation. The use of many levels of include files requires more storage during compilation than if the same files were included directly in the main program (at one level). Include files can contain a `goal` or `domains` and `predicates` declarations, provided the restrictions on program structure are observed (see page 130). In the example in Figure 11-3 a file is included in a program, and that file in turn contains an *include* directive.

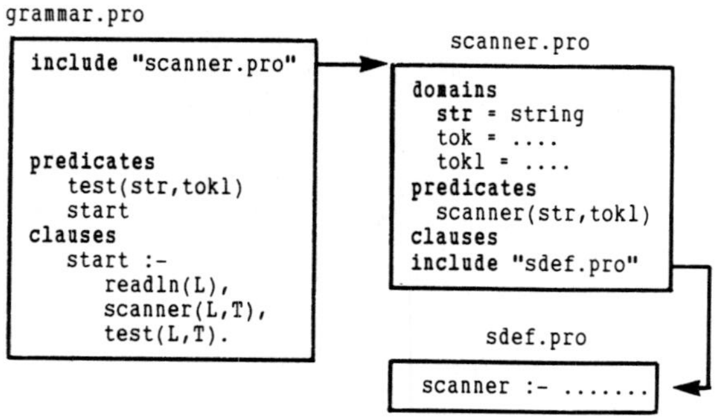

Figure 11-3 Example Use of the Include Directive

nobreak

In the *absence* of the *nobreak* compiler option, code will be generated to check the keyboard before each predicate call to ensure that the Ctrl Break or Ctrl C key combination has not been pressed. This slows down program execution slightly and takes up a little extra program space. *nobreak* stops this automatic generation of code. When the *nobreak* option is in operation, the only way to escape an endless loop is to reboot the entire operating system. It should only be used, therefore, when a program has been thoroughly tested.

nowarnings

nowarnings suppresses the warnings given when a variable occurs only once in a clause, and when a variable is not bound on return from a clause.

project

project is used in modular programming. All Turbo Prolog modules involved in a project need to share an internal symbol table. *project* must appear on the first line of a module to specify which project it belongs to. For example:

```
project "MYPROJ"
```

See page 152 for complete details about modular programming.

trace and shorttrace

trace prevents Turbo Prolog from carrying out the elimination of tail recursion (see page 145) and various other optimizing tricks so that the trace shows all *RETURNs*. *shorttrace* shows a trace with these optimizations being used.

If either *trace* or *shorttrace* is specified, all predicates will be traced. If *trace* or *shorttrace* is followed by a list of predicate names, only those predicates in the list will be traced. Turbo Prolog displays the information shown in Table 11-2.

Table 11-2 Trace Window Messages

CALL	Each time a predicate is called, the predicate's name and the values of its parameters are displayed in the trace window.
RETURN	*RETURN* is displayed in the trace window when a clause is satisfied and the predicate returns to any calling predicate. If there are further clauses that match the input parameters, an asterisk will be displayed to indicate that this clause is at a backtracking point.
FAIL	When a predicate fails, the word *FAIL* is displayed, followed by the name of the failing predicate.
REDO	*REDO* indicates that backtracking has taken place. The name of the predicate that is being retried, together with the values of its parameters, are displayed in the trace window.

For example, given

```
trace
domains
     list=integer*
predicates
     eq(integer,integer)
     member(integer,list)
clauses
     member(X,[X|_]).
     member(X,[_|L]):-member(X,L).
     eq(X,X).
```

and a goal that uses the *eq* predicate to determine whether 2 is a *member* of the list [*1*,2], we obtain the trace shown in Figure 11-4.

```
dialog
Goal:   member(X,[1,2]), eq(X,2)
X = 2
1 Solution

Goal:
```

```
trace
CALL:   member(_,[1,2])
RETURN:*member(1,[1,2])
CALL:   eq(1,2)
FAIL:   eq(1,2)
REDO:   member(_,[1,2])
CALL:   member(_,[2])
RETURN:*member(2,[2])
CALL:   eq(2,2)
RETURN: eq(2,2)
REDO:   member(_,[2])
CALL:   member(_,[])
FAIL:   member(_,[])
```

Figure 11-4 Use of *trace*

trail

trail is used to specify the size of the internal *trail* array. The format is:

```
trail= Number_of_words
```

The *trail* array is used to register side effects (primarily bindings of reference variables). Since, by default, there is no *trail* array, if *reference* variables (see page 149) have been used, a trail size must be given explicitly; otherwise, a trail overflow error will result. For most purposes

```
trail = 100
```

will be adequate.

DYNAMIC DATABASES IN TURBO PROLOG

Because Turbo Prolog represents a relational database as a collection of facts, the Turbo Prolog language can be utilized as a powerful query language for dynamic databases. Its unification algorithm automatically selects facts with the correct values for the known parameters and assigns values to any unknown parameters, and its backtracking algorithm gives all the solutions to a given query.

In this section we'll talk about how to update a dynamic database—insert new information and remove the old during execution. To increase speed when processing large databases, facts belonging to dynamic databases are treated differently from normal predicates. Dynamic database predicates are distinguished from normal predicates by declaration in a separate `database` section.

Declaration of the Database

The keyword `database` marks the beginning of a sequence of predicate declarations for predicates describing a *dynamic database*. A dynamic database is a database to which facts can be added during execution, or fetched from a disk file by a call to the standard predicate *consult*. A `database` declaration must precede all normal predicate declarations, as shown in this code excerpt:

```
domains
     name,address = string
     age = integer
     sex = male ; female
database
     person(name,address,age,sex)
predicates
     male(name,address,age)
     female(name,address,age)
     child(name,age,sex)
clauses
     male(Name,Address,Age) if
     person(Name,Address,Age,male).
     ...
```

The predicate *person* can be used in precisely the same way as the other predicates, the only difference being that it is possible to insert and remove facts for the *person* predicate during execution. Facts added in this way are stored in internal memory.

Manipulation of a database is carried out by three standard predicates. `asserta` inserts a new fact *before* any existing facts for a given relation, `assertz` inserts a new fact *after* all existing facts for the given relation, and `retract` removes a fact from the database.

For example, the first of the following two goals inserts a fact about *"John"* for the *person* predicate. The second retracts the first fact about *"Fred"*:

```
assertz( person("John","New York",35) ).
retract( person("Fred",_,_) ).
```

To modify a fact in the database, the fact is first retracted and then the new version of the fact is asserted.

The whole database can be saved in a text file by calling the predicate *save* with the name of the text file as its parameter. For example, after the call to

```
save("mydata.dba")
```

the file mydata.dba will resemble an ordinary Turbo Prolog program with a fact on each line. Such a file can later be read into memory using the *consult* predicate:

```
consult("mydata.dba")
```

consult succeeds if the program in the file does not contain errors; otherwise, it fails.

Handling Facts

The `readterm` predicate makes it possible to access facts in a file. `readterm` can read any object written by the *write* predicate and takes the form

```
readterm(<name>,TermParam).
```

where ⟨*name*⟩ is the name of a domain. The following code excerpt shows how `readterm` might be used.

```
domains
     name,addr = string
     one_data_record = p(name,addr)
     file = file_of_data_records
predicates
     person(name,addr)
     moredata(file)
clauses
     person(Name,Addr):-
                    openread(file_of_data_records,"dd.dat"),
                    readdevice(file_of_data_records),
                    moredata(file_of_data_records),
                    readterm(one_data_record,p(Name,Addr)).
     moredata(_).
     moredata(File):-not(eof(File)),moredata(File).
```

Provided the file *dd.dat* contains facts belonging to the *description* domain, such as

```
p("Peter","28th Street")
p("Curt","Wall Street")
```

the following is an example of a dialog that retrieves information from that file:

```
Goal : person("Peter",Address).
Address="28th Street"
1 Solution
Goal : person("Peter","Not an address").
False
Goal : _
```

Facts that describe database predicates can also be manipulated as though they were terms. This is made possible by the *dbasedom* domain, which is automatically declared by the Turbo Prolog system and constitutes one alternative for each predicate in the database. It describes each database predicate by a functor and by the domains of the arguments in that predicate.

As an example, consider the declarations

```
database
     person(name,telno)
     city(cno,cname)
```

The Turbo Prolog system generates the corresponding *dbasedom*:

```
domains
     dbasedom = person(name,telno) ; city(cno,cname)
```

This domain can be used like any other predefined domain. Thus, if it were not already supplied as part of the Turbo Prolog system, a predicate *my_consult*, similar to the standard predicate *consult*, could be constructed as follows:

```
domains
     file = dbase
database
     ...
predicates
     my_consult(string)
     repeat(file)
clauses
     my_consult(FileName):-
               openread(dbase,FileName),
               readdevice(dbase),
               repeat(dbase),
               readterm(dbasedom,Term),
               assertz(Term),
               fail.
     my_consult(_):- eof(dbase).
     repeat(_).
     repeat(File):-not(eof(File)), repeat(File).
```

If, for example, the `database` program section contains the declaration

```
p(string,string)
```

and a file called *dd.dat* exists with contents as described on page 141 we could obtain the following dialog:

```
Goal:my_consult("dd.dat").
True
Goal:p(X,Y).
X = "Peter", Y = "28th Street"
X = "Curt", Y = "Wall Street"
2 solutions
```

Extending the Database onto Files

The next example program illustrates how to implement new predicates that are like `assertz` and `retract` except that *the resulting database is maintained in files, rather than in RAM*. This extends the normal database facility, since database facts are part of a Prolog program and are therefore restricted by the size of available RAM. With the database in files, the only limit is the size of available disk space. This means that your Turbo Prolog database could be anything up to 100M bytes.

In the program, two new predicates, *dbassert* and *dbretract*, are implemented using an index file to record the positions of the facts in the data file. Each position is represented by a real number specifying where that fact is stored relative to the beginning of the *datafile*. The use of an index file in this way is not essential, but it could be the basis for binary search or hashing techniques to speed up access to the facts in the database.

```
domains
     file          = datafile; indexfile
     name, address = string
     age           = integer
     sex           = m or f
     interest      = symbol
     interests     = interest*
database
     person(name,address,age,sex,interests)
predicates
     dbassert(dbasedom)
     dbretract(dbasedom)
     dbread(dbasedom)
     dbass(dbasedom,string,string)
     dbaaccess(dbasedom,real)
     dbret(dbasedom,string,string)
     dbret1(dbasedom,real)
     dbrd(dbasedom,string,string)
clauses

/* Entry routines. These can be changed to fit the actual
application: for example, extended to a pool of open files in
order to access several databases at a time, or to allow more
than one datafile. */

dbassert(Term):-   dbass(Term,"dba.ind","dba.dat").

dbretract(Term):-  dbret(Term,"dba.ind","dba.dat").

dbread(Term):-     dbrd(Term,"dba.ind","dba.dat").

/* dbass appends a term to the data file and updates the
   index file  */

dbass(Term,IndexFile,DataFile ):-
     existfile( DataFile ), existfile( IndexFile ),!,
     openappend( datafile, Datafile ),
     writedevice( datafile ),
     filepos( datafile, Pos, 0 ),
     write( Term ),nl,
     closefile( datafile ),
     openappend( indexfile ,IndexFile ),
     writedevice( indexfile ),
     writef( "%7.0\n",Pos ),
     closefile( indexfile ).

dbass( Term, IndexFile, DataFile ) :-
     openwrite( datafile, Datafile ),
     writedevice( datafile ),
     filepos( datafile, Pos, 0 ),
     write( Term ),nl,
     closefile( datafile ),
     openwrite( indexfile ,IndexFile ),
     writedevice( indexfile ),
     writef( "%7.0\n",Pos ),
     closefile( indexfile ).
```

```
/* dbrd returns terms from the database. The files are closed
after the database has been read. */

dbrd( Term, IndexFile, DataFile ) :-
     openread( datafile, DataFile ),
     openread( indexfile, IndexFile ),
     dbaaccess( Term, -1 ).

dbrd(_,_,_) :-
     closefile( datafile ), closefile( indexfile ), fail.

dbaaccess( Term, Datpos ):-
     Datpos>=0,
     filepos( datafile,Datpos,0 ),
     readdevice( datafile ),
     readterm( Dbasedom, Term ).

dbaaccess(Term,_) :-
     readdevice( indexfile ),
     readreal( Datpos1 ),
     dbaaccess( Term, Datpos1 ).

/* dbret retracts terms from the database. A term is retracted
   by writing a negative number in the index file. */

dbret(Term,Indexfile,Datafile):-
     openread( datafile, DataFile ),
     openmodify( indexfile, IndexFile ),
     dbret1( Term, -1 ).

dbret1( Term, Datpos ):-
     Datpos>=0,
     filepos( datafile,Datpos,0 ),
     readdevice( datafile ),
     readterm( dbasedom, Term ),!,
     filepos( indexfile, -9, 1 ),
     flush(indexfile),
     writedevice(indexfile),
     writef( "%7.0\n", -1 ),
     writedevice(screen).

dbret1(Term,_) :-
     readdevice( indexfile ),
     readreal( Datpos1 ),
     dbret1( Term, Datpos1 ).
```

CONTROL OF INPUT AND OUTPUT PARAMETERS: FLOW PATTERNS

Most standard predicates can be used to perform several functions depending on how the predicate is called. In one situation, a particular parameter may have a known value; in a different situation some other parameter may be known; and for certain purposes all of the parameters may be known at the time of the call.

We can call the known parameters the **i**n parameters for a predicate, and the unknown parameters the **o**ut parameters. The pattern of the **i**n and **o**ut parameters in a given predicate call indicates the behavior of that predicate for that call. This pattern is called a *flow pattern*. If a predicate is to be called with two arguments, there are four possibilities for its flow pattern:

```
(i,i)
(i,o)
(o,i)
(o,o)
```

It may not make sense to use a certain predicate in as many ways as there are flow patterns. For example, there would be no point in a call to *readchar* like

```
readchar(X)
```

with the variable X bound (i.e., with an **i**n parameter).

However, as the following example shows, it is possible to produce predicates (in this case, the *plus* predicate), which can be called with any combination of free and bound parameters:

```
                    /* Program 61 */
predicates
   plus(integer,integer,integer)
   numb(integer)
clauses
    plus(X,Y,Z):- bound(X),bound(Y),Z=X+Y.
    plus(X,Y,Z):- bound(Y),bound(Z),X=Z-Y.
    plus(X,Y,Z):- bound(X),bound(Z),Y=Z-X.
    plus(X,Y,Z):- free(X),free(Y),bound(Z),numb(X),Y=Z-X.
    plus(X,Y,Z):- free(X),free(Z),bound(Y),numb(X),Z=X+Y.
    plus(X,Y,Z):- free(Y),free(Z),bound(X),numb(Y),Z=X+Y.
    plus(X,Y,Z):-
        free(X),free(Y),free(Z),numb(X),numb(Y),Z=X+Y.
/* Generator of numbers starting from 0 */
    numb(0).
    numb(X) :- numb(A) , X=A+1.
```

PROGRAMMING STYLE

This section provides some comprehensive guidelines for writing good Turbo Prolog programs. We open with a discussion of tail recursion, and follow with a number of rules for efficient programming style.

Stack Considerations and Eliminating Tail Recursion

To conserve space and for faster execution, Turbo Prolog eliminates tail recursion wherever possible. Consider the definition of the predicate *member*:

```
member(X,[X|_]).
member(X,[_|Y]):-member(X,Y).
```

The essentially iterative operation of checking or generating elements of a given list one by one has been implemented in a recursive manner, with recursion's attendant demands on stack space (and therefore on execution time).

Tail recursion elimination is a technique for replacing such forms of recursion with iteration, and in spite of its name, it is also useful in situations in which there is no direct recursion or even no recursion at all—just a long chain of procedure calls.

To see how it works, suppose we had defined *demopred*, which uses *member* as follows:

```
demopred(X,Y):-...,member(A,B),test(A),....
```

When *member* is first activated, the system must remember that once *member* has been successfully evaluated, control must pass to the predicate *test*. This means that the address of *test* must be saved on the stack.

Likewise, for each recursive call of *member*, the system must remember the address the *member* predicate needs to return to after successful evaluation—namely, itself. Since there are no backtracking points between

```
member(X,[_|Y]) :-
```

and the recursive call

```
member(X,Y)
```

there is no need to stack the address of *member* several times. It is enough to remember that on successful termination of *member*, control should pass to *test*. This is tail recursion elimination. Where the system itself cannot eliminate recursion, the programmer can do a lot to limit its effect (and limit demand on the stack) by adopting a few rules of thumb about programming style.

Rule 1. *Use more variables rather than more predicates.* This rule is often in direct conflict with program readability, so a careful matching of objectives is required to achieve programs that are efficient both in their demands upon relatively cheap machines and upon relatively expensive human resources.

Thus, if writing a predicate to reverse the elements of a list,

```
reverse(X,Y):- reverse1([],X,Y).
reverse1(Y,[],Y).
reverse1(X1,[U|X2],Y):- reverse1([U|X1],X2,Y).
```

makes less demands upon the stack than

```
reverse([],[]).
reverse([U|X],Y):-reverse(X,Y1),append(Y1,[U],Y).

append([],Y,Y).
append([U|X],Y,[U|Z]):- append(X,Y,Z).
```

which uses the extra predicate *append*.

Rule 2. *When ordering subgoals in a rule, those with the most bound variables should come first.* Thus, if writing a Turbo Prolog predicate to solve the simultaneous equations

```
X + 1 = 4
X + Y = 5
```

and using a "generate and test" method,

```
solve(X,Y):-
     numb(X),plus(X,1,4),
     numb(Y),plus(X,Y,5).
```

is better than

```
solve(X,Y):-
     numb(X),numb(Y),
     plus(X,Y,5),plus(X,1,4).
```

(The *numb* and *plus* predicates are imported from Program 61). *numb* generates numbers and *plus(X,Y,Z)* is a predicate that works for all possible flow patterns and succeeds if *Z* is bound to the sum of the values to which *X* and *Y* are bound, etc.

Rule 3. *Try to ensure that execution fails efficiently when no solutions exist.* Suppose we want to write a predicate *singlepeak* that checks the integers in a list to see if, in the order given, they ascend to a single maximum and then descend again. Thus

```
singlepeak([1,2,5,7,11,8,6,4]).
```

would succeed and

```
singlepeak([1,2,3,9,6,8,5,4,3]).
```

would fail.

Definition 1 disobeys rule 3, since the failure of a list to have a single peak is only recognized when *append* has split the list into every possible decomposition:

Definition 1

```
singlepeak(X):-append(X1,X2,X),up(X1),down(X2).

up[_].
up([U,V|Y]):- U<V,up([V|Y]).
down([]).
down([U]).
down([U,V|Y]):- U>V, down([V|Y]).

append([],Y,Y).
append([U|X],Y,[U|Z]):- append(X,Y,Z).
```

On the other hand, definition 2 recognizes failure at the earliest possible moment:

Definition 2

```
singlepeak([]).
singlepeak([U,V|Y]):-U<V,singlepeak([V|Y]).
singlepeak([U,V|Y]):-U>V,down([V|Y]).
down([]).
down([U]).
down([U,V|Y]):- U>V, down([V,Y]).
```

Definition 3 shortens *singlepeak* further by observing rule 1. Thus, using definition 3

```
singlepeak(Y,up)
```

succeeds if *Y* is bound to a single peaked list appended to an ascending list and

```
singlepeak(Y,down)
```

succeeds if *Y* is bound to a descending list.

Definition 3

```
singlepeak([],_).
singlepeak([U,V|W],up):-
     U<V,singlepeak([V|W],up).
singlepeak([U,V|W],_):-
     U>V,singlepeak([V|W],down).
```

Rule 4. *Let Turbo Prolog's unification mechanism do as much of the work as possible.* At first thought, you might think to define a predicate *equal* to test two lists for equality as

```
equal([],[]).
equal([U|X],[U|Y]):- equal(X,Y).
```

but this is unnecessary. Using the definition

```
equal(X,X).
```

Turbo Prolog's unification mechanism does all the work!

Rule 5. *Use backtracking instead of recursion to effect repetition.* Backtracking decreases stack requirements. The idea is to use the *repeat . . . fail* combination instead of recursion. This is so important that the next section is dedicated to the technique.

Use of the Fail Predicate

To have a particular sequence of subgoals evaluated repeatedly, it is often necessary to define a predicate like *run* with a clause of the form

```
run:-      readln(X),
           process(X,Y),
           write(Y),
           run.
```

thus incurring unnecessary tail recursion overheads that cannot be automatically eliminated by the system because *process(X,Y)* involves backtracking.

In this case, the *repeat . . . fail* combination avoids the need for the final recursive call. Given

```
repeat.
repeat:-repeat.
```

we can redefine *run* without tail recursion as follows:

```
run:-      repeat,
           readln(X),
           process(X,Y),
           write(Y),
           fail.
```

fail causes Turbo Prolog to backtrack to *process*, and eventually to *repeat*, which always succeeds.

Determinism, Non-determinism and How to Set the Cut

The compiler directive *check_determ* is useful when you need to decide where to place the cut, since it marks those clauses which give rise to non-deterministic predicates. If you want to make these predicates deterministic, the cut will have to be inserted to stop the backtracking (which causes the non-determinism). As a general rule in such cases, the cut should always be inserted as far to the left as possible without destroying the underlying logic of the program.

Domains Containing References

Consider the predicate *lookup* in Program 62 during the evaluation of the goal

```
lookup(tom,27,Tree),
lookup(dick,28,Tree),
lookup(harry,26,Tree).
```

```
                    /* Program 62 */
domains
    tree = reference t(id,val,tree,tree)
    id = symbol
    val = integer
predicates
    lookup(id,val,tree)
clauses
   lookup(ID,VAL,t(ID,VAL,_,_)):-!.
   lookup(ID,VAL,t(ID1,_,TREE,_)):-
        ID<ID1,!,lookup(ID,VAL,TREE).
   lookup(ID,VAL,t(_,_,_,TREE)):-lookup(ID,VAL,TREE).
```

After matching with the first rule, the compound object to which *Tree* is bound takes the form

```
t("tom",27,_,_)
```

and even though the last two parameters in *t* are not bound, *t* must be carried forward to the next subgoal evaluation

```
lookup("dick",28,Tree)
```

which in turn binds *Tree* to

```
t("tom",28,t("dick",28,Tree,_),_)
```

Finally, the subgoal

```
lookup("harry",26,Tree)
```

binds *Tree* to

```
t("tom",28,t("dick",28,_,t("harry",26,_,_),_),_)
```

which is the result returned by the goal.

Because an unbound variable is passed from one subgoal to another, the domain *tree* has been declared as a *reference* to a compound object. This indicates that—internally—Turbo Prolog will have to pass references (or, loosely, addresses) rather than values. If *t* had not been declared as a reference object, Turbo Prolog would display a warning at runtime saying that references must be passed.

In many cases, the use of reference objects is avoidable. If they are used, however, they must be declared as such; otherwise, Turbo Prolog will display a warning, "The variable is not bound in this clause" during compilation. Program 63 uses several reference declarations to implement a Turbo Prolog interpreter which, given the goal

```
call(atom(likes,[symb(tom),X]))
```

will respond

```
X = symb("baseball")
1 Solution
```

The program contains clauses representing Program 1 (see "The Structure of a Turbo Prolog Program" in Chapter 3) except for the fact

```
likes(tom,baseball).
```

which will be inserted dynamically in the clause database during the dialog below. Notice that the fact

```
likes(mark,tennis).
```

is represented in the interpreter as

```
clauses(atom(likes,[symb(mark),symb(tennis)]),[]).
```

As given, the interpreter does not understand all of regular Turbo Prolog syntax. That would require a parser that reads a string and transforms it into a "parse tree" according to the domains in the program. However, it can produce the following dialog:

```
Goal: call(atom(likes,[symb(bill),X]))
No  solution
Goal:assertz(clause(atom(likes,[symb(tom),symb(baseball)]),[])).
True

Goal: call(atom(likes,[X,Y]))
X = symb("ellen"), Y = symb("tennis")
X = symb("john"),  Y = symb("football")
X = symb("eric"),  Y = symb("swimming")
X = symb("mark"),  Y = symb("tennis")
X = symb("bill"),  Y = symb("baseball")
X = symb("tom"),   Y = symb("baseball")
6 Solutions
```

```
                    /* Program 63 */
code=1000 trail=1000
domains
  term  = reference var(vid);symb(symbol);cmp(fid,terml)
  terml = reference term*
  atom  = atom(aid,terml)
  atoml = atom*
  e = e(vid,term)
  env = reference e*
  fid,aid,vid = symbol
database
  clause(atom,atoml)
```

```
predicates
  call(atom)
  unify_term(term,term,env)
  unify_terml(terml,terml,env)
  unify_littl(atoml,env)
  member(e,env)
clauses
             /*The clauses below form the Turbo Prolog interpreter*/
  call(atom(Id,Terml)):-
     clause(atom(Id,Terml1),Body),
     free(E),unify_terml(Terml,Terml1,E),unify_littl(Body,E).
  unify_terml([],[],_).
  unify_terml([Trm1|TL1],[Trm2|TL2],E):-
       unify_term(Trm1,Trm2,E),unify_terml(TL1,TL2,E).
  unify_term(Term,var(X),Env):-member(e(X,Term),Env),!.
  unify_term(symb(X),symb(X),_).
  unify_term(var(X),var(X),_)
  unify_term(cmp(ID,L1),cmp(ID,L2),E):-unify_terml(L1,L2,E).
  unify_littl([],_).
  unify_littl([atom(Id,Terml)|Atoml],Env):
        unify_terml(Call,Terml,Env),call(atom(Id,Call)),
        unify_littl(Atoml,Env).
  member(X,[X|_]).
  member(X,[_|L]):-member(X,L).

/* These are the clauses that represent the
part of a program already entered into the interpreter's
database. They could all be asserted instead of being
included statically as part of the program body. */

clause(atom(likes,[symb(ellen),symb(tennis)]) , []).
clause(atom(likes,[symb(john),symb(football)]), []).
clause(atom(likes,[symb(eric),symb(swimming)]), []).
clause(atom(likes,[symb(mark),symb(tennis)]) , []).
clause(atom(likes,[symb(bill),var(X)]),
       [atom(likes,[symb(tom),var(X)])]).
```

The warning "The variable is not bound in this clause (F10=Ok, Esc=Abort)", as well as the warnings 3001, 3009, 3011, warn that the variable used does not have a value. If you press F10, the domain of that variable is automatically retyped to a reference domain unless you are compiling to object modules that are part of a project. In this case, you must explicity declare that the domain of that variable is a reference domain. For example:

```
domains refInt = reference integer.
```

GENERATING EXECUTABLE STAND-ALONE PROGRAMS

A Turbo Prolog program can be compiled and linked to form a stand-alone executable file. Turbo Prolog actually does this for you: just set the Compile switch in the Options pull-down menu to "Compile to EXE file", and then give a Compile command. Provided the program is error free, an OBJ file is generated (with the same name as the source program text) and the linker is automatically invoked.

To ensure a successful link process, the following conditions must be satisfied:

- COMMAND.COM must be present.
- There must be enough memory available to contain the complete linked program. If memory resources are limited, you can compile the program to an OBJ file, exit from the Turbo Prolog system via the **Q**uit command, and finally start the link process by hand without the Turbo Prolog system resident. To do so, you will need a Microsoft or compatible linker.

  ```
  Link init MYPROG MYPROG.Sym,,Prolog
  ```

  where *MYPROG* is the name of the Turbo Prolog program to be linked.

MODULAR PROGRAMMING

A powerful feature of the Turbo Prolog system is its ability to handle programs that are broken up into modules. Modules can be written, edited, and compiled separately, and then linked together to create a single executable program. If you need to change the program, you need only edit and recompile one of the modules, not the entire program—a feature you will appreciate when you write large programs. Also, modular programming allows you to take advantage of the fact that, by default, all predicate and domain names are local. This means different modules can use the same name in different ways.

Turbo Prolog uses two concepts to manage modular programming: *projects* and *global* declarations. Among other things, these features make it possible to keep a record of which modules make up a program (called a *project*), and to perform type checking across module boundaries. In this section, we'll define the two concepts and then, by way of a simple example, show how some modules can be combined into a single, stand-alone program.

Projects

When a program is to be made up of several modules, Turbo Prolog requires a *project* definition specifying the names of the modules involved. You must create a file (called the LIBRARIAN) containing the list of the module names. The contents of the librarian file take the form

```
name_of_firstmodule+
name_of_secondmodule+
 ...
```

Each module is specified by its first name only (no file type) followed by a +. The file name of the project definition file becomes the name of the project, and it must have file type *PRJ*.

The first step in modular programming is to make up a name for the project and then create a corresponding LIBRARIAN file containing the names of the modules in the project. This is done via the **M**odule list option in the **F**iles pull-down menu. Each project is associated with a unique LIBRARIAN.

The project concept has two purposes:

1. The contents of the LIBRARIAN file are used during linkage; the names of the modules are inserted into the link command (given via PLINK.BAT) from that file.
2. The project name is used during compilation to identify a symbol table shared by all modules in that project. The symbol table is stored in a file in the OBJ directory with the same name as the project and file type *.SYM* . This file is automatically generated and updated during compilation.

To achieve the second purpose, the name of the project must be given *in each module* via the *project* compiler directive, which takes the form

```
project "MYPROJ"
```

Global Domains and Global Predicates

By default, all names used in a module are local. Turbo Prolog programs communicate across module boundaries using predicates defined in a `global predicates` section. The domains used in global predicates must be defined as global domains, or else be domains of standard types.

All the modules in a project need to know exactly the same global predicates and global domains. The easiest way to achieve this is by writing all global declarations in one single file, which can then be included in every relevant module via an *include* directive.

global domains

A domain is made global by writing it in a `global domains` program section. In all other respects, `global domains` are the same as ordinary (local) domains.

global predicates

global predicate declarations differ from ordinary (local) predicate declarations in that they must contain a description of the flow pattern(s) in which each given predicate may be called. A `global predicates` declaration must follow the scheme

```
mypred(d1,d2,..,dn) - (f,f,...,f)(f,f,..,f)...
```

where *d1,d2,...,dn* are global domains and each group

```
(f,f,...,f)
```

denotes a flow pattern where each *f* is either **i** (input parameter) or **o** (**o**utput parameter).

Note that if any global definition is changed, *all* modules in that project must be recompiled.

Compiling and Linking the Modules

Before compiling and linking the modules, the following conditions must be fulfilled:

1. Each module must be headed with the two compiler directives *project* and *include*. For example:

   ```
   project "MYPROJ"
   include "GLOBALS.PRO"
   ```

   (assuming that the project name is MYPROJ and that the global declarations are saved in the file GLOBALS.PRO)

2. One and only one module must contain a `goal` section! This module is regarded as the main module. Any facts describing a database predicate given in the program text must be written in the main module.
3. PLINK.BAT, LINK.EXE, and COMMAND.COM must satisfy the conditions necessary for successful linking, as described on pages 151 and 152.

The modules in the project can be compiled with the compile option switch set to either "Compile to **O**BJ" or "Compile to **E**XE". Once you have compiled all the other modules in a project, the best way to compile the last module is by using the compile **O**ption set to "Compile to **E**XE". This automatically invokes the linker and runs the compiled program. Otherwise, if memory resources are limited, all modules should first be compiled with the compile **O**ption set to "Compile to **O**BJ." By exiting the Turbo Prolog system, control can then be given to DOS and the DOS linker will handle the job.

The link process can be initiated for MYPROJ by giving the command

```
PLINK MYPROJ
```

(see Appendix C).

An Example

Now let's look at the steps involved in combining two modules into a single program. Assume that the two modules and the project are called MAIN.PRO, SUB1.PRO, and MYPROJ respectively, and that the necessary global declarations are saved in the file GLOBDEF.PRO.

Step 1. Create a project file via the **M**odule list entry in the **F**iles menu by giving the name *MYPROJ* to the "Name of module list?" prompt and then edit the contents to:

```
main+sub1+
```

Step 2. Create, edit, and save the global declarations file so that it appears as follows:

```
/* GLOBDEF.PRO */

global domains
name=string
global predicates
welcome(name)-(i)
```

Step 3. Create, edit, and save the main module file so that it appears as follows:

```
/* MAIN.PRO */

project "MYPROJ"
include "globdef.pro"
predicates
   test

goal
   test.
clauses
   test:-clearwindow,
         write("Please write your name"),
         nl,nl,nl,
         readln(ThisName),
         welcome(ThisName).
```

Step 4. Set the Compile Switch in the **O**ptions pull-down menu to "Compile to OBJ" and give a **C**ompile command, thus generating the files MAIN.OBJ and MYPROJ.SYM.

Step 5. Create, edit, and save the sub-module file as follows:

```
/* SUB1.PRO */

project "MYPROJ"
include "globdef.pro"
clauses
   welcome(Name):-
       write("Welcome ",Name),
       write(" Nice to meet you."),
       sound(100,200).
```

Step 6. Set the Compile Switch in the **O**ptions pull-down menu to "Compile to EXE" and give a **C**ompile command, thus generating the file SUB1.OBJ and performing an autolink process.

This link process links the files

```
INIT.OBJ, SUB1.OBJ, MAIN.OBJ, MYPROJ.SYM and PROLOG.LIB
```

to give the file

```
MYPROJ.EXE
```

Alternately, it is now possible to automatically compile all modules in a project. Select **P**roject from the **O**ptions pull-down menu, give the name of the project, select the **C**ompile option, and all modules will be compiled. The Prolog modules should reside in the .PRO directory, and the .PRJ file should reside in the .OBJ directory.

PC-DOS linker version 2.14 (or later) or PLINK86™ version 1.48 overlay linker from Phoenix Software Associates, Ltd. can be used as external linkers.

INTERFACING PROCEDURES WRITTEN IN OTHER LANGUAGES

Although Turbo Prolog is an excellent tool for many purposes, there are still reasons to use other languages. For example, it's easier to perform numeric integration in

FORTRAN; interrupt handling is probably done better in assembly language; and, of course, if someone has developed a large program in Pascal that already solves some aspect of the problem, this work should not be wasted. For these reasons, Turbo Prolog allows interfacing with other languages. Currently, the languages supported are Pascal, C, FORTRAN, and assembler.

Declaring External Predicates

To inform the Turbo Prolog system that a global predicate is implemented in another language, a *language* specification is appended to the global predicate declaration:

```
global predicates
     add(integer,integer,integer)-(i,i,o),(i,i,i) language C
     scanner(string,token)-(i,o) language Pascal
```

Turbo Prolog makes the interfaced language explicit to simplify the problems of activation record and parameter format, calling and returning conventions, segment definition, and linking and initialization.

Calling Conventions and Parameters

The 8086 processor family gives the programmer a choice between NEAR and FAR subroutine calls. Turbo Prolog requires that *all calls to and returns from subroutines be FAR.*

When interfacing to a routine written in C, *the parameters are pushed onto the stack in reverse order* and, after return, the stack pointer is automatically adjusted. When interfacing to other languages, the parameters are pushed in the normal order and *the called function is responsible for removing the parameters from the stack.*

In many language compilers for the 8086 family, there is a choice between 16-bit and 32-bit pointers, where the 16-bit pointers refer to a default segment. To access all of memory, Turbo Prolog always uses 32-bit pointers.

Turbo Prolog types are implemented in the following way:

```
integer    2 bytes
real       8 bytes (IEEE format)
char       1 byte (2 bytes when pushed on the stack)
string     4 byte dword pointer to a null terminated string
symbol     4 byte dword pointer to a null terminated string
compound   4 byte dword pointer to a record
```

An output parameter is pushed as a 32-bit pointer to a location where the return value must be assigned.

For input parameters, the value is pushed directly and the size of the parameter depends on its type.

Naming Conventions

The same predicate in Turbo Prolog can have several type variants and several flow variants. *A separate procedure is called for each type and flow variant.* To call these different procedures, a separate name must be assigned to each procedure. This is done by numbering the different procedures with the same predicate name from 0 upwards. For example, given the declaration

```
global predicates
     add(integer,integer,integer)-
                         (i,i,o),(i,i,i) language pascal
```

the first variant with flow pattern (*i,i,o*) is named *add_0* and the second with flow pattern (*i,i,i*) is named *add_1*.

An Assembler Routine Called from Turbo Prolog

Suppose an assembly language routine is to be called into operation via the clause

```
double(MyInVar,MyOutVar)
```

with *MyInVar* bound to an integer value before the call so that, after the call, *MyOutVar* is bound to twice that value.

The "activation record" placed on top of the stack when *double* is activated will take the form shown in Figure 11-5. The basic assembly language outline is

```
MOV     AX,[BP]+10              ;get the value to which
                                ;MyInVar is bound
ADD     AX,AX                   ;double that value
LDS     SI,DWORD PTR [BP]+6     ;Store the value to
                                ;which MyOutVar is to
                                ;be bound in the
                                ;appropriate address.
MOV     [SI],AX
```

[BP]+10 →	The value to which MyInVar is bound. SIZE = 2 bytes
[BP]+6 →	Address in which the value for MyOutVar must be placed. SIZE = 4 bytes
[BP]+2 →	Address from which execution is to continue after double has been executed. SIZE = 4 bytes
[BP]+0 →	Previous BP setting before execution of double began. SIZE = 2 bytes

Figure 11-5 Activation Record

After adding the statements necessary to preserve Turbo Prolog's *SP* and *BP* registers, and to be able to combine the assembly language fragment with a Turbo Prolog .OBJ module, we obtain the following code:

```
A_PROG       SEGMENT BYTE
             ASSUME CS:A_PROG
PUBLIC       double_0
double_0     PROC   FAR
             PUSH   BP
             MOV    BP,SP
             MOV    AX, [BP]+6
             ADD    AX,AX
             LDS    SI,DWORD PTR [BP]+10
             MOV    [SI],AX
             POP    BP
             MOV    SP,BP
             RET    6
double_0     ENDP
A_PROG       ENDS
END
```

The Turbo Prolog program containing the call to *double* must contain the `global predicates` declaration

```
global predicates
     double(integer,integer) - (i,o) language asm
```

but otherwise is no different from any other program.

If this assembly language program module is assembled into the file MYASM.OBJ and the calling Turbo Prolog object module is MYPROLOG.OBJ, the two can be linked via

```
LINK INIT+MYPROLOG+MYASM+MYPROLOG.SYS,MIXPROG,,PROLOG
```

and thus produce an executable stand-alone program in the file MIXPROG.EXE (using the Turbo Prolog library in PROLOG.LIB). It is important that MYPROLOG.SYS appear last in the above *link* command.

In general, the format of an activation record will depend upon the number of parameters in the calling Turbo Prolog predicate and the domain types corresponding to those parameters. Thus, if we wanted to define

```
add(Val1,Val2,Sum)
```

with *Val1*, *Val2* and the *Sum* belonging to domains of integer type, the activation record would take the form shown in Figure 11-6.

Notice that each parameter occupies a corresponding number of bytes. For output parameters, the size is always 4 bytes (used for segment address and offset). For input parameters, the size is determined by the value actually pushed onto the stack and is thus dependent on the corresponding domain type.

Thus, *Val1* and *Val2*—belonging to a domain of integer type and being used with an (**i**) flow pattern—both occupy 2 bytes, whereas *Sum*—being used with an (**o**) flow pattern—occupies 4 bytes.

Note also that, within the Turbo Prolog compiler, a call to an external predicate takes the form

```
/* push parameters */
MOV  AX,SEGMENT DATA
MOV  DS,AX
CALL FAR PTR EXTERNAL_PREDICATE_IMPLEMENTATION
```

so that the data segment addressed while a procedure for an external predicate is being executed is the one called *DATA*.

[BP]+10 →	Address in which the value for Sum must be placed. SIZE = 4 bytes
[BP]+8 →	The value to which Val2 is bound. SIZE = 2 bytes
[BP]+6 →	The value to which Val1 is bound. SIZE = 2 bytes
[BP]+2 →	Address from which execution is to continue after add has been executed. SIZE = 4 bytes
[BP]+0 →	Previous BP setting before execution of add began. SIZE = 2 bytes

Figure 11-6 Activation Record

Calling C, Pascal and FORTRAN Procedures from Turbo Prolog

Program 64 demonstrates how to access a subroutine written in C from a Turbo Prolog program. The process with Pascal and FORTRAN is similar.

```
              /* Program 64 */
global predicates
        treble(integer,integer) - (i,o) language c
goal
     write("Type an integer"),readint(A),
     treble(A,T),
     write("Treble that number is ",T),nl.
```

In the Turbo Prolog program that contains the call to *treble*, the *language* used to implement it must be specified in the `global` predicates section. In the C source (shown in Program 65), you must use the Turbo Prolog naming convention for the names of the C-subroutines. The name of the predicate (*treble*) must be followed by an integer corresponding to the flow pattern.

```
              /* Program 65 */

treble_0(x,y) int x; int *y
    {
      *y=3*x;  /*The value of x can be used in treble */
    }
```

Low-Level Support

The Turbo Prolog standard predicate *bios* gives the programmer access to the low-level bios (**b**asic **i/o** **s**ystem) routines. These routines are documented in the *IBM DOS*

Reference Manual. Information is passed to and from the bios functions via the predefined compound object *reg(..)*, so that, using the variables *AXi, BXi, CXi, DXi, SIi, DIi, DSi, ESi* to represent the register values passed to *bios* and *AXo, . . . , ESo* for those returned by the bios, the Turbo Prolog predicate takes the form

```
bios(IntNo,reg(AXi,BXi,CXi,DXi,SIi,DIi,DSi,ESi),
     reg(AXo,BXo,CXo,DXo,SIo,DIo,DSo,ESo))
```

The domain for the compound object *reg(AX,BX,...)* is predefined as

```
regdom = reg(integer,integer,integer,....)
```

Program 66 uses the *bios* standard predicate and three of the other four low-level support standard predicates: *ptr_dword, memword, membyte*, and *portbyte*. These take the following formats:

```
ptr_dword(StringVar,Segment,Offset)
portbyte(PortNo,Byte)
memword(Segment,Offset,Word)
membyte(Segment,Offset,Byte)
```

ptr_dword returns the internal *Segment* and *Offset* address of *StringVar*. *portbyte* sets or returns the value at *PortNo*, depending on whether *Byte* is bound or free. *memword* sets or returns the value of the *Word* at the memory address given by *Segment* and *Offset*, depending on whether *Word* is bound or free. *membyte* acts the same as *memword*, but for a single byte.

Program 66 defines four predicates:

- *dosver* returns the actual DOS version number.
- *diskspace* returns the total number of bytes and number of available bytes on the given *Disk*. The *Disk* is specified by a number: 0 denotes the default disk, 1 denotes drive A:, 2 denotes drive B:, and 3 denotes drive C:.
- *makedir* creates a subdirectory.
- *removedir* removes a subdirectory.

In light of Program 66, try out the following three goals:

```
dosver(DosVersionNumber).
diskspace(DriveNumber,TotalSpace,RemainingSpace).
makedir("testdir"),
readchar(_),system("dir"),removedir("testdir"),
readchar(_),
system("dir").
```

```
                    /* Program 66 */
predicates
  dosver(real)
  diskspace(real,real)
  makedir(STRING)
  removedir(STRING)
```

```
clauses
  dosver(VERSION):-
     AX=48*256,

     bios(33,reg(AX,0,0,0,0,0,0,0),reg(VV,_,_,_,_,_,_,_)),
     /* you could use her notation, bios($21...)
        instead of bios(33...) */
     L=VV/256, H=VV-256*L, VERSION=H+L/100.

    diskspace(DISK,TOTALSPACE,FREESPACE):-
        AAX=54*256,
        bios(33,reg(AAX,0,0,DISK,0,0,0,0),
               reg(AX,BX,CX,DX,_,_,_,_)),
        FREESPACE=1.0*BX*CX*AX, TOTALSPACE=1.0*DX*CX*AX.

     makedir(NAME):-
        ptr_dword(NAME,DS,DX),
        AX=256*57,
        bios(33,reg(AX,0,0,DX,0,0,DS,0),_).

     removedir(NAME):-
        ptr_dword(NAME,DS,DX),AX=256*58,
        bios(33,reg(AX,0,0,DX,0,0,DS,0),_).
```

ACCESSING THE EDITOR FROM WITHIN A TURBO PROLOG PROGRAM

The following predicates are used to call the Turbo Prolog editor.

edit(InStringParam,OutStringParam)

The Turbo Prolog editor is invoked in the active window. All the usual editor facilities are now available. (The operation of the editor is described in Chapters 2 and 12.) The editor will be used on the text given in *InStringParam*, and *OutStringParam* will receive the edited result. Thus, the following call could be used to start editing an empty screen:

```
edit("",Text).
```

display(String)

The Turbo Prolog editor is invoked in the active window. The text in *String* can be examined under editor control but cannot be altered (and therefore only a subset of the editor's facilities are available in "display" mode).

editmsg(InString,OutString,LeftHeader,RightHeader, Message,Position,HelpFileName,Code)

The Turbo Prolog editor is called, and *InString* can then be edited in the currently active window to form *OutString*. Two texts are inserted in the header given by *LeftHeader* and *RightHeader*. The cursor is located at the *Position*-th character in *InString* and the indicated *Message* is displayed at the bottom of the window. The file loaded when the "help" key [F1] is pressed is *HelpFileName*. The value returned in *Code* is used to indicate how the editing was terminated (*Code=0* if terminated by [F10] and *Code=1* if aborted by [Esc]).

DIRECTORY AND FORMATTING FACILITIES

The following predicates can be used to access the Turbo Prolog file directory and to format output.

dir(Path,FileSpec,Filename)

The Turbo Prolog file directory facilities are invoked. The indicated *Path* and *FileSpec* define the files to appear in the directory. Cursor keys can then be used to select one of the filenames. Pressing [↵] selects the file to which the cursor is currently pointing. An example of a call could be

```
dir("\mydir","*.pro",NameOfSelectedProgram)
```

writef(FormatString,Arg1,Arg2,Arg3, ...)

This predicate allows the production of formatted output. *Arg1* to *ArgN* must be constants or variables that belong to domains of standard type. It is not possible to format compound domains. The format string contains ordinary characters, which are printed without modification, and format specifiers of the form:

```
%-m.p
```

where the optional (−) indicates that the field is to be left-justified (right-justified is the default). The optional *m* field is a decimal number specifying a minimum field, with the optional *.p* field specifying the precision of a floating-point image or the maximum number of characters to be printed from a string. For real numbers, *p* can be qualified by one of the letters: *f*, e, or *g* with the following denotation:

f Reals in fixed decimal notation.
e Reals in expoenntial notation.
g Use the shortest format (this is the default)

For example:

```
Goal: person(N,A,I),
writef("Name= %-15, Age= %2, Income=$%9.2f \n",N,A,I).
```

would produce output such as the following:

```
Name= Pete Ashton   , Age= 20, Income=$ 11111.11
Name= Marc Spiers   , Age= 32, Income=$ 22222.22
Name= Kim Clark     , Age= 28, Income=$ 33333.33
```

12 *Reference Guide*

This chapter provides a comprehensive reference to all aspects of the Turbo Prolog system. We'll discuss files on the distribution disk, the menu system, the editor, and how to calculate screen attributes. The remainder of the chapter is a classified, alphabetical lookup for all functions, predicates, and compiler directives.

FILES ON THE DISTRIBUTION DISK

The distribution disk contains the following files:

PROLOG.EXE contains the editor, compiler, file handler and runtime package.

PROLOG.ERR contains error messages. This text file need not be present if you don't mind the absence of explanatory compile-time error messages. If the file isn't present, errors will be indicated only by an error number; Appendix B contains explanations for all error messages. If you want complete error messages to be displayed, these can either be in a disk file (which must be called PROLOG.ERR) or can be stored in memory (for the details, see Appendix B).

PROLOG.HLP is an ASCII text file containing help messages. If you wish, you can edit the help text to your liking.

READ.ME (if present) contains the latest updates and suggestions about Turbo Prolog. It may also contain addenda or corrections to this manual.

***.PRO** files contain the source text for sample Turbo Prolog programs.

PROLOG.LIB is the library needed when OBJect files are linked to form EXEcutable files.

INIT.OBJ must be included as the first OBJ file in all LINK commands when creating executable files. INIT.OBJ contains code to initialize the computer before processing the actual Turbo Prolog program code.

PROLOG.OVL contains the overlays required during development and compilation.

FILES NEEDED WHEN USING TURBO PROLOG

To start Turbo Prolog. The only files necessary to load Turbo Prolog are PROLOG.EXE and PROLOG.OVL. However, if during a previous Turbo Prolog session the system configuration was changed, a file PROLOG.SYS will have been created (using the **S**ave configuration option on the **S**etup menu). If such a file exists, its contents will be used to define system parameters (such as size of windows) when Turbo Prolog is started up.

To give error messages. Error messages (rather than just error code numbers) will only be displayed if PROLOG.ERR is present in the same directory as PROLOG.EXE.

To use DOS commands within Turbo Prolog programs. DOS commands can be used from within a Turbo Prolog program, provided that the directory specified via a path in the **S**etup pull-down menu contains the same version of COMMAND.COM as was used to boot the computer.

When generating .EXE files. PPROLOG.OVL must be accessible via the path or from within the Turbo directory. PROLOG.LIB and INIT.OBJ must be in the Turbo directory.

INSTALLATION

Installation of colors, directories, windows, and other features can be performed via the **S**etup pull-down menu described on page 168. Any changes made can be saved in a .SYS file in the same directory as the Turbo Prolog system (the Turbo directory). The default .SYS file is PROLOG.SYS but several .SYS files can be maintained via the **S**etup menu. When a .SYS file is read via the "Read Configuration" command, the system is automatically configured from the named file. .SYS files contain ASCII text that can be modified directly with a text editor. The contents of .SYS files are explained in detail in Appendix D.

THE MAIN MENU

This section is a functional reference to the Turbo Prolog menu system. If you need help with the keystrokes required to use the menus, see Chapter 2.

The Run Command

The **R**un command is used to execute a program residing in memory. If a compiled program is already in memory, and the source of that program has not been modified in the editor since the last **R**un, it will be executed immediately. If not, the source program in the editor will first be compiled, after which the resulting program will be executed.

Turbo Prolog programs can be executed in two ways:

1. If the program contains a goal, the goal is executed, and any output from Turbo Prolog appears in the dialog window. After execution, the user can press the space bar to return to the main menu.
2. If the goal is not internal (written in the program), the user can try several goals; the "conversation" between the user and Turbo Prolog will appear in the dialog window.

During program execution, some of the function keys have special meanings:

F8	Automatically retypes the previous goal on the next line in the dialog window.
F9	Calls the editor.
⇧ F9	Selects a system window to be resized.
⇧ F10	Re-sizes or moves the dialog window.
Ctrl S (toggle)	Temporarily halts the output of a program to the screen. Pressing Ctrl S again continues output.
Ctrl C Ctrl Break	Interrupts program execution and returns control to the main menu or the dialog window.
Ctrl P (toggle)	Automatically echoes any output sent to the screen to the printer. Pressing Ctrl P again stops output to the printer.

The Compile Command

The Compile command compiles the program currently in the editor. Compilation may result in a program resident in memory (default), in an OBJ file, or an EXE file, depending on the current setting of the compile option switch in the Options pull-down menu.

When compiling to an EXE file, all linking is performed automatically. If the compiled program is part of a project, the linking process depends on the project definition. (See page 152.)

When compiling to OBJ files, if the program is part of a project, it must begin with the keyword project and the name of that project (see page 152). The project must have been defined via the Librarian entry in the Setup menu.

Instead of using the automatic linking process, you can give the LINK commands in DOS. This might be desirable, for example, if there is not enough memory to allow linkage with the Turbo Prolog system resident. To link in DOS, quit the Turbo Prolog system, switch to the OBJ directory, and give a PLINK command in one of the following ways:

```
PLINK PROGRAM
```

or

```
PLINK PROJECT1
```

The first command links a single compiled program (where the source was in PROGRAM.PRO) to an executable file. The second command links a project called PROJECT1 to an executable file.

The Options Menu

The **O**ptions pull-down menu is shown in Figure 12-1.

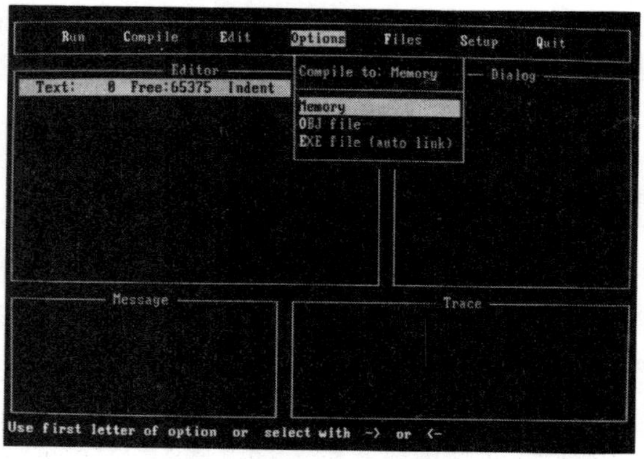

Figure 12-1 Options Menu

The current compile setting is shown as the first (non-selectable) entry. You can select either of the other two options if desired. Compilation to OBJ and EXE files is described under the **C**ompile Command (see previous section).

The Edit Command

The **E**dit command invokes the built-in editor for editing the file defined as the workfile (via the **F**ilename entry in the **F**iles pull-down menu). If no workfile file name has been specified, WORK.PRO is assumed.

In addition to editing the current workfile, you can also edit another file from inside the editor without disturbing the editing of the workfile. Also, you can incorporate some or all of the contents of another file into the one being edited. For more information about the editor, see page 172.

The Files Menu

The **F**iles pull-down menu is shown in Figure 12-2.

Load

Load selects a workfile from the PRO directory. The workfile can then be edited, compiled, executed, or saved.

After issuing a **L**oad command, you will be prompted for a file name. You can enter either of the following:

1. Any legal file name. If the period and file type (extension) are omitted, the .PRO extension is automatically assumed. To specify a file name with no extension, enter the name followed by a period.

2. A file name from a directory. The directory facility is consulted when the *File name:* prompt is answered either by pressing ↵ or with a pattern containing wildcards followed by ↵. If no file pattern is given, all files with the .PRO extension will be listed. In either case, the cursor can then be moved up and down in the resulting list of file names by the arrow keys, Home, End, PgUp and PgDn. Choose a file by pressing ↵. If Esc is pressed, the cursor will return to the *File name:* prompt.

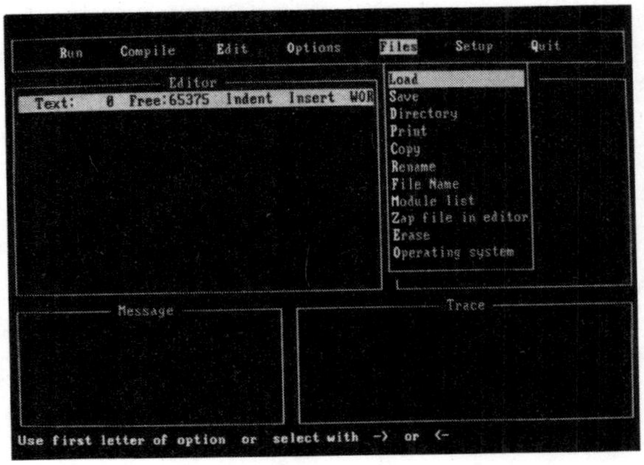

Figure 12-2 Files Menu

Save

Save saves the current workfile on disk. The old version of the named file, if any, is given a .BAK extension.

Directory

Directory is used to select the default directory for .PRO files. It can also be used to browse in the .PRO directory. After issuing the **D**irectory command, you will be prompted for a directory path. Any legal path name can be given. See the **S**etup command, page 168 for a description of the other directories used by the system.

File Name

File is used to rename the workfile (by default, WORK.PRO). This operation does not affect any files on disk. This is useful, for example, for saving an edited program, so that the program previously saved under the current workfile name is not erased.

Module list

When you select **M**odule list, you will be asked for the name of the file containing the list of modules in a given project. Type in a name, or select it from a catalog of project names found in the OBJ directory. For example, if you specify the name APROJECT, any existing module list of that name can be edited; otherwise, an empty file is prepared for editing. In either case, once the new module list is complete, exiting the editor with the F10 key automatically updates the module list file APROJECT.PRJ in the OBJ directory.

Zap File in Editor

Zap erases the text currently in the editor. The current workfile name is maintained.

Print

Print sends the program to the printer. It will initiate a dialog in which the user is asked to mark the program block to be printed.

Erase

Erase erases a disk file. The file can be specified by name, or it can be selected from the directory as described on page 167.

Rename

Rename renames a disk file. After issuing the **R**ename command, you will be asked for the name of the original file by the *From:* prompt; respond with a legal file name (possibly prefixed with a path). Then type the new name after the *To:* prompt. As with the **E**rase command, files can be specified by name, or selected from the directory.

Operating System

Operating system calls the DOS operating system; Turbo Prolog remains resident in memory. The version of DOS used during the boot process must be available in the DOS directory. Once DOS has been called, any DOS commands can be executed, including MD and FORMAT. Control is returned to the resident Turbo Prolog system with the EXIT command.

Setup Menu

Setup should be selected when any of the setup parameters are to be inspected, temporarily changed, or recorded permanently in a .SYS file. The **S**etup menu is shown in Figure 12-3.

Defining Directories

The **P**, **O**, **E**, **T**, and **D** entries define a drive and path for each of the five directories used by the system.

When you select a directory, you will be prompted for a drive and a path. Type in the drive and/or path, press [↵], and Turbo Prolog will accept your specification; if you change your mind and want to start over, press [Esc].

The **P**RO directory is used by default in all file-handling operations performed from the **F**iles pull-down menu. This includes **L**oading and **S**aving Turbo Prolog programs.

OBJ directory is used for files of .OBJ and .PRJ type.

The **E**XE directory is used for the files generated by the Turbo Prolog system of .EXE type.

The **T**URBO directory is used for the Turbo Prolog system itself, i.e., for the system files PROLOG.EXE, PROLOG.ERR, PROLOG.HLP, PROLOG.SYS, PROLOG.OVL and PROLOG.LIB.

The **D**OS directory should contain the version of COMMAND.COM that was used when the computer was booted. Whenever the **O**perating system entry in the **F**iles menu is selected or when **Q**uitting the Turbo Prolog system, COMMAND.COM is consulted again. This directory is also used as the default for any DOS command issued from within the Turbo Prolog system.

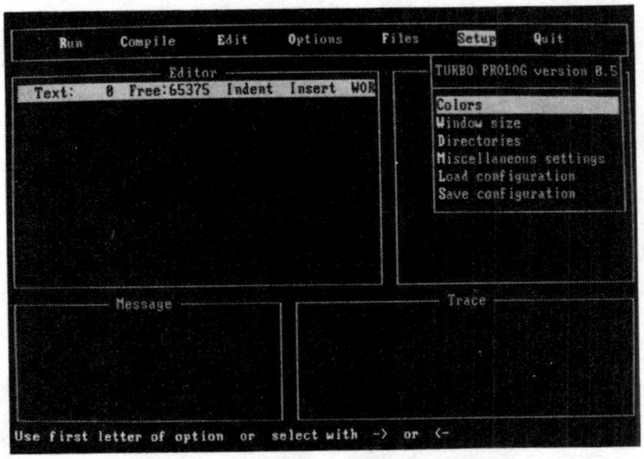

Figure 12-3 Setup Menu

Window Definition

Window activates another menu, shown in Figure 12-4. Select **E**, **D**, **M**, **T**, or **A**, then do the following to define the selected window:

Window Width	Press ← to make the width smaller, or → to make it larger.
Window Length	Press ↑ or ↓ to decrease or increase the length of the window. To make changes in larger increments, hold down the Ctrl key at the same time.
Window Position	Move the window to a new position by holding down the ⇧ key and pressing the arrow keys.

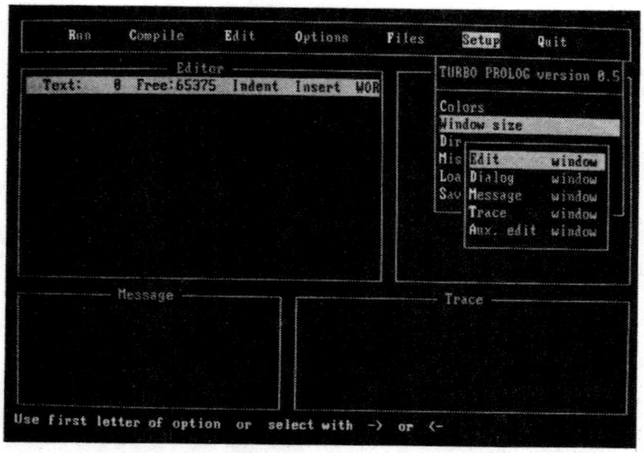

Figure 12-4 Window Definition Menu

Color Setting

This entry is used to define the background and foreground colors of one or more system windows. When selected, a new pop-up menu appears (Figure 12-5) to enable you to select which window will be affected:

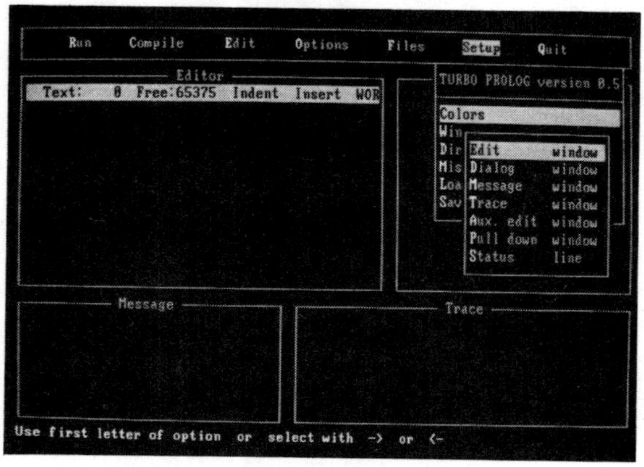

Figure 12-5 Color Settings Menu

Choose **E**, **D**, **M**, **T**, **A**, **P**, or **S** to select a window. Then use the arrow keys to alter the foreground and background colors. The status line at the bottom of the screen reflects the current meanings of these keys:

```
<--, --> :Background color ↑^, ↓v:Foreground color Any other:End Attr = 7 ^[&k12H
```

The ← and → keys can be used to increase or decrease the selected window's background attribute value in steps, and ↑ and ↓ can be used similarly to control the foreground color. The actual attribute value selected is shown to the right of the status line.

Miscellaneous

Miscellaneous is used to define more specialized parameters. When selected, the pop-up menu shown in Figure 12-6 appears.

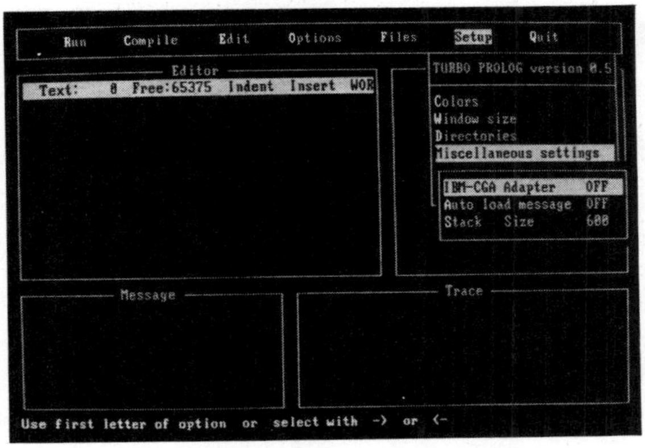

Figure 12-6 Miscellaneous Menu

I toggles special synchronization to improve performance on a color screen driven by the IBM Color/Graphics Adapter. By default, no special synchronization is provided.

A toggles whether the text file containing error messages is to be loaded into memory (Autoload messages ON), or whether each error message is to be loaded from PROLOG.ERR each time an error occurs. By default, Autoload messages are OFF.

S is used to (re)define the stack size. The default is 600 paragraphs (1 paragraph is 16 bytes). When you issue the **S** command, you will be prompted for a new stack size in the interval 600-4000 paragraphs.

Load Configuration

Press **L** to load a .SYS file from the Turbo directory and reset the system according to the parameters it contains.

Save Configuration

S saves the current setup in a .SYS file in the Prolog directory. The configuration can be given any name, but the default PROLOG.SYS is automatically used when the Turbo Prolog system is first started up.

Note: To have a configuration included into a stand-alone program, use the *config* compiler directive.

Quit Command

Use the **Q**uit command to leave the Turbo Prolog system. If the workfile has been edited since it was loaded, Turbo Prolog will ask you if you want to save the workfile before quitting.

THE TURBO PROLOG EDITOR

The Turbo Prolog editing commands can be grouped into the following four categories:

- Cursor movement commands
- Insert and delete commands
- Block commands
- Miscellaneous commands

Each group will be described separately in the sections that follow. Table 12-1 provides an overview of the commands available. In the following sections, each of the descriptions consists of a heading defining the command, followed by the keystrokes used to activate the command. In some cases, there are two ways to give a command, using either the PC's function keys or WordStar-like commands; both will be shown.

Table 12-1 Editing Command Overview

Cursor Movement Commands	
Character left	Beginning of line
Character right	End of line
Word left	Top of file
Word right	End of file
Line up	Beginning of block
Line down	End of block
Page up	Bottom of page
Page down	Top of page
Insert and Delete Commands	
Insert mode on/off	Delete right word
Delete left character	Delete line
Delete character under cursor	Delete to end of line

Table 12-1 Editing Command Overview (continued)

Block Commands	
Mark block begin	Mark block end
Copy block	Repeat the last copy
Move block	Delete block
Read block from disk	Hide/display block
Miscellaneous Editing Commands	
Call the auxiliary editor	Go to line
Which line number	End edit
Auto indent on/off	Find
Repeat last find	Find & replace
Repeat last find & replace	

Cursor Movement Commands

These commands are used to move the cursor to different areas in a text file.

Character left ← or Ctrl S
Moves the cursor one character to the left without affecting the character there. This command does not work across line breaks; when the cursor reaches the left edge of the window, it stops.

Character right → or Ctrl D
Moves the cursor one character to the right without affecting the character there. When the cursor reaches the right edge of the window, the text scrolls horizontally until the cursor reaches the extreme right of the line; it then moves to the beginning of the next line (if there is one).

Word left Ctrl ← or Ctrl A
Moves the cursor to the beginning of the word to the left.

Word right Ctrl → or Ctrl F
Moves the cursor to the beginning of the word to the right. This command works across line breaks.

Line up ↑ or Ctrl E
Moves the cursor to the line above. If the cursor is on the top line, the window scrolls down one line.

Line down ↓ or Ctrl X
Moves the cursor to the line below. If the cursor is on the last line, the window scrolls up one line.

Page up PgUp or Ctrl R
Moves the cursor one page up with an overlap of one line. The cursor moves one window, less one line, backward in the text.

Page down PgDn or Ctrl C
Moves the cursor one page down with an overlap of one line. The cursor moves one window, less one line, forward in the text.

Beginning of line Home or Ctrl Q S

Moves the cursor all the way to the left edge of the window (column one).

End of Line End or Ctrl Q D

Moves the cursor to the end of the line, i.e., to the position following the last printable character on the line.

Top of file Ctrl PgUp or Ctrl Q R

Moves to the first character of the text.

End of file Ctrl PgDn or Ctrl Q C

Moves to the last character of the text.

Beginning of block Ctrl Q B

Moves the cursor to the block begin marker set with Ctrl K B. The command works even if the block is not displayed (see page 175), or the block end marker is not set.

End of block Ctrl Q K

Moves the cursor to the block end marker set with Ctrl K K. The command works even if the block is not displayed (see page 175), or the block begin marker is not set.

Insert and Delete Commands

These commands let you insert and delete characters, words, and lines. They can be divided into two types: one command that controls the text entry mode (insert or overwrite), and a number of simple delete commands.

Insert mode on/off Ins or Ctrl V

Toggles between insert (default) and overwrite modes. The current mode is displayed on the status line at the top of the window.

Insert mode is the default value when the editor is activated. In this mode, existing text to the right of the cursor moves to the right as you type in the new text.

Overwrite mode is used to replace old text with new. In this mode, characters are replaced by the new characters typed over them.

Delete left character ←

This is the backspace key directly above the ↵ key. It moves one character to the left and deletes the character there. Any characters to the right of the cursor move to the left.

Delete character under cursor Del

Deletes the character under the cursor and moves any character to the right of the cursor one position to the left. This command works across line breaks.

Delete right word Ctrl T

Deletes the word to the right of the cursor.

Delete line Ctrl Y

Deletes the line containing the cursor and moves any lines below one line up.

Delete to end of line Ctrl Q Y

Deletes all text from the cursor position to the end of the line.

Block Commands

These commands are used to mark and manipulate blocks of text.

Mark block begin Ctrl K B

Marks the beginning of a block. You can also use the begin block marker as a reference point to move to with the Ctrl Q B command.

Mark block end Ctrl K K

Marks the end of a block. You can also use the end block marker as a reference point to jump to with the Ctrl Q K command.

Copy block F5 or Ctrl K C

F5 Marks the start and end of the block, then copies the block to the cursor position. First, press F5 to mark the beginning of the block. Then move the cursor to the end of the block, and press F5 again to mark the end of the block. Finally, move the cursor where you want to insert the block. Press F5 again to copy the block.

Ctrl K C Places a copy of a marked and highlighted block at the cursor position. The original block is left unchanged, and the markers are placed around the new copy of the block.

Repeat the last copy ⇧ F5

The block previously marked with F5 is inserted at the cursor position.

Move block F6 or Ctrl K V

F6 Marks the start and end of the block, then moves the block to the cursor position. First, press F6 to mark the beginning of the block. Then move the cursor to the end of the block and press F6 again to mark the end of the block. Finally, move the cursor to where you want to insert the block. Press F6 again to move the block.

Ctrl K V Moves a marked and highlighted block from its original position to the cursor position. The block disappears from its original position and the markers remain around the block at its new position.

Delete block F7 or Ctrl K Y

F7 Marks the start and end of the block, then deletes it. First, press F7 to mark the beginning of the block. Then move the cursor to the end of the block and press F7 again to mark the end of the block. Finally, press F7 to delete the block.

Ctrl K Y Deletes a marked and highlighted block.

Read block from disk F9 or Ctrl K R

Opens the **F**iles menu and selects the **L**oad option. You can then load the file and view it as though in the editor. The text to be copied is selected either by pressing F9 at the beginning and end of the block, or by marking the block with Ctrl K B and Ctrl K K. The block is then inserted in the main edit text at the current cursor position.

Hide/display block Ctrl K H

Causes block highlighting to be toggled off and on. Ctrl K block manipulation commands (copy, move, delete, or write to a file) work only when the block is highlighted. Block-related cursor movements (jump to beginning/end of block) work whether the block is highlighted or not.

Miscellaneous Commands

Call the auxiliary editor F8

Establishes a separate window for temporary editing of another text file (before copying a block from it, for example). Functionally, the auxiliary editor is exactly the same as the ordinary editor, and is especially useful when include files must be edited. After terminating the temporary edit of a file with the F10 key, you can save the edited version of that file.

Go to line F2

When you press F2, you will be prompted for a line number. Enter a line number, but don't press ↵. Press F2 again to move the cursor to the beginning of the indicated line.

Which line number ⇧ F2

Displays the line number of the cursor at the bottom of the screen. Press another key to continue editing.

End Edit Esc or F10

F10 Terminates editing and, if the editing was due to a program syntax error, automatically recompiles the program.

Esc Terminates editing.

Auto indent Ctrl Q I

Provides automatic line indentation. When auto indent is active, the indentation of the current line is repeated on all subsequent lines. When you press ↵, the cursor does not return to column one, but to the starting column of the line you just terminated.

When you want to change the indentation, simply move the cursor to select the new column. When auto indent is active (the default), the message *indent* is displayed at the top of the editor window.

Find F3 or Ctrl Q F

Searches for any string up to 25 characters long. When you issue this command, you are prompted for a search string. Type in the search string. Then, if F3 was used as the find command, press F3 again. If Ctrl Q F was used, press ↵.

The find operation can be repeated with the Repeat last find command.

Repeat last find ⇧ F3 or Ctrl L

Searches for the next occurrence of the search string.

Find and Replace F4 or Ctrl Q A

Searches for any string up to 25 characters long, then replaces it with any other string up to 25 characters long.

When you issue this command, you are prompted for the search string. Type in the search string. If you used F4, press F4 again. If Ctrl Q A was used, press ↵. Next, enter the string to replace the search string, terminated in the same way as the search string.

Then you are asked if you want a global or local find and replace. If local is specified, only one find and replace operation is carried out. Otherwise the find and replace operation is repeatedly carried out throughout the text, from the current cursor position onwards.

Finally, you are asked if you want to be prompted before a replacement is carried out. If you answer **N**o, the find and replace operation is carried out without further ado. If you answer **Y**es, the find string may or may not be found. If it is found (and the **Y** option is specified), you are asked the question: Replace (Y/N)? Press **Y** to replace or **N** to skip. You can also abort the search and replace operation by pressing Esc. The find and replace operation can be repeated with the Repeat last find and replace command.

Repeat last find and replace ⇧ F4 or Ctrl L

This command repeats the latest Find and replace operation exactly as if all information had been re-entered.

Function Key Summary

Function Keys	
F1	Help
F2	Go to Line Actual Line
F3	Search Search Again*
F4	Replace Replace Again*
F5	Copy Copy Again*
F6	Move Text
F7	Delete Text
F8	Auxiliary Edit
F9	External Copy
F10	End editor
Special Combinations	
Ctrl ←	Move to word at left
Ctrl →	Move to word at right
Ctrl Home	Go to start of text
Ctrl End	Go to end of text
Alt ←	Delete line to left
Alt →	Delete line to right
Ctrl ⟵	Delete line
Ctrl V	Toggle indentation
Ins	Insert/Overwrite

*These functions are activated when ⇧ is pressed at the same time as the function key.

THE CALCULATION OF SCREEN ATTRIBUTES

Turbo Prolog allows you to specify the colors and/or attributes for your particular screen type. The methods for a monochrome and color/graphics screen are outlined in the following sections.

Monochrome Display Adapter

1. Choose the integer representing the required foreground and background combination from Table 12-2.
2. Add 1 if you want characters to be underlined in the foreground color.
3. Add 8 if you want the white part of the display to be in high intensity.
4. Add 128 to this value if you want the character to blink.

Table 12-2 Monochrome Display Adapter Attribute Values

Black characters on a black background (i.e., blank)	0
White characters on a black background (normal video)	7
Black characters on a white background (inverse video)	112

Color/Graphics Adapter

1. Choose one foreground color and one background color.
2. Add the corresponding integer values from Table 12-3.
3. Add 128 if you want whatever is displayed with this attribute to blink.

Table 12-3 Color/Grapics Adapter Attribute Values

Foreground colors		Background colors	
Black	0	Black	0
Gray	8	Blue	16
Blue	1	Green	32
Light Blue	9	Cyan	48
Green	2	Red	64
Light Green	10	Magenta	80
Cyan	3	Brown	96
Light Cyan	11	White	112
Red	4		
Light Red	12		
Magenta	5		
Light Magenta	13		
Brown	6		
Yellow	14		
White	7		
White (High Intensity)	15		

ARITHMETIC FUNCTIONS AND PREDICATES

Table 12-4 Turbo Prolog Arithmetic Predicates and Functions

Functional Predicate	Description
bitand(X,Y,Z) *bitnot(X,Z)* *bitor(X,Y,Z)* *bitxor(X,Y,Z)*	If X and Y are bound to integer values, Z will be bound to an integer that is the result of (1) representing the values of X and Y as signed 16-bit numbers and (2) performing the corresponding logical operation AND, OR, NOT, XOR on those numbers.
bitleft(X,N,Y) *bitright(X,N,Y)*	If X and N are bound to integer values, Y is bound to the integer that is the result of representing X as a signed 16-bit number and shifting left or right the number of places specified by N.
random(X)	Binds X to a pseudo-random number x with $0 <= x < 1$.
X mod Y	Returns the remainder of X divided by Y.
X div Y	Returns the quotient of X divided by Y.
abs(X)	If X is bound to a positive value *v*, *abs(X)* returns that value; otherwise it returns $-1 * v$.
round(X)	Returns the rounded value of X.
cos(X), sin(X), tan(X)	The trigonometric functions require that X be bound to a value representing an angle in radians.
arctan(X)	Returns the *arctan* of the real value to which X is bound.
exp(X)	e raised to the value to which X is bound.
ln(X)	Logarithm to base e.
log(X)	Logarithm to base 10.
sqrt(X)	Square root.

CLASSIFIED INDEX OF STANDARD PREDICATES

Below is a classified index of all standard predicates. Predicates are grouped by function. Detailed descriptions are given in alphabetical order on the pages that follow this index.

Page

Reading

Writing

ALPHABETICAL DIRECTORY OF STANDARD PREDICATES

This section lists all Turbo Prolog standard predicates in alphabetical order. Each predicate is described in the following format:

- predicate name and a typical invocation
- types of the parameters in corresponding positions of the predicate
- list of the possible flow patterns for this predicate
- description of the outcome of a call to the predicate for each of the allowed flow patterns.

asserta(⟨fact⟩) (dbasedom) : (i)

Inserts a ⟨*fact*⟩ in the RAM database before any other stored clauses for the corresponding predicate. The ⟨*fact*⟩ must be a term belonging to the domain *dbasedom*, which is internally generated.

assertz(⟨fact⟩) (dbasedom) : (i) (o)

Inserts a ⟨*fact*⟩ in the RAM database after all other stored clauses for the corresponding predicate. The ⟨*fact*⟩ must be a term belonging to the domain *dbasedom*, which is internally generated.

attribute(Attr) (integer) : (i) (o)

`(i)`
Sets the default attribute value for all screen positions.

`(o)`
Binds *Attr* to the current default attribute value for all screen positions.

back(Step) (integer) : (i)

Indicates how many *Steps* the turtle is to move from its current position along its current direction. *back* fails if the movement leads to a position outside the screen (screen is 32000 horizontal and 32000 vertical steps). The current position of the turtle will only be updated if *back* is successful.

beep

Beeps the computer's speaker.

bios(InterruptNo,RegsIn,RegsOut)

(integer,regdom,regdom) : (i,i,o)

Causes BIOS interrupt *InterruptNo* with register values indicated in the parameter *RegsIn* and binds the parameter *RegsOut* to the register values after the interrupt has been executed. *RegsIn* and *RegsOut* both belong to the internal domain *regdom*, which is defined as:

```
regdom = reg(AX,BX,CX,DX,SI,DI,DS,ES)
```

where *AX*, *BX*, *CX*, *DX*, *SI*, *DI*, *DS* and *ES* are all of integer domain type.

bound(Variable) — ((variable)) : (o)

Succeeds if *Variable* is bound.

char_int(CharParam,IntParam) — (char,integer) : (i,o) (o,i) (i,i)

`(i,o)`
Binds *IntParam* to the decimal ASCII code for *CharParam*.

`(o,i)`
Binds *CharParam* to the character having the decimal ASCII code specified by *IntParam*.

`(i,i)`
Succeeds if *IntParam* is bound to the decimal ASCII code for *CharParam*.

clearwindow

Clears the currently active window of text by filling it with its background color.

closefile(SymbolicFileName) — (file) : (i)

Closes the named file. *closefile* succeeds even if the named file has not been opened.

comline(Line) — (string):(0)

Reads the command line parameters used when invoking a program you have written.

concat(String1,String2,Longstring)

(string,string,string):(i,i,o)(o,i,i)(i,o,i)(i,i,i)

Obtains *Longstring* by concatenating *String1* and *String2*.

consult(DOSFileName) — (string) : (i)

Adds a text file (created, for example, by saving a database with the *save* predicate) to the current database. The predicate succeeds by loading the facts (describing declared database predicates) from the file *DOSFileName* into memory. If the file contains any syntactic errors, *consult* fails.

cursor(Row,Column) (integer,integer) : (i,i) (o,o)

`(i,i)`

Moves the cursor to the indicated position (relative to the top left corner at row 0, column 0) in the currently active window.

`(o,o)`

Binds *Row* and *Column* to the current cursor position.

cursorform(Startline,Endline) (integer,integer) : (i,i)

Sets the height and vertical position of the cursor within a single-character display area. Each character occupies 8 scan lines of the screen, so *Startline* and *Endline* must be bound to values between 1 and 8, inclusive. (Note that color systems only have 8 scan lines.)

date(Year,Month,Day) (integer,integer,integer) : (i,i,i) (o,o,o)

`(o,o,o)`

Reads the date from the computer's internal clock.

`(i,i,i)`

Sets the date used by the computer's internal clock.

deletefile(DosFileName) (string) : (i)

Deletes the file *DosFileName* from the currently active disk.

dir(Pathname,FileSpecString,DosFileName) (string,string,string) : (i,i,o)

Calls the Turbo Prolog file directory command. The indicated *PathName* and *FileSpec-String* define the files to appear in the directory window. The user can select a name (returned in *DosFileName*) with the cursor keys, followed by ↵ when the desired filename is highlighted. *dir* fails if it is aborted with the Esc key.

disk(DosPath) (string) : (i) (o)

`(i)`

Sets the current default drive and path.

`(o)`

Returns the current default drive and path.

display(String) (string) : (i)

Displays the contents of *String* in the currently active window. The contents can be inspected (but not altered) using the editor's cursor control keys.

dot(Row,Column,Color) (integer,integer,integer) : (i,i,i) (i,i,o)

`(i,i,i)`

Provided the screen is initialized to graphics mode, *dot* puts a dot at the point determined by the values of *Row* and *Column*, in the specified *Color*. The coordinates are both integers from 0 to 31999 and are independent of the current screen mode.

`(i,i,o)`

When used with *Color* as a free parameter, *dot* reads the color value at the point determined by *Row* and *Column*.

edit(InputString,OutputString) (string,string) : (i,o)

Calls the Turbo Prolog editor. *InputString* can then be edited in the currently active window to form *OutputString*.

editmsg(InStr,OutStr,LeftHeader,RightHeader,Message, Position,HelpFileName,Code) (string,string,string,string,string,integer,string,integer) :(i,o,i,i,i,i,i,o)

Calls the Turbo Prolog editor. *InStr* can then be edited in the currently active window to form *OutStr*. Two texts are inserted in the header given by *LeftHeader* and *RightHeader*. The cursor is located at the *Position*-th character in *InStr* and the indicated *Message* is displayed at the bottom of the window. The name of the file loaded when the "Help" key F1 is pressed is *HelpFileName*. The value returned in *Code* indicates how editing was terminated (*Code*=0 if terminated by F10 and *Code*=1 if aborted by Esc).

⟨expression⟩ = ⟨expression⟩ (equals) (i,o);(o,i);(i,i);(o,o)

Equal (=) will accept any expression of a standard domain type or any user-defined structure, including functors or lists.

`(i,i)`

Tests for equality. If the left side is equal to the right, the operator succeeds.

`(i,o) (o,i)`

If the left side and right side can be unified, the bindings are made and the operator succeeds. If unification fails, the operator fails.

For arithmetic, expressions are evaluated and variables are bound.

`(o,o)`

If the left side and right side can be unified, the bindings are made and the operator succeeds. If unification fails, the operator fails.

eof(SymbolicFileName) (file) : (i)

Checks whether the pointer to the current file position (see *filepos*) is pointing to the end of the file. If so, *eof* succeeds; otherwise it fails.

existfile(DosFileName) (string) : (i)

Succeeds if the file *DosFileName* appears in the directory of the currently active disk (see *disk*).

exit

Stops program execution and returns control to the Turbo Prolog menu system.

fail

Forces *fail*ure of a predicate and, hence, backtracking.

field_attr(Row,Column,Length,Attr) (integer,integer,integer,integer) : (i,i,i,i) (i,i,i,o)

`(i,i,i,i)`
If *Row* and *Column* refer to a position within the currently active window (see *makewindow* and *shiftwindow*) and a field of the given *Length* starting at that position can be contained inside that window, all the positions in that field are given attribute *Attr.*

`(i,i,i,o)`
The attribute of the field occupying *Length* characters at position *Row, Column* of the currently active window is bound to *Attr.* As above, the specified field must fit inside this window.

field_str(Row,Column,Length,String) (integer,integer,integer,string) : (i,i,i,i) (i,i,i,o)

`(i,i,i,i)`
If *Row* and *Column* refer to a position within the currently active window (see *makewindow* and *shiftwindow*) and a field of the given *Length* starting at that position can be contained inside that window, the value to which *String* refers will be written at that position, subject to these conditions:

If *String* is bound to a value that contains more characters than *Length* indicates, only the first *Length* characters are written. If *String* is shorter than *Length*, the rest of the field will be filled with blank spaces.

`(i,i,i,o)`
The text occupying the field of *Length* characters at position *Row, Column* of the currently active window is read into *String*. As above, the specified field must fit inside this window.

filemode(SymbolicFileName,FileMode) (file,integer) : (i,i) (i,o)

Accesses binary files, where *FileMode* specifies text mode:0 or binary mode:1.

Text mode: The character CR (ASCII 13) is suppressed using standard input routines (*readchar, readln...*). A CR will be asserted before each LF with output predicates. Both CTRL-Z and physical EOF can mark EOF of a text file.

Binary mode: no transformations will be done at all in this mode. Standard predicates work normally in this mode.

filepos(SymbolicFileName,FilePosition,Mode)

(file,real,integer) : (i,i,i) (i,o,i)

`(i,i,i)`

Selects the position in the named file where a value is to be written by *write*. Positions are calculated according to the type of element stored in the file and the value of *Mode*.

Thus, if *SymbolicFileName* refers to a file of bytes, and *FilePosition* and *Mode* are bound to 11 and 0 respectively, the next byte written into the file will be at byte position 11 (from the beginning of the file).

`(i,o,i)`

Returns the position relative to the beginning of the file where the next *write* will take place. Reading the file position therefore requires that *Mode*=0.

Mode	Position
0	Relative to the start of the file
1	Relative to the current position
2	Relative to the end of the file

file_str(DosFileName,StringVariable) (string,string) : (i,o)(i,i)

Reads characters (maximum 64K) from the named file into the string until an end-of-file character (decimal ASCII code 26, normally Ctrl Z) is received.

findall(Variable,⟨atom⟩,ListVariable)

Collects the values from backtracking into a list. Thus, if ⟨*atom*⟩ is a predicate with its arguments represented by valid Turbo Prolog variable names, and *Variable* is the name of one of the variables in the predicate, *ListVariable* will be bound to the list of values for that variable that was obtained from instances when the predicate can succeed due to backtracking.

flush(SymbolicFileName) (file) : (i)

Forces the contents of the internal file buffer to be written to the current *writedevice*. *flush* is useful when output is directed to a serial port and it may be necessary to send the data to the port before the buffer is full. (Normally file buffers are *flush*ed automatically).

forward(Step) (integer) : (i)

Provided the screen is initialized to graphics mode, *forward* moves the pen from its current position the indicated number of *Steps* along its current direct. *forward* fails if the movement leads to a position outside the screen (screen is 32000 horizontal and vertical steps). The current position of the turtle will only be updated if *forward* is successful. If the pen is activated, *forward* leaves a trail in the current pen color.

free(Variable) **(⟨variable⟩) : (o)**

Succeeds if *Variable* is not bound.

frontchar(String,FrontChar,RestString)
(string,char,string) : (i,o,o) (i,i,o) (i,o,i) (i,i,i) (o,i,i)

Operates as if it were defined by the equation

```
String=(the concatenation of FrontChar and RestString)
```

so that either *String* must be bound or both *FrontChar* and *RestString* must be bound.

frontstr(NumberOfChars,String1,StartStr,String2)
(integer,string,string,string) : (i,i,o,o)

Splits *String1* into two parts. *StartStr* will contain the first *NumberOfChars* characters in *String1* and *String2* will contain the rest.

fronttoken(String,Token,RestString)
(string,string,string) : (i,o,o) (i,i,o) (i,o,i) (i,i,i) (o,i,i)

Operates as if it were defined by the equation

```
String = (the concatenation of Token and RestString)
```

so that either *String* must be bound or both *Token* and *RestString* must be bound. Thus, *fronttoken* succeeds if *Token* is bound to the first token of *String* and *RestString* is bound to the remainder of the *String*. A group of one or more characters constitutes a token in one of the following cases:

- they constitute a ⟨name⟩ according to Turbo Prolog syntax.
- they constitute a valid string representation of a Turbo Prolog integer or real (a preceding sign is returned as a separate token).
- it is a single character, but not the ASCII space character (decimal code 32).

gotowindow(WindowNo) **(integer) : (i)**

where *WindowNo* is the number assigned to a window with the *makewindow* predicate.

graphics(ModeParam,Palette,Background)
(integer,integer,integer) : (i,i,i)

Initializes the screen in medium, high or extra-high resolution graphics. *ModeParam* selects the resolution. The resulting screen formats are shown in Table 12-5.

Table 12-5 Graphics Screen Formats

ModeParam	Cols	Rows	Adapter and Resolution
1	320	200	CGA, medium resolution 4 colors.
2	640	200	CGA, high resolution, black and white.
3	320	200	EGA, medium resolution, 16 colors.
4	640	200	EGA, high resolution, 16 colors.
5	640	350	EGA, enhanced resolution, 3 colors.

CGA: The standard Color/Graphics Adapter
EGA: Enhanced Graphics Adapter

Background (also an integer value) selects a background color. In screen modes 1 and 2, the choice is made according to Table 7-1.

inkey(Char) (char) : (o)

inkey reads a single character from the standard input, if one is present. If there is nothing on the standard input, *inkey* fails.

isname(StringParam) (string) : (i)

Succeeds if *StringParam* is a ⟨*name*⟩ according to Turbo Prolog syntax.

keypressed

It is possible to test for a key pressed without reading the keystroke. The predicate *keypressed* succeeds if any key has been pressed; otherwise, it fails.

left(Angle) (integer) - (i) (o)

`(i)`
Turns the turtle the indicated *Angle* (in degrees) to the left (counterclockwise).

`(o)`
Binds *Angle* to the current direction of the turtle.

line(Row1,Col1,Row2,Col2,Color) (integer,integer,integer,integer,integer) : (i,i,i,i,i)

Provided the screen is initialized to graphics mode, *line* draws a *Color* line between the points defined by *Row1*, *Col1*, and *Row2*, *Col2*, respectively. The coordinates are integers from 0 to 31999 and are independent of the current screen mode.

makewindow(WindowNo,ScrAtt,FrameAttr,Header, Row,Col,Height,Width) (integer,integer,integer,string,integer,integer,integer,integer) : (i,i,i,i,i,i,i,i) (o,o,o,o,o,o,o)

`(i,i,i,i,i,i,i,i)`

Defines an area of the screen as a window. Each window is identified by a number (*WindowNo*) which is used when selecting which window is to be active. If *FrameAttr* is less than or greater than zero, a border is drawn around the defined area (i.e. the window is framed) and the upper border line will include the *Header* text. Once defined, the window is "cleared" and the cursor is moved to its top left corner. The row and column positions of the left corner of the window—relative to the whole screen—are specified by parameters *Row* and *Col*, respectively, and *Height* and *Width* give the dimensions of the window. It is important that *Row*, *Col*, *Height* and *Width* be compatible with the size of the display—normally 25 rows of 80 characters. The size of the display can be changed using the *graphics* standard predicate.

`(o,o,o,o,o,o,o)`

This flow pattern allows the *makewindow* predicate to return the current values of a window.

membyte(Segment,Offset,Byte) (integer,integer,integer) : (i,i,i) (i,i,o)

`(i,i,i)`

When *Byte* is bound, *membyte* stores the value of the Byte at the memory address given by *Segment* and *Offset* (calculated as *Segment**16+*Offset*).

`(i,i,o)`

When *Byte* is free, *membyte* reads the value of the byte at the memory address given by *Segment* and *Offset* (calculated as *Segment**16+*Offset*).

memword(Segment,Offset,Word) (integer,integer,integer) : (i,i,i) (i,i,o)

`(i,i,i)`

When *Word* is bound, *memword* stores the value of the *Word* at the memory address given by *Segment* and *Offset* (calculated as *Segment**16+*Offset*).

`(i,i,o)`

When *Word* is free, *memword* reads the value of the word at the memory address given by *Segment* and *Offset* (calculated as *Segment**16+*Offset*). (Values in the range 32768 to 65536 are taken as negative integers).

nl

Causes a carriage-return, line-feed sequence to be sent to the current writedevice.

not(⟨atom⟩)

Succeeds if ⟨*atom*⟩ represents a goal that fails when evaluated.

openappend(SymbolicFileName,DosFileName) (file,string) : (i,i)

Opens the disk file *DosFileName* for appending, and attaches the *SymbolicFileName* to that file for future reference within the Turbo Prolog program containing this call.

openmodify(SymbolicFileName,DosFileName) (file,string) : (i,i)

Opens the disk file *DosFileName* for both reading and writing, and attaches the *SymbolicFileName* to that file for future reference within the Turbo Prolog program containing this call. This predicate can be used in conjunction with *filepos* to update a random access file.

openread(SymbolicFileName,DosFileName) (file,string) : (i,i)

Opens the disk file *DosFileName* for reading, and attaches the *SymbolicFileName* to that file for future reference within the Turbo Prolog program containing this call.

openwrite(SymbolicFileName,DosFileName) (file,string) : (i,i)

Opens the disk file *DosFileName* for writing and attaches the *SymbolicFileName* to that file for future reference within the Turbo Prolog program containing this call. If a file called *DosFileName* already exists on the disk, it is deleted.

pencolor(Color) (integer) : (i)

Determines the *Color* of the trail left by the pen. For the standard Color/Graphics Adapter, the color is determined according to Table 7-2.

pendown

Activates the pen used by the *forward* and *back* predicates.

penpos(X,Y,A)

`(i,i,i)`
If all parameters are bound before calling *penpos*, the predicate sets the position and direction of the turtle (and its pen).

`(o,o,o)`
If all parameters are free, they will be bound to the values determined by the current position of the turtle.

penup

De-activates the pen used by the *forward* and *back* predicates.

portbyte(PortNo,Value) (integer,integer) : (i,i) (i,o)

`(i,o)`

Binds *Value* to the decimal equivalent of the byte value at I/O port *PortNo*.

`(i,i)`

Sends the *Value* to I/O port *PortNo*.

ptr_dword(StringVar,Segment,Offset) (string,integer,integer) : (i,o,o) (o,i,i)

`(i,o,o)`

When *StringVar* is bound, *ptr_word* returns the internal *Segment* and *Offset* address of *StringVar.*

`(o,i,i)`

When *Segment* and *Offset* are bound, *ptr_word* returns the contents of location *Segment**16+Offset* and following as a string. The string consists of the characters with the given ASCII values and is terminated at the first location containing a NUL byte (i.e., a byte set to 0).

readchar(CharVariable) (char) : (o)

Reads a single character from the current read device (the *keyboard* unless the default is changed via *readdevice*).

readdevice(SymbolicFileName) (symbol) : (i) (o)

`(i)`

Reassigns the current read device to the file opened with the given *SymbolicFileName*, which may be the pre-defined symbolic file *keyboard* or any user-defined symbolic file name for a file opened for reading or modifying.

`(o)`

Binds *SymbolicFileName* to the name of the current read device, which may be the pre-declared *keyboard* or a file (see, for example, *openread*).

readint(IntVariable) (integer) : (o)

Reads an integer from the current read device (the *keyboard* unless the default is changed via *readdevice*) terminated by an ASCII carriage-return character.

readln(StringVariable) (string) : (o)

Reads characters from the current read device (the *keyboard* unless the default is changed via *readdevice*) until an ASCII carriage-return character is read.

readreal(RealVariable) **(real) : (o)**

Reads a real from the current read device (the *keyboard* unless the default is changed via *readdevice*) terminated by an ASCII carriage-return character.

readterm(Domain,Term) **(⟨name⟩,⟨variable⟩) : (i,o)**

Reads any object written by the *write* predicate. *Term* is bound to the object read, provided it conforms with the declaration of *Domain*. *readterm* allows facts to be accessed on files.

removewindow

Removes the currently active window from the screen.

renamefile(OldDosFileName,NewDosFileName)
(string,string) : (i,i)

Renames the file *OldDosFileName* (on the currently accessed disk) to *NewDosFileName*.

retract(⟨fact⟩) **(dbasedom) : (i)**

Deletes the first ⟨*fact*⟩ in the database that matches the given ⟨*fact*⟩.

right(Angle) **(integer) : (i) (o)**

`(i)`
Turns the turtle the indicated *Angle* (in degrees) to the right (clockwise).

`(o)`
Binds *Angle* to the current direction of the turtle.

save(DOSFileName) **(string) : (i)**

Saves all the clauses for database predicates in the text file to which *DOSFileName* refers. *save* saves a fact on each line in the file. The file can later be read into memory by the *consult* predicate. The text file—and thus the entire *database*, can also be inspected and manipulated using the editor.

scr_attr(Row,Col,Attr) **(integer,integer,integer) : (i,i,i) (i,i,o)**

`(i,i,i)`
Sets the attribute of the character at screen position *Row, Col* to the value referred to by *Attr*.

`(i,i,o)`
Returns the value of the attribute setting for the character at position *Row, Col*.

scr_char(Row,Column,Char) (integer,integer,char) : (i,i,i) (i,i,o)

`(i,i,i)`
Writes the character *Char* on the screen with the current attribute at the position given by *Row* and *Column*.

`(i,i,o)`
Reads a character from the specified position.

Scroll(NoOfRows,NoOfCols) (integer,integer) : (i,i)

NoOfRows indicates the number of lines to be scrolled up or down. A positive number scrolls up, a negative number scrolls down.

NoOfCols indicates the number of columns to be scrolled left or right. A positive number scrolls left and a negative number scrolls right.

shiftwindow(WindowNo) (integer) : (i) (o)

`(i)`
Changes the currently active window to the one referred to by *WindowNo*. (Any previously active window is stored in its current state.) The cursor returns to the position it was in when window *WindowNo* was last active.

`(o)`
Binds *WindowNo* to the number of the currently active window.

sound(Duration,Frequency) (integer,integer) : (i,i)

Plays a note through the speaker with given *Frequency* for *Duration* hundredths of a second.

storage(StackSize,HeapSize,TrailSize) (real,real,real) : (o,o,o)

Returns the available size of the three run-time memory areas used by the Turbo Prolog system.

str_char(StringParam,CharParam) (string,char) : (i,o) (o,i) (i,i)

`(i,o)`
Binds *CharParam* to the single character contained in the string to which *StringParam* is bound.

`(o,i)`
Binds *StringParam* to the character specified by *CharParam*.

`(i,i)`
Succeeds if *CharParam* and *StringParam* are both bound to representations of the same character.

str_int(StringParam,IntParam) (string,integer) : (i,o) (o,i) (i,i)

`(i,o)`
Binds *IntParam* to the internal (binary) equivalent of the decimal integer to which *StringParam* is bound.

`(o,i)`
Binds *StringParam* to a string of decimal digits representing the value to which *IntParam* is bound.

`(i,i)`
Succeeds if *IntParam* is bound to the internal (binary) representation of the decimal integer to which *StringParam* is bound.

str_len(String,Length) (string,integer) : (i,i) (i,o)

`(i,i)`
Succeeds if *String* has *Length* characters.

`(i,o)`
Succeeds by binding *Length* to the number of characters in *String*.

str_real(StringParam,RealParam) (string,real) : (i,o) (o,i) (i,i)

`(i,o)`
Binds *RealParam* to the internal (binary) equivalent of the decimal real number to which *StringParam* is bound.

`(o,i)`
Binds *StringParam* to a string of the decimal digits representing the value to which *RealParam* is bound.

`(i,i)`
Succeeds if *RealParam* is bound to the internal (binary) representation of the decimal real number represented by the string to which *StringParam* is bound.

system(DosCommandString) (string) : (i)

`(i)`
Sends *DosCommandString* to DOS for execution.

text

Resets the screen in text mode. The call has no effect if the screen was already in text mode.

time(Hours,Minutes,Seconds,Hundredths) (integer,integer,integer,integer) : (i,i,i,i) (o,o,o,o)

`(i,i,i,i)`

Sets the *time* used by the computer's internal clock.

`(o,o,o,o)`

Reads the *time* from the computer's internal clock.

trace(Status) (symbol) : (i) (o)

`(i)`

trace(on) turns tracing on (in whichever mode has been selected by the corresponding compiler directive—*trace* or *shorttrace*); *trace(off)* turns tracing off.

`(o)`

Binds *Status* to on or off, indicating whether tracing is being performed or not.

upper_lower(StringInUpperCase,StringInLowerCase) (string,string) : (i,i) (i,o) (o,i)

`(i,o)`

Binds *StringInLowerCase* to the lowercase equivalent of the string to which *StringIn-UpperCase* is bound.

`(o,i)`

Binds *StringInUpperCase* to the uppercase equivalent of the string to which *StringIn-LowerCase* is bound.

`(i,i)`

Succeeds if *StringInLowerCase* and *StringInUpperCase* are bound to lower and uppercase versions of the same string.

window_attr(Attr) (integer) : (i)

Gives the currently active window the attribute value to which *Attr* is bound.

window_str(ScreenString) (string) : (i) (o)

`(i)`

Binds *ScreenString* to the string currently displayed in the active window; therefore *ScreenString* has the same number of lines as there are lines in the active window. The length of each line is determined by the last non-blank character in that line.

`(o)`

ScreenString is written in the window according to the following criteria:

- If there are more lines in the string than there are lines in the window, lines will be written until the window space is exhausted.
- If there are fewer lines in the string than in the window, the remaining lines in the window will be filled out with blank spaces.

- If there are more characters on a string line than are available on a window line, the string line will be truncated to fit.
- If there are fewer characters in a line than there are columns in the window, the line will be filled out with blank spaces.

write(e1,e2,e3, ... ,eN) ((i)*)

Writes the given constants or values in the currently active window on the current writedevice. Can be called with an optional number of arguments *ei*, which can either be constants or variables bound to values of the standard domain types.

writedevice(SymbolicFileName) (symbol) : (i) (o)

`(i)`
Reassigns the current *writedevice* to the file opened with the given *SymbolicFileName*, which may be one of the predefined symbolic files (*screen* and *printer*) or any user-defined symbolic filename for a file opened for writing or modifying.

`(o)`
Binds *SymbolicFileName* to the name of the current *writedevice*, which may be the pre-declared *screen* or *printer*, or a file (see, for example, *openwrite*).

writef(FormatString,Arg1,Arg2,Arg3, ...) (i,(i)*)

Produces formatted output. *Arg1* to *ArgN* must be constants or variables that belong to domains of standard type. The format string contains ordinary characters, which are printed without modification, and format specifiers of the form:

```
%-m.p
```

- "-" indicates left justification; right justification is the default.
- The optional *m* field specifies the minimum field width.
- The optional *.p* field determines the precision of a floating-point image (or the maximum number of characters to be printed from a string). This field can also contain one of the letters *f*, e or g denoting:

  f — Reals in fixed decimal notation (default).
  e — Reals in exponential notation.
  g — Use the shortest format.

COMPILER DIRECTIVES

Table 12-6 Compiler Directives

`check_cmpio`	Check for use of compound flow patterns.
`check_determ`	Warn about the presence of nondeterministic clauses.
`code=nnnnn`	Size of the code array in paragraphs (1 paragraph is 16 bytes).
`config`	Allows a stand-alone .EXE application to read a configuration file that defines default window attributes and code size.
`diagnostics`	Print compiler diagnostics.
`include "filename"`	Include a Turbo Prolog file during compilation.
`nobreak`	Predicates should not scan the keyboard to see if Ctrl Break has been pressed.
`nowarnings`	Suppress warnings.
`shorttrace`	Trace all predicates, but without destroying any system optimization.
`shorttrace p1,p2`	*shorttrace* predicates *p1,p2* only.
`trace`	Display complete trace information by removing various optimizations carried out by the compiler. For example, *trace* stops automatic elimination of tail recursion so that all RETURNs from predicate calls can be inspected.
`trace p1,p2,..`	*Trace* predicates *p1,p2,..* only.
`trail=nnn`	Size of the trail in bytes.

BNF SYNTAX FOR TURBO PROLOG

The following BNF notation is used to define Turbo Prolog syntax:

`<term>`	Names of language constructs are surrounded by "⟨" and "⟩".
`{ X }*`	Represents zero or more repetitions of *X*.
`[X]`	Means that *X* is optional.
`X ! Y`	Indicates that *X* and *Y* are alternatives and that either *X* or *Y* must be used.

Names

A Turbo Prolog ⟨*name*⟩ is defined by

```
<name> ::= (<letter> ! _ ) { <letter> ! <digit>! _}*
```

⟨*name*⟩s must start with a letter or an underscore, followed by a contiguous sequence of letters, digits and underscore characters. A list of names separated by commas is defined by

```
<name-list>          ::= <name> ! <name> , <name-list>
```

Similarly,

```
<variable>          ::= ( <capital-letter> ¦ _ ) [<name>]
<functor>           ::= <small-letter> [<name>]
```

Note that a leading capital letter (or underscore) denotes a variable and a leading small letter denotes a constant.

```
<letter>            ::= <small letter> ¦ <capital letter>
<small-letter>      ::= a ¦ b ¦ ... x ¦ y ¦ z
<capital-letter>    ::= A ¦ B ¦ ... X ¦ Y ¦ Z
<digit>             ::= 0 ¦ 1 ¦ ... 8 ¦ 9
```

Program Section

```
<program>           ::= { <directives> }* { <program section> }*
<program section>   ::= <domain section>     ¦
                        <predicate section>  ¦
                        <clause section>     ¦
                        <goal section>       ¦
                        <database section>   ¦
                        <include-directive>
```

(This syntax is subject to the restrictions on program sections.)

Directives

```
<directive>         ::= check_cmpio                  ¦
                        check_determ                 ¦
                        code= <integer>              ¦
                        diagnostics                  ¦
                        <include-directive>          ¦
                        nobreak                      ¦
                        nowarnings                   ¦
                        shorttrace                   ¦
                        trace                        ¦
                        trail=<digits>

<include-directive>::= include "<filename>"
```

Domains Section

```
<domain-section>    ::= [global] domains { <domain-definition> }*
<domain-definition>::= <name-list> = [reference] <righthand>
                        ¦ file = <name-list>
<righthand>         ::= <domain type> ¦
                        <name> *      ¦
                        <d-alternatives>
```

```
<domain-type>        ::= char    ¦
                         integer ¦
                         symbol  ¦
                         string  ¦
                         real    ¦
<d-alternatives>     ::= <d-alternative> ¦
                          <d-alternative> <or> <d-alternatives>
<d-alternative>      ::= <functor> [ ( [ <name-list> ] ) ]
```

Predicate and Database Section

```
<database-section> ::= database { <predicate-def>}*

<predicate-section>::= predicates { <predicate-def> }* ¦ global
                                 predicates {<global-predicate-def>}*

<global-predicate-def>::=<predicate-def>[-{<flow-
                           spec>}*[language<language>]]
<flow-spec>         ::=(<flow-param-list>)

<flow-param-list>   ::=<flow-param>¦ <flow-param>, <flow-param-list>

<flow-param>        ::=i¦o

<language>          ::=assembler¦c¦pascal¦fortran

<predicate-def>     ::= <name> [ ( [ <name-list> ] ) [.]
```

Clause Section

```
<clause-section>    ::= clauses { <clause> }*

<clause>            ::= <fact> . ¦ <rule> .

<fact>              ::= <relational-expr>

<rule>              ::= <relational-expr> <if> <alternatives>

<alternatives>      ::= <subgoal-list> [<or> <subgoal-list> ]

<subgoal-list>      ::= <subgoal> ¦
                        <subgoal> <and> <subgoal-list>

<subgoal>           ::= <relational-expr>          ¦
                        <comparison>               ¦
                        <findall-literal>          ¦
                        <database-literal>         ¦
                        <flow-literal>             ¦
                        not( <relational-expr> )   ¦
                        !

<relational-expr>   ::= <name> [ ( [<term-list>] ) ]

<findall-literal>   ::= findall(<variable>,<relational-expr>,
                        <variable>)

<database-literal> ::= asserta( <fact> ) ¦
                       assertz( <fact> ) ¦
                       retract( <fact> )
```

```
<flow-literal>      ::= free( <variable> ) |
                          bound( <variable> )

<and>               ::= and | ,

<or>                ::= or  | ;

<if>                ::= if  | :-
```

Goal Section

```
<goal>              ::= <subgoal-list> .
```

Terms

```
<term-list>         ::= <term> | <term> , <term-list>

<term>              ::= [<sign>] <number> |
                        <char>            |
                        <list>            |
                        <string>          |
                        <variable>        |
                        <compound term>

<number>            ::= <digits> [. <digits> [<exponent>] ]

<digits>            ::= <digit> | <digit><digits>

<exponent>          ::= e [sign] <digits>

<sign>              ::= + | -

<char>              ::= '<character>' | '\<character>'

<string>            ::= " {<character>}* "

<list>              ::= [ ] |
                        [ <element-list> ]

<element-list>      ::= <term>[|<term>]|
                        <term> , <element-list>

<compound-term>     ::= <functor> [ ( [<term-list>] ) ]
```

Comparisons

```
<comparison>        ::= <ascii> <compare> <ascii> |
                        <arithmetic> <compare> <arithmetic>

<ascii>             ::= <functor> | <string> | <char> |<variable>
<arithmetic>        ::= <multexp> <adding> <arithmetic> |
                        <multexp>

<multexp>           ::= <factor> <multiplying> <arithmetic> |
                        <factor>
```

```
<factor>            ::= <variable>      |
                        <number>        |
                        (<arithmetic>) |
                        <function> ( <arithmetic> )

<compare>           ::= = | <= | >= | >< |<> |=<|=>|<|>

<adding>            ::= + | -

<multiplying>       ::= * | / | div | mod

<function>          ::= abs    | cos | sin | tan |
                        arctan | exp | ln  | log |
                        sqrt
```

SYSTEM LIMITS

- A ⟨*name*⟩ may consist of a maximum of 250 characters.
- A string constant may consist of a maximum of 250 characters.
- A string variable may be bound to a string containing a maximum of 64K characters.
- The range of allowable integer values is −32768 to +32767.
- The range and format of real numbers follows the 8-byte IEEE standard. The exponent must be an integer between −308 and +308.
- No more than 50 parameters may be used in a predicate.
- It is not possible to give a goal for a submodule.
- The maximum number of include files is 10.
- The maximum number of domain names is 250.
- The maximum number of alternatives in a domain declaration is 250.
- The maximum number of predicate names is 300.
- The maximum number of variables in a clause is 100.
- The maximum number of literals in a clause is 100.
- The maximum number of clauses in each predicate is 500.

A ASCII Character Codes

Following are the ASCII character codes as understood by Turbo Prolog.

ASCII Character Set

Special Characters (group 1)

char	code	char	code	char	code	char	code
!	33	%	37	)	41	−	45
"	34	&	38	'	39	*	42	.	46

Digits

char	code	char	code	char	code	char	code
0	48	3	51	6	54	9	57
1	49	4	52	7	55		
2	50	5	53	8	56		

Special Characters (group 2)

char	code	char	code	char	code	char	code
:	58	<	60	>	62	@	64
;	59	=	61	?	63		

Uppercase Letters

char	code	char	code	char	code	char	code
A	65	H	72	O	79	V	86
B	66	I	73	P	80	W	87
C	67	J	74	Q	81	X	88
D	68	K	75	R	82	Y	89
E	69	L	76	S	83	Z	90
F	70	M	77	T	84		
G	71	N	78	U	85		

ASCII Character Set (continued)

Special Characters (group 3)

char	code	char	code	char	code	char	code
[	91	]	93	_	95		
\	92	^	94		96		

Lowercase Letters

char	code	char	code	char	code	char	code
a	97	h	104	o	111	v	118
b	98	i	105	p	112	w	119
c	99	j	106	q	113	x	120
d	100	k	107	r	114	y	121
e	101	l	108	s	115	z	122
f	102	m	109	t	116		
g	103	n	110	u	117		

Special Characters (group 4)

char	code	char	code	char	code	char	code
{	123	|	124	}	125	~	126

The following characters are non-printable.

Unprintable ASCII Characters

Code	Key Combination	Effect
1	Ctrl A	
2	Ctrl B	
3	Ctrl C	Halt execution
4	Ctrl D	
5	Ctrl E	
6	Ctrl F	
7	Ctrl G	
8	Ctrl H	Backspace
9	Ctrl I	Tabulate character
10	Ctrl J	
11	Ctrl K	
12	Ctrl L	
13	Ctrl M	⟨RETURN⟩
14	Ctrl N	
15	Ctrl O	
16	Ctrl P	Toggles echoing to printer
17	Ctrl Q	Continue printout
18	Ctrl R	
19	Ctrl S	Temporarily stops printout
20	Ctrl T	Turn tracing on and off
21	Ctrl U	
22	Ctrl V	
23	Ctrl W	
24	Ctrl X	
25	Ctrl Y	
26	Ctrl Z	End-Of-File character
27	Esc	Escape
28		
29		
30		
31		
32	SPACE	Space character

B Error Messages

Following is a comprehensive list of the error codes returned by Turbo Prolog.

1	Illegal character
3	Illegal keyword
4	Use the format CODE=dddd or TRAIL=ddd
5	This size must not exceed 64
10	Illegal character
11	Character constants should be terminated by a '
12	The comment is not terminated by */
14	The name is too long. (max. 250 characters)
15	The textstring is too long. (max. 250 characters)
16	The textstring should be terminated with a " in the same line
17	Real constant is out of range
100	Undeclared domain (or misspelling)
102	Standard domains must not be declared
103	This domain was declared previously
104	Syntax error: = or , expected
105	Name expected (either a domain or a functor)
106	Alternatives in a list declaration are illegal
107	This functor has already been used in the domain declaration
108	Functor name expected
109	Domain name expected
110	Syntax error in domain declaration:) or , expected
111	WARNING: Domain used as a functor (F10=Ok, Esc=Abort)
112	WARNING: Domain declaration with a single functor (F10=Ok, Esc=Abort)
200	Illegal start of domain declaration
201	This name is reserved for a standard predicate
202	This predicate is already declared
204	Domain name or) expected
205	Undeclared domain or misspelling
206	Too many parameters used in this predicate

208 Syntax error in predicate declaration:) or , expected
209 Illegal number of parameters
210 Only one database predicate declaration is allowed
211 This predicate is declared as a database predicate
220 Syntax error in declaration of global predicates: - expected
221 Syntax error: (expected
222 Syntax error in flow pattern: i or o expected
223 Flow pattern has the wrong length
226 Syntax error: predicates or domains expected
227 Project name expected
228 At most one internal goal may be specified
229 The include file does not exist
230 Include files may not be used recursively; this file is already included
231 Too many include files; the maximum is 10
232 The include file is too big
233 database declarations must precede predicates
234 Global predicates must be declared first

400 Syntax error (Illegal start of predicate declaration)
401 No clauses for this predicate
402 Syntax error. AND , or . expected
403 Predicate name expected
404 Undeclared predicate or misspelling
405 (expected
406) or , expected
407 Illegal number of parameters: refer to declaration
408 This sign should be followed by a number
409 Syntax error—this token is misplaced
410 Variable expected
411 , expected
412 Syntax error
413 Syntax error: , | or] expected
414 Number or variable expected
415 Clauses for the same predicate should be grouped
416 Comparison operator expected i.e., one of < <= >= >< <>
417 Text after . is prohibited here
418 Unexpected end of text
419 Syntax error in clause body
420 WARNING: the variable is only used once. (F10=Ok, Esc=Abort)
421 The parameter is missing
422 . :- or IF expected
423 , or) expected
424 This facility is not implemented in this version
425 A list should be terminated by a]
426 Initializing a "database" is not allowed in a submodule
427 To generate an object module the program must contain a goal
450 Syntax error

600 Too many domain names
601 Too many alternatives in the domain declaration
602 Too many predicate names
603 Too many parameters in this clause
604 Too many literals in this clause
605 Too many clauses
606 Too many arguments
607 Too many domain names on the left side of a domain declaration
608 Too many database predicates
610 Code array too small: use code=size to get more space
611 Trail array too small: use trail=size to get more space
612 Overflow: too many structures in clause

701 An internal system error has occurred; please contact your dealer

1000 The parameters in makewindow are illegal
1001 The cursor values are illegal
1002 Stack overflow; re-configure with Setup if necessary
1003 Heap overflow; not enough memory or an endless loop
1004 Arithmetic overflow.
1005 The window referred to is unknown
1006 There is not enough room in the editor for the text
1007 Heap overflow; not enough memory or an endless loop
1008 Code overflow; use code=size to get more space
1009 Trail overflow; use trail=size to get more space
1010 Attempt to open a previously opened file
1011 Attempt to re-assign input device to a unopened file
1012 Attempt to re-assign output device to a unopened file
1013 'system' call tries to execute a program which is too big or resident
1014 Division by zero
1015 Illegal window number
1016 Maximum number of windows exceeded
1018 The file isn't open
1020 Free variables are not allowed here

2000 Not enough storage space for the text
2001 Can't execute a write operation
2002 Impossible to open
2003 Impossible to erase
2004 Illegal disk
2005 ⟩⟩⟩ Text buffer full ⟨⟨⟨
2006 Can't execute a read operation
2200 Type error
2201 Free variable in expression
2202 The free variable in findall can only be used inside findall
2203 The free variable in findall does not occur in the predicate
2204 This is the first occurrence of this variable
2205 Type error: illlegal variable type for this position

2206 Type error: the functor does not belong to the domain
2207 Type error: the compound object has the wrong number of arguments
2208 Expressions may not contain objects of this type
2209 Comparisons may only be made between standard types
2210 Objects from these domains cannot be compared
2211 There is no corresponding list domain
2212 Type error: This parameter can't handle compound objects
2213 Type error: This argument can't be a real

3001 WARNING: Variable used twice with output flow pattern. (F10=Ok, Esc=Abort)
3002 WARNING: Composite flow pattern. (F10=Ok, Esc=Abort)
3003 This flow pattern doesn't exist for the standard predicate
3004 Free variable in NOT
3005 Free variables are not allowed in WRITE
3006 The last variable in FINDALL must be free
3007 WARNING: The variable is not bound in this clause (F10=Ok, Esc=Abort)
3008 Free variable in expression
3009 WARNING: two free variables in expression. (F10=Ok, Esc=Abort)

3010 Loop in the flow analysis; don't use a compound flow pattern here
3011 WARNING: this will create a free variable. (F10=Ok, Esc=Abort)
4001 WARNING: non-deterministic clause. (F10=Ok, Esc=Abort)
4002 WARNING: non-deterministic predicate. (F10=Ok, Esc=Abort)

5001 Error in reading symbol table
5003 Error in writing symbol table
5103 Row number too small
5104 Row number too big
5105 Column number too small
5106 Column number too big
5107 Illegal screen mode (should be in range 1–6)
5109 Direction should be 0 or 1
5114 The line is outside the window

C PROLOG.SYS

The table below describes the contents of the system-generated text file PROLOG. SYS. The first two columns give the meanings of the parameters in the order in which they appear in PROLOG.SYS. The third column gives an example value for each parameter.

No.	Meaning	Example Value
1	Screen synchronization activated (1=active, 0=not active)	0
2	Autoload error messages into RAM (1=active, 0=not active)	0
3	Stack size in paragraphs (1 paragraph is 16 bytes)	600
4	Screen attribute for the message window	120
5	Screen attribute for the trace window	32
6	Screen attribute for the dialog window	67
7	Screen attribute for the status line (options window)	15
8	Screen attribute for the edit window	7
9	Screen attribute for the auxiliary edit window	112
10	Screen attribute for areas outside the system windows, etc.	112
11	Screen attribute for pull-down and pop-up menus and catalogs	7
12	Edit window format: TOP ROW coordinate	4
13	Edit window format: BOTTOM ROW coordinate	22
14	Edit window format: LEFT COLUMN coordinate	1
15	Edit window format: RIGHT COLUMN coordinate	78
16	Message window format: TOP ROW coordinate	18
17	Message window format: BOTTOM ROW coordinate	22
18	Message window format: LEFT COLUMN coordinate	1
19	Message window format: RIGHT COLUMN coordinate	32

No.	Meaning	Example Value
20	Dialog window format: TOP ROW coordinate	4
21	Dialog window format: BOTTOM ROW coordinate	14
22	Dialog window format: LEFT COLUMN coordinate	35
23	Dialog window format: RIGHT COLUMN coordinate	78
24	Trace window format: TOP ROW coordinate	18
25	Trace window format: BOTTOM ROW coordinate	22
26	Trace window format: LEFT COLUMN coordinate	35
27	Trace window format: RIGHT COLUMN coordinate	78
28	Auxiliary edit window format: TOP ROW coordinate	6
29	Auxiliary edit window format: BOTTOM ROW coordinate	22
30	Auxiliary edit window format: LEFT COLUMN coordinate	1
31	Auxiliary edit window format: RIGHT COLUMN coordinate	78
32	Path for the OBJ-directory	C:\objdir
33	Path for the EXE-directory	C:\exedir
34	Path for the TURBO-directory	C:\prolog
35	Path for the DOS-directory	C:\dosdir

D Using Turbo Prolog with Turbo Pascal

The Turbo Prolog system allows you to create .OBJ files. However, Turbo Pascal versions 1, 2, and 3 do not allow the linking of Turbo Pascal programs with such .OBJ modules. This means that for the time being, there is no simple way of interfacing Turbo Prolog modules with Turbo Pascal programs.

However, Borland plans to release Turbo Pascal 4.0 by the second quarter of 1987. Turbo Pascal 4.0 will allow the inclusion of Turbo Pascal modules within Turbo Prolog programs. We at Borland look forward to these exciting new possibilities.

E Glossary

anonymous variable The variable "_" used in place of an ordinary variable when the values that the ordinary variable may become bound to are of no interest.

arguments Collective name for the objects and variable names in a relation.

atom A relation, possibly involving objects or variables.

attribute A positive whole number that determines the characteristics of the display in a given window, including color, blinking/non-blinking and normal/inverse video.

backtracking The mechanism built into Turbo Prolog whereby, when evaluation of a given sub-goal is complete, Turbo Prolog returns to the previous sub-goal and tries to satisfy it in a different way.

bound variable A variable that refers to a known value.

calling a sub-goal (or predicate) An expression denoting that Turbo Prolog is now trying to satisfy a certain sub-goal (belonging to the given predicate).

char An arbitrary character enclosed between two single quotation marks.

compiler directives Instructions to the Turbo Prolog compiler to take special actions.

clause A fact or rule for a particular predicate, followed by a period (.).

compound goal A goal containing at least two sub-goals.

compound object An object consisting of a functor and a list of objects separated by commas and enclosed in parentheses.

current input device The currently assigned readdevice from which standard predicates take input by default.

current output device The currently assigned writedevice to which standard predicates send output by default.

cut (or !) The cut commits Turbo Prolog to all the choices made so far in the evaluation of the predicate containing the cut. Once the cut has been evaluated as a sub-goal, Turbo Prolog may not backtrack past it.

database predicates Predicates for which facts can be added to or deleted from the Turbo Prolog system during execution.

dialog window The system window in which external goals are given and the results of those goals recorded.

domain Specifies the types of values objects may take in relation.

editor window The window where text currently in the workfile can be edited.

element of a list Either an object or another list.

expert system A computer system that mimics the ability of an expert in a certain (usually very narrow) field.

external goal A goal entered in the dialog window by the user and given to the program currently in the workfile.

fact A relation between objects. In the fact

```
likes(john,mary)
```

likes is the name of the relation and *john* and *mary* are objects.

fail A sub-goal that Turbo Prolog cannot satisfy.

field A contiguous sequence of character display positions occurring on the same row of the screen display.

filename Either a symbolic file name starting with a lowercase letter and appearing on the righthand side of a *file* domain declaration, or one of the predefined symbolic file names *printer, screen, keyboard,* and *com1.*

flow pattern The pattern formed according to whether the parameters in a predicate call are used for input (i.e., are known) or for output (i.e., are unknown).

flow variant If a predicate is associated with several different flow patterns, a separate internal implementation of the routines corresponding to that predicate will exist for each flow pattern. These different implementations are called flow variants of the predicate.

free variable A variable that does not currently refer to any value.

functor A name for a compound object.

global Qualifier used to allow more than one program module access to certain domains and predicates.

goal The collection of sub-goals that Turbo Prolog attempts to satisfy.

goal tree A diagrammatic representation of the possible choices that can be made in the evaluation of the constituent sub-goals of a goal.

hand trace A trace produced by the programmer working with pen and paper rather than by the computer.

head of a list The first element of a list.

heap That part of memory used by Turbo Prolog for building structures, storing strings and inserting facts for database predicates.

infix notation Writing arithmetic expressions with the operators between the two values or expressions on which they are to operate.

integer A whole number in the range −32,768 to 32,767.

internal goal A goal contained in the goal section of a program.

iterative method A method that involves repeating the same basic action(s) over and over again until the desired objective is achieved.

list A special sort of object consisting of a collection of elements enclosed in square brackets and separated by commas.

message window The window in which messages related to the operation of the Turbo Prolog system appear.

module A Turbo Prolog program with global declarations forming part of a *project*.

multiple predicate declarations Any one predicate can have several declarations, each involving different domain specifications for the argument(s) of the relevant relation.

name Any contiguous sequence of letters, digits, and underscore characters that start with a lowercase letter or underscore.

object The name of an individual element of a certain type.

operator priority The hierarchy that determines the order in which operators are obeyed in arithmetic expressions.

parameters Collective name for the objects and variable names in a relation.

pointer The device by which Turbo Prolog keeps a record of the next place in its database of facts and rules to which to backtrack.

predicate Every Turbo Prolog fact or rule belongs to some predicate, which specifies the name of the relation involved and the types of objects involved in the relation.

project A Turbo Prolog program consisting of more than one module.

real A decimal number in the range $\pm 1.0E-307$ to $\pm 1.0E+308$.

recursion The technique whereby an entity is defined in terms of itself.

reference objects and domains If an unbound variable is passed from one sub-goal to another, the domain containing the values to which the variable will eventually become bound must be declared as a *reference* domain. Elements of such a domain are *reference* objects.

relation A name describing the manner in which a collection of objects (or objects and variables referring to objects) belong together.

repeat..fail combination A technique that can be used to avoid tail recursion by using Turbo Prolog's backtracking mechanism instead.

return from a sub-goal (or predicate) An expression used to denote that Turbo Prolog has now finished evaluating a certain sub-goal (belonging to the given predicate).

rule A relationship between a "fact" and a list of sub-goals which must be satisfied for that "fact" to be true.

satisfying a sub-goal The process by which Turbo Prolog chooses values for any unbound variables (if possible) in such a way that the sub-goal is true according to the given clauses for the corresponding predicate.

search principle One of four basic rules that Turbo Prolog follows in attempting to satisfy a goal.

stack The part of memory used by Turbo Prolog for parameter transfer.

stand-alone programs Programs that can be run from DOS independently of the Turbo Prolog system.

standard predicate A predicate already defined internally in Turbo Prolog.

standard type (of domain) A domain containing objects of a single type chosen from integer, real, char, string, symbol and file.

string An arbitrary number of characters enclosed by a pair of double quotation marks.

sub-goal A relation, possibly involving objects or variables, which Turbo Prolog must attempt to satisfy.

sub-object One of the objects in a compound object.

symbol A name starting with a lowercase letter.

tail of a list The list that remains when the first element of a given list (and its separating comma) are removed.

tail recursion elimination Action taken internally by the Turbo Prolog system to reduce the space/time overhead of tail recursion in rules.

term Either an object from one of the domains of standard type, a list, a variable, or a compound term, i.e., a functor followed by a list of terms enclosed in parentheses and separated by commas.

token A name, an unsigned (real or integer) number, or a non-space character.

trace The production of a step-by-step report on the execution of a program showing all relevant details.

trace window The window in which Turbo Prolog can generate a trace of program execution.

trail The part of memory used by Turbo Prolog to register the binding and unbinding of reference variables.

type system The means by which all objects in a relation or all variables used as arguments in a relation are constrained to belong to domains corresponding to those used in the relevant predicate's declaration(s).

unification The process by which Turbo Prolog tries to match a sub-goal against facts and the left hand side of rules in order either to satisfy that sub-goal, or to determine one or more further sub-goals necessary to evaluate the original sub-goal.

variable A name beginning with a capital letter that can be used to represent the (possibly unknown) value of a certain object.

variable binding(s) The status—free or bound—of one or more variables.

workfile The file in which a Turbo Prolog source program text is held ready for compilation or execution.

Index

Borland Software

TURBO PASCAL

EDITOR TOOLBOX™

It's All You Need To Build Your Own Text Editor Or Word Processor

Build your own lightning-fast editor and incorporate it into your Turbo Pascal® programs. Turbo Editor Toolbox gives you easy-to-install modules. Now you can integrate a fast and powerful editor into your own programs. You get the source code, the manual, and the know-how.

Create your own word processor. We provide all the editing routines. You plug in the features you want. You could build a WordStar®-like editor with pull-down menus like Microsoft's® Word, and make it work as fast as WordPerfect.®

To demonstrate the tremendous power of Turbo Editor Toolbox, we give you the source code for two sample editors:

Simple Editor A complete editor ready to include in your programs. With windows, block commands, and memory-mapped screen routines.

MicroStar A full-blown text editor with a complete pull-down menu user interface, plus a lot more. Modify MicroStar's pull-down menu system and include it in your Turbo Pascal programs.

The Turbo Editor Toolbox gives you all the standard features you would expect to find in any word processor:

- Wordwrap
- UN-delete last line
- Auto-indent
- Find and Find/Replace with options
- Set left and right margin
- Block mark, move, and copy
- Tab, insert and overstrike modes, centering, etc.

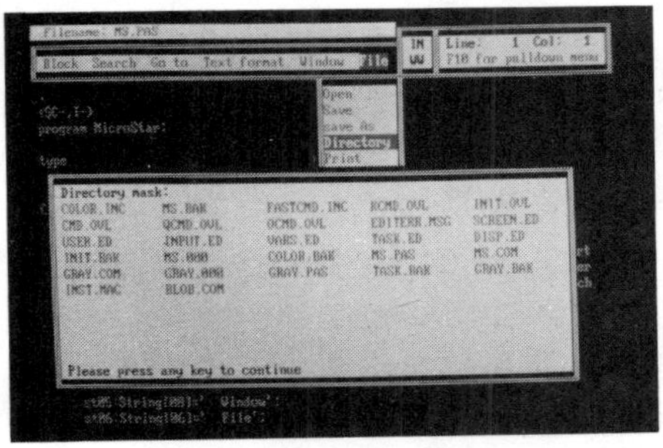

MicroStar's pull-down menus.

And Turbo Editor Toolbox has features that word processors selling for several hundred dollars can't begin to match. Just to name a few:

- ☑ ***RAM-based editor***. You can edit very large files and yet editing is lightning fast.
- ☑ ***Memory-mapped screen routines.*** Instant paging, scrolling, and text display.
- ☑ ***Keyboard installation.*** Change control keys from WordStar-like commands to any that you prefer.
- ☑ ***Multiple windows.*** See and edit up to eight documents—or up to eight parts of the same document—all at the same time.
- ☑ ***Multitasking.*** Automatically save your text. Plug in a digital clock, an appointment alarm—see how it's done with MicroStar's "background" printing.

Best of all, **source code is included for everything in the Editor Toolbox.**

Suggested Retail Price: $69.95 (not copy protected)

Minimum system configuration: IBM PC, XT, AT, 3270, PCjr, and true compatibles. PC-DOS (MS-DOS) 2.0 or greater. 192K RAM. You must be using Turbo Pascal 3.0 for IBM and compatibles.

BORLAND INTERNATIONAL

TURBO PASCAL

GRAPHIX TOOLBOX®

A Library of Graphics Routines for Use with Turbo Pascal®

High-resolution graphics for your IBM® PC, AT,® XT,® PCjr®, true PC compatibles, and the Heath Zenith Z-100.™ Comes complete with graphics window management.

Even if you're new to Turbo Pascal programming, the Turbo Pascal Graphix Toolbox will get you started right away. It's a collection of tools that will get you right into the fascinating world of high-resolution business graphics, including graphics window management. You get immediate, satisfying results. And we keep Royalty out of American business because you don't pay any—even if you distribute your own compiled programs that include all or part of the Turbo Pascal Graphix Toolbox procedures.

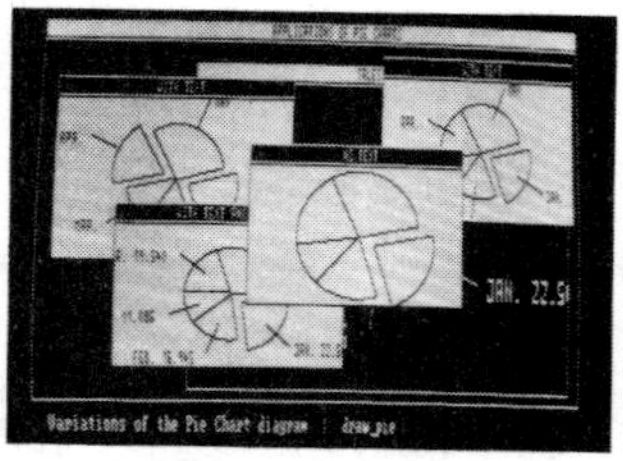

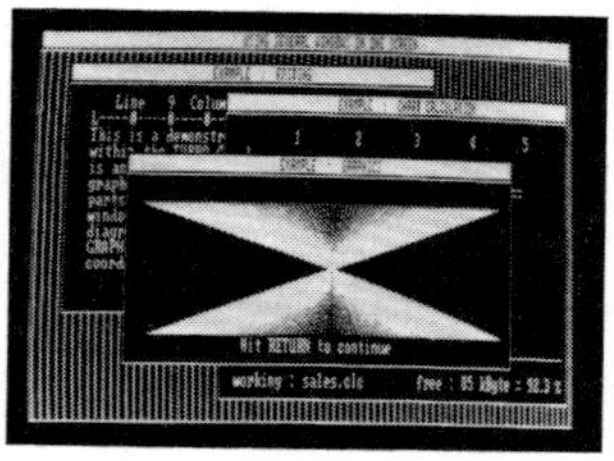

What you get includes:

- Complete commented source code on disk.
- Tools for drawing simple graphics.
- Tools for drawing complex graphics, including curves with optional smoothing.
- Routines that let you store and restore graphic images to and from disk.
- Tools allowing you to send screen images to Epson-compatible printers.
- Full graphics window management.
- Two different font styles for graphic labeling.
- Choice of line-drawing styles.
- Routines that will let you quickly plot functions and model experimental data.
- And much, much more . . .

"While most people only talk about low-cost personal computer software, Borland has been doing something about it. And Borland provides good technical support as part of the price."

John Markov & Paul Freiberger, syndicated columnists.

If you ever plan to create Turbo Pascal programs that make use of business graphics or scientific graphics, you need the Turbo Pascal Graphix Toolbox.

Suggested Retail Price: $69.95 (not copy protected)

Minimum system configuration: IBM PC, XT, AT, PCjr, true compatibles and the Heath Zenith Z-100. Turbo Pascal 3.0 or later. 192K RAM minimum. Two disk drives and an IBM Color Graphics Adapter (CGA), IBM Enhanced Graphics Adapter (EGA), Hercules Graphics Card or compatible.

BORLAND
INTERNATIONAL

If you use an IBM® PC, you need

TURBO Lightning®

Turbo Lightning teams up with the Random House® Concise Dictionary to check your spelling as you type!

Turbo Lightning, using the 83,000-word Random House Dictionary, checks your spelling *as you type*. If you misspell a word, it alerts you with a beep. At the touch of a key, Turbo Lightning opens a window on top of your application program and suggests the correct spelling. Just press one key and the misspelled word is instantly replaced with the correct word. It's that easy!

Turbo Lightning works hand-in-hand with the Random House Thesaurus to give you instant access to synonyms

Turbo Lightning lets you choose just the right word from a list of alternates, so you don't say the same thing the same way every time. Once Turbo Lightning opens the Thesaurus window, you see a list of alternate words, organized by parts of speech. You just select the word you want, press ENTER and your new word will instantly replace the original word. Pure magic!

If you ever write a word, think a word, or say a word, you need Turbo Lightning

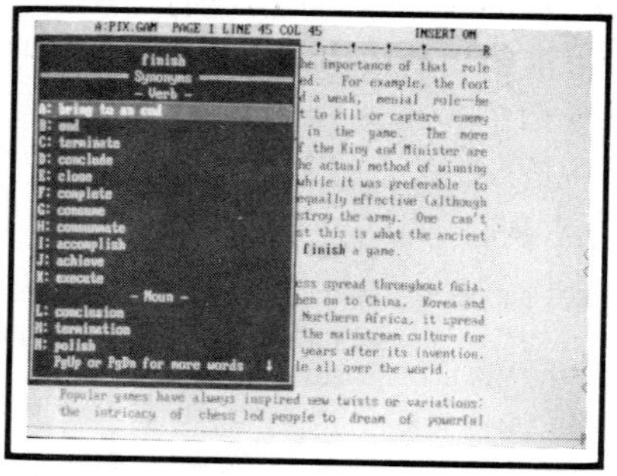

The Turbo Lightning Dictionary

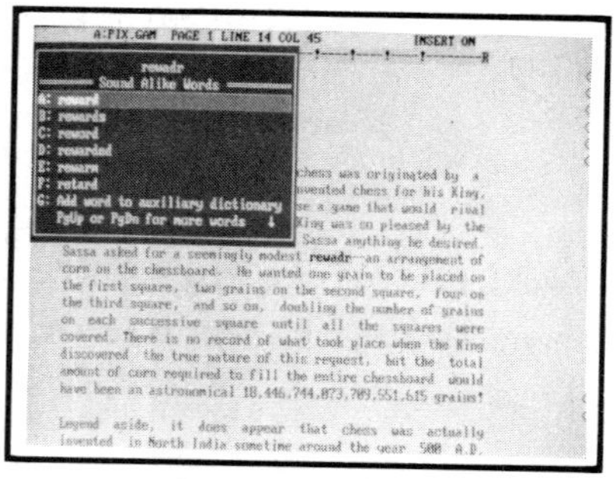

The Turbo Lightning Thesaurus

Turbo Lightning's intelligence lets you teach it new words. The more you use Turbo Lightning, the smarter it gets

You can also *teach* your new Turbo Lightning your name, business associates' names, street names, addresses, correct capitalizations, and any specialized words you use frequently. Teach Turbo Lightning once, and it knows forever.

Turbo Lightning is the engine that powers Borland's Turbo Lightning Library™

Turbo Lightning brings electronic power to the Random House Dictionary and Random House Thesaurus. They're at your fingertips—even while you're running other programs. Turbo Lightning will also "drive" soon-to-be-released encyclopedias, extended thesauruses, specialized dictionaries, and many other popular reference works. You get a head start with this first volume in the Turbo Lightning Library.

And because Turbo Lightning is a Borland product, you know you can rely on our quality, our 60-day money-back guarantee, and our eminently fair prices.

Suggested Retail Price: $99.95 (not copy protected)

Minimum system configuration: IBM PC, XT, AT, PCjr, and true compatibles with 2 floppy disk drives. PC-DOS (MS-DOS) 2.0 or greater. 256K RAM. Hard disk recommended.

BORLAND INTERNATIONAL

REFLEX FOR THE MAC™

The easy-to-use relational database that thinks like a spreadsheet. Reflex for the Mac lets you crunch numbers by entering formulas and link databases by drawing on-screen lines.

5 free ready-to-use templates are included on the examples disk:

- A sample 1040 tax application with Schedule A, Schedule B, and Schedule D, each contained in a separate report document.
- A portfolio analysis application with linked databases of stock purchases, sales, and dividend payments.
- A checkbook application.

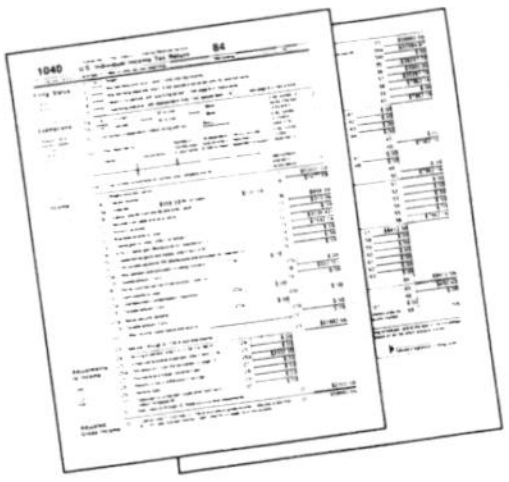

- A client billing application set up for a law office, but easily customized by any professional who bills time.
- A parts explosion application that breaks down an object into its component parts for cost analysis.

Reflex for the Mac accomplishes all of these tasks without programming—using spreadsheet-like formulas. Some other Reflex for the Mac features are:

- Visual database design.
- "What you see is what you get" report and form layout with pictures.
- Automatic restructuring of database files when data types are changed, or fields are added and deleted.
- Display formats which include General, Decimal, Scientific, Dollars, Percent.
- Data types which include variable length text, number, integer, automatically incremented sequence number, date, time, and logical.
- Up to 255 fields per record.
- Up to 16 files simultaneously open.
- Up to 16 Mac fonts and styles are selectable for individual fields and labels.

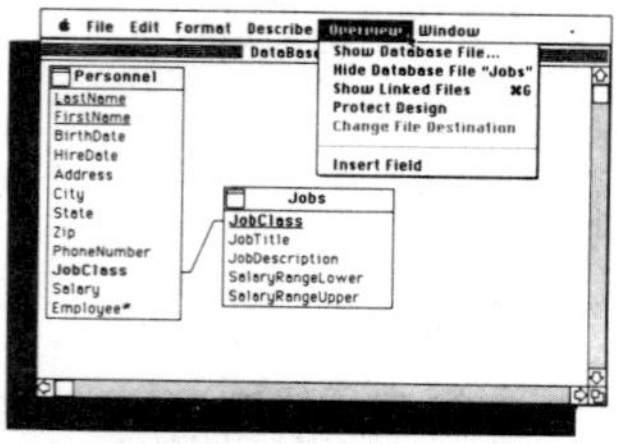

After opening the "Overview" window, you draw link lines between databases directly onto your Macintosh screen.

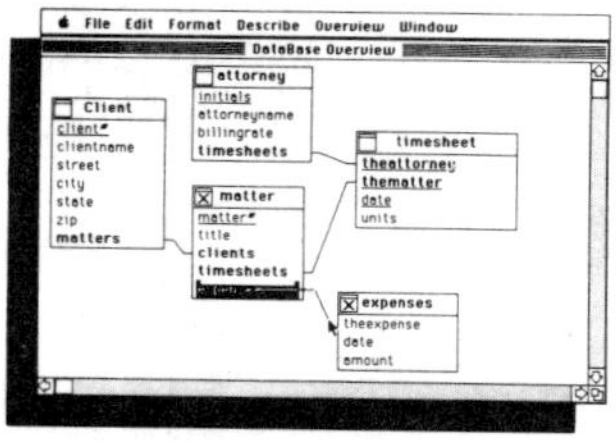

The link lines you draw establish both visual and electronic relationships between your databases.

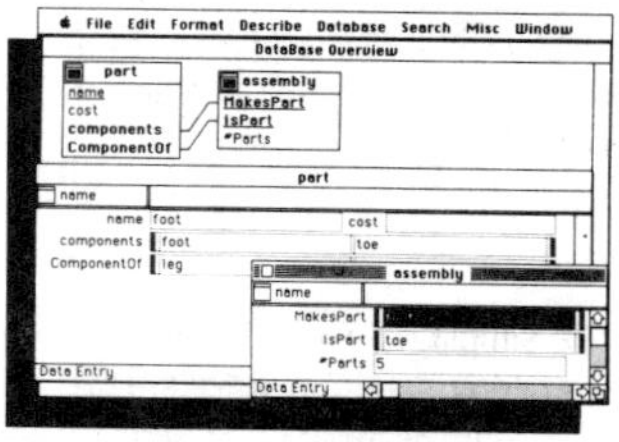

You can have multiple windows open simultaneously to view all members of a linked set—which are interactive and truly relational.

Critic's Choice

"... a powerful relational database ... uses a visual approach to information management." **InfoWorld**

"... gives you a lot of freedom in report design; you can even import graphics." **A+ Magazine**

"... bridges the gap between the pretty programs and the power programs." **Stewart Alsop, PC Letter**

BORLAND INTERNATIONAL

Suggested Retail Price: $99.95*

*Introductory offer through 1-15-87

Minimum System Requirements: *512K*

Reflex for the Mac is a trademark of Borland/Analytica, Inc. Macintosh is a trademark of McIntosh Laboratory, Inc. and is used with express permission of its owner.

BOR 0149

How To Buy Borland Software

NOTES

NOTES

NOTES

NOTES

NOTES